International Socialism 128

Autumn 2010

Contributors

Jamie Allinson is completing a PhD at the University of Edinburgh. He is a corresponding editor of the journal *Historical Materialism*.

Jairus Banaji has worked with the trade unions in India. His Marxist work includes *Theory as History: Essays on Modes of Production and Exploitation* (Brill, 2010).

Esme Choonara is a health worker in east London and author of *A Rebel's Guide to Trotsky*.

Estelle Cooch is a socialist activist based in London.

Gareth Dale is currently writing a biography of Karl Polanyi.

Neil Davidson is a Senior Research Fellow with the Faculty of Applied Social Science at the University of Strathclyde.

Jess Edwards is a primary school teacher and assistant secretary of Lambeth NUT.

Panos Garganas is the editor of the Greek newspaper *Workers' Solidarity*.

Christakis Georgiou is currently doing doctoral research on European integration. He is a member of France's New Anticapitalist Party associated with the magazine *Que Faire?*

Jane Hardy is Professor of Political Economy at the University of Hertfordshire and author of *Poland's New Capitalism*.

Tom Hickey is Principal Lecturer in Philosophy and Politics at the University of Brighton.

Phil Marfleet is Professor of Migration and Refugee Studies at the University of East London.

John Molyneux has written extensively on Marxism, politics and art. His books include *What is the Real Marxist Tradition?* and *Rembrandt and Revolution*, and much of his work can be found on johnmolyneux.blogspot.com

Simon Pirani is is a researcher and journalist, author of *The Russian Revolution in Retreat 1920-1924* and *Change in Putin's Russia: Power Money and People*.

Beccy Reese works at the TUC and has long been fascinated with science fiction.

Austerity politics

Fiscal austerity is more and more securely locked into place in the advanced capitalist countries. This is despite all the signs that the world economy faces, at best, a weak and unsteady recovery. The financial markets spent the summer agonising over the probability of a double-dip recession. But Robert Reich, labour secretary under Bill Clinton, summed up the view of many economists of different political and intellectual allegiances who believe the data actually point to a grimmer reality:

> It's nonsense to think of the economy heading downward again into a double-dip recession when most Americans never emerged from the first dip. We're still in one long big dipper.
>
> More people are out of work today than were last year, counting everyone too discouraged even to look for work... Not since the government began to measure the ups and downs of the business cycle has such a deep recession been followed by such anaemic job growth. Jobs came back at a faster pace even in March 1933 after the economy started to "recover" from the depths of the Great Depression. Of course, that job growth didn't last long. That recovery wasn't really a recovery at all. The Great Depression continued. And that's exactly my point. The Great Recession continues.[1]

Another Keynesian economist, Paul Krugman, argues that "we are now, I fear, in the early stages of a third depression", comparable in scale

---

1: Reich, 2010.

and length to those of the late 19th century and of the 1930s.[2] Recent data from the US Census Bureau seem to bear this out. In 2009 those living below the poverty line in the US rose by four million to 44 million, 14.3 percent of the population, the highest level since 1994. Median household income was 4.2 percent lower than in 2007 and 5 percent lower than in 1999.[3]

Yet the imperative to cut budget deficits boosted by the bank bailouts and by the economic slump is becoming ever more strongly entrenched politically. Even France—supposedly the centre of resistance to German demands for austerity within the eurozone—is heading towards "a new era of budgetary discipline", finance minister Christine Lagarde told the *Financial Times*, promising €40 billion of spending cuts and tax increases.[4] The biggest holdout against the G20 consensus on austerity—Barack Obama's administration—is besieged by a Republican right reinvigorated by the Tea Party movement and the Democrats' growing unpopularity. Meanwhile, an increasing number of US states face Greek-style fiscal crises as aid from Washington dries up.

The destabilising consequences of budget-cutting are worrying even the high priests of neoliberalism in the International Monetary Fund. In a joint report with the International Labour Organisation, the IMF documents what it calls the

> Dire state of labour markets: Over 210 million people across the globe are estimated to be unemployed at the moment, an increase of more than 30 million since 2007. Three quarters of the increase in the number of unemployed people has occurred in the advanced economies and the remainder among emerging market economies. Within the advanced countries, the problem is particularly severe in the United States—the epicentre of the Great Recession and the country with the highest increase in the number of unemployed: an increase of 7.5 million unemployed people since 2007.[5]

The report warns that "high and long-lasting unemployment... represents risks to the stability of existing democracies and hinders the development of new democracies in countries undergoing political transitions". Moreover,

---

2:   Krugman, 2010.
3:   Eckholm, 2010.
4:   Hall, Hollinger and Barber, 2010.
5:   ILO-IMF, 2010, p4.

a premature fiscal retrenchment could damage growth and lead to even larger deficits and debts. Abrupt shifts in fiscal policy stances, in many countries at the same time, could destabilise recovery and weaken future growth. A credible and gradual return to fiscal stability over several years is likely to be a more successful strategy, not only for recovery and growth, but also for deficit and debt reduction... Social dialogue is essential to avoiding an explosion of social unrest.[6]

Fear of an "explosion of social unrest" is also beginning to pervade the Conservative-Liberal Democrat coalition government in Britain as it psychs itself up for the announcement on 20 October of what are expected to be the most severe cuts in public expenditure since the "Geddes Axe" of 1922 under Lloyd George's Liberal-Unionist coalition.

Claims, for example by chancellor of the exchequer George Osborne, that "fiscal responsibility is both fair and progressive" look increasingly hollow. The *Financial Times* quotes an OECD study that found that

Sweden—alongside Finland—suffered the sharpest rise in income inequality among developed countries in the late 1990s, a period when both were also carrying out the most aggressive programmes to improve the state of their public finances... Income inequality also rose in Canada, as well as in the UK and several other countries that moved to cut big deficits. Poverty rates in Sweden, Canada and Finland between 1995 and the mid-2000s were among the highest in the OECD.[7]

As the scale of what is in prospect begins to sink in, there are signs that public opinion is beginning to turn against the government. An IPSOS-Mori poll in mid-September showed Labour on level pegging with the Tories at 37 percent, the Lib Dems down eight points from their general election performance at 15 percent, and dissatisfaction with the coalition for the first time outweighing satisfaction (47:43 percent).[8] The government is sticking by its guns, and one can detect a tone of naked class revenge in remarks such as Nick Clegg's that welfare isn't "a giant cheque written by the state to compensate the poor for their predicament".[9]

But, predictably enough, Andrew Rawnsley reports, the pressures

---

6:   ILO-IMF, 2010, pp22, 8.
7:   Pimlott, 2010.
8:   http://www.ipsos-mori.com/researchpublications/researcharchive/poll.aspx?oItemId=2672
9:   Press Association, 2010.

on the coalition are causing fierce conflicts involving the Treasury and min-isters running spending departments that have been told to plan for cuts of between 25 and 40 percent:

> Relations between the Treasury and the biggest of the spenders, the Department for Work and Pensions, are becoming especially bitter. George Osborne pre-empted his own review last week when the chancellor declared that he had already identified an additional reduction in benefits worth £4 billion on top of the £11 billion of cuts announced in the budget. That was news to Iain Duncan Smith [Secretary of State for Work and Pensions]. Early in the process, Mr Osborne tried to put peer pressure on Mr Duncan Smith when the chancellor suggested that other departments would not have to suffer so much if more swingeing cuts were made to welfare benefits. "We're relying on you to find us the money," one of Mr Duncan Smith's ministers was told by a minister from another department. "Fine," replied the DWP minister. "So long as you don't mind having a lynch mob outside your constituency office."

> Yes, it has already got to the point where ministers are threatening each other with lynch mobs. One Lib Dem member of the cabinet recently gave me his private estimate of where the opinion polls will be in about a year's time. His forecast was: "25-5". By that, he meant the Tories will slump to 25 percent over the next 12 months and the Lib Dems will collapse to 5 percent. This was not a frivolous forecast, but a deadly serious one.[10]

In reaction, the labour movement has begun to stir into life. The Trades Union Congress voted in September for a campaign of coordi-nated action and a national demonstration in March. This isn't anything like enough, particularly if one compares it to the general strikes that have been mounted in France and Greece. Nevertheless, the TUC campaign pro-vides a framework in which serious resistance to the coalition can develop. Meanwhile, the Labour leadership election saw Ed Miliband, one of the can-didates who had sought to distance themselves from New Labour, narrowly beat his brother David.

What this shows is that, however much the eras of Neil Kinnock and Tony Blair may have drained the political life out of the Labour Party and weakened its social roots, the mechanism that has come into action during past periods of opposition, when the party leadership came under

---

10: Rawnsley, 2010.

strong internal pressure to move leftwards, is still, albeit feebly, operative. Anyone who thinks that this is likely to lead to anything comparable to the Bevanite movement in the 1950s or Bennism in the late 1970s and early 1980s is kidding themselves. The Labour left today is a pale shadow of what it once was and Ed Miliband will, precisely because he had triumphed over the Blairite candidate, come under enormous pressure to prove himself a safe, business-friendly "moderniser".

But, as we argued in the last issue's Analysis, Labour retains sufficient roots in working class communities and, via the trade union bureaucracy, in the organised working class, to reflect and, at least partially, to accommodate moods in the class. Doing so in the present situation in any case fits with Labour's electoral interests: protesting, however hypocritically, against the coalition's cuts and targeting the Lib Dems in the cities are obvious first steps towards political recovery. This underlines the importance of the path taken by the Right to Work campaign of building a broad coalition of resistance that critically involves Labour supporters at both national and local levels.

These developments have led one radical left commentator, Seumas Milne, to announce that "a new centre of gravity is emerging in British politics which Labour—and the trade unions, for that matter—can tap into…there's no reason to believe that the coalition can't be forced from power in five years—or before".[11] But Milne also argues that resistance in the forms of strikes and demonstrations isn't enough:

> Campaigns and strikes may reduce or shift the burden of cuts here and there. But only if the coalition is compelled to change direction by the force of opinion, pressure and events can the wider threat to jobs, living standards and economic recovery be lifted. As Len McCluskey, the broad-left favourite to win next month's election to become general secretary of Britain's biggest union, Unite, puts it: "We have no alternative to resistance, but the ultimate solution is political."… What direction the Labour leadership now takes on the economy will have far-reaching consequences not only for the party, but for the campaign of resistance unions are trying to build. If the cuts really are to be derailed, there has to be an alternative.[12]

Milne, like McCluskey, seems to be placing his hopes in a revived Labour Party under Ed Miliband. This seems, to put it mildly, a trifle optimistic. If Aneurin Bevan and Tony Benn weren't able to transform Labour

---

11:   Milne, 2010b.
12:   Milne, 2010a.

in periods when the party was much more democratic and working class organisation stronger, what chances are there for a real change now under the leadership of Gordon Brown's ex-gofer? Nevertheless, Milne is absolutely right to pose the question of political alternatives. This isn't simply a matter of electoral politics, though this is important.

The ideological stakes involved in resisting austerity are very high. The drive to "fiscal consolidation" is more than anything else a political attempt to clamp back into place and indeed, if possible, to strengthen neoliberalism after the immense shock it suffered during the financial crash and the return to the state that this compelled.[13] Rejecting the necessity of the cuts requires, not simply a critique of the ideological assumptions used to justify it, but also some sort of account of another way out of the crisis. Simply falling back onto some version of Keynesianism, as Krugman, Reich and other mainstream critics of austerity do, isn't sufficient, most immediately because this approach fails to confront the fact that conflicting class interests are at play in different economic strategies.

The logic of resisting the cuts thus demands the formulation of an alternative economic programme. This is clear from the experience of Greece, where the severity of the austerity offensive mounted by the government of George Papandreou and the scale of workers' opposition have led, as Panos Garganas explains in the interview that follows, to a widespread discussion of the desirability of Greece defaulting on its foreign debt and withdrawing from the eurozone and possibly also from the European Union itself. The most detailed outline of what this would involve is to be found in a new report by Research on Money and Finance (RMF), a group of researchers based at the School of Oriental and African Studies in London.

The possibility of Greece defaulting on its massive foreign debt—nearly €300 billion in government bonds—is in any case on the agenda. The Greek finance minister, George Papaconstantinou, made a point of ruling it out during a tour of Western European financial centres in mid-September: "Restructuring [of Greece's debt] is not going to happen... It would be a fundamental break to the unity of the eurozone".[14] There is, however, widespread scepticism in the financial markets that default can be avoided, given the burden of debt on a shrinking economy.

RMF argues for what it calls "debtor-led default". In other words, rather than allowing the Western European banks that are the main holders

---

13: This ideological crisis is one of the main themes of Callinicos, 2010.
14: Oakley and Hope, 2010.

of Greek bonds to respond to the failure of austerity by imposing a debt restructuring in which the burden would still fall mainly on working people, Greece should unilaterally suspend debt repayments. This should be accompanied by withdrawal from the euro to remove the obstacle posed by the neoliberal and unaccountable European Central Bank's control of monetary policy and banking in the eurozone:

> First, it would be more difficult for the defaulting country to confront a domestic banking crisis without full command over monetary policy. More broadly, if banks were placed under public ownership following default but continued to remain within the Eurosystem, it would be practically impossible to deploy them in order to reshape the economy. Second, continued membership of the eurozone would offer little benefit to the defaulter in terms of accessing capital markets, or lowering the costs of borrowing. Third, the option of devaluation would be impossible, thus removing a vital component of recovery.[15]

But suspending debt repayments and withdrawing from the euro should be accompanied by a broader shift in economic policy to the left:

> From the perspective of working people, but also of society as a whole, the answer would be a broad programme of public ownership and control over the economy, starting with the financial system. Public ownership over banks would guarantee their continuing existence, preventing a run on deposits. Capital and foreign exchange controls would also be imposed to prevent export of capital and to minimise speculative transactions. A set of conditions would thus be created allowing for the adoption of industrial policy which would alter the balance of the domestic economy by strengthening the productive sector. The sources of growth in the medium term would be found in the decisive restructuring of the economy, rather than the expansion of exports through devaluation. [16]

This programme bears some resemblance to that adopted by the radical-left People Before Profit Alliance in Southern Ireland in April 2009. Though People Before Profit's "Alternative Economic Agenda" doesn't directly address the question of the euro, it calls for the nationalisation of the banks, the creation of a state banking system, a State Construction

---

15:   Lapavitsas and others, 2010b, p52.
16:   Lapavitsas and others, 2010b, p53.

Agency to organise a programme of public works, the development of new strategic industries, and genuine tax and pension reform to end the Irish economy's dangerous dependence on neoliberal financialisation.[17]

The RMF proposals, as sketched out by their principal author, Costas Lapavitsas, have attracted widespread discussion—and opposition—on the Greek radical left in recent months. Two main criticisms have been made. The first is that withdrawing from the euro represents a regression towards nationalism. This isn't a ridiculous concern. A strongly nationalist version of Euroscepticism for long predominated on the Greek left—in the social democratic Pasok till it first took office in 1981 and in the powerful but Stalinist Communist Party up to the present. It is underlain by a view of Greece as a "dependent" country oppressed by the US and the EU, rather than the relatively developed metropolitan capitalism that it is today (a similar view of Southern Ireland as a "neocolony" has been commonplace on the Republican left as well).[18]

Nevertheless, the reality of the eurozone needs to be acknowledged. Not simply is neoliberalism hard-wired into its institutional structure, but, as successive RMF reports have shown and is discussed by Christakis Georgiou elsewhere in the present issue, it involves a hierarchy in which relatively peripheral economies such as Greece, Portugal, Spain and southern Ireland serve as markets and debtors for the stronger Western European states, above all Germany.[19] Moreover, the current efforts to "reform" the eurozone are intended further to entrench a neoliberal policy regime and the subordination of the supposedly profligate peripheral economies.

The logic of resisting austerity leads ineluctably to stopping paying the debt and withdrawing from the euro. The idea that this involves an abandonment of internationalism implies a view of history in which there is a linear movement from the national to the European and then to the global levels. But history develops dialectically, with sudden twists and turns, and not in a straight line. A break with the euro in Greece or elsewhere that led to a successful defence of jobs, services and living standards could act as a beacon for a new, fighting internationalism that could start to create a very different Europe.

The second objection is more serious. Breaking with the euro wouldn't necessarily benefit working people. The return to the old Greek currency,

---

17: People Before Profit Alliance, 2009. For supporting analysis and argument, see Allen, 2009.

18: For a critique of the Irish version, see Allen, 1990.

19: Lapavitsas and others, 2010a and 2010b.

the drachma, would in all likelihood lead to a substantial devaluation. Indeed, as RMF points out, this is one of the main attractions of leaving the euro-zone: weaker economies such as Greece have been crucified by being tied to a German economy whose labour costs have fallen sharply relative to those of the rest of the eurozone without their having the traditional tool of devaluation to maintain their competitiveness.

Devaluation would reduce the price of Greek exports compared to those of their competitors. But, because devaluation also raises import prices, the result would be likely to be an increase in the rate of inflation and hence, unless workers respond effectively, a cut in real wages. At key moments in the history of British capitalism—1931, 1967, 1992, 2007—devaluation has served as a means of restoring competitiveness and raising the rate of exploitation. A version of Keynesianism (not necessarily that of Keynes himself) has seen devaluation and inflation as a more effective way of cutting real wages and boosting profitability than orthodox attempts to cut money wages.[20]

No doubt if the Papandreou government's austerity programme looked like it was failing, substantial sections of Greek capital might be attracted to default and devaluation to improve their competiveness and profitability. After all, as the latest RMF report shows, this is precisely the strategy pursued by Russia in 1998 and by Argentina in 2001 when confronted by financial crashes. But what this shows is that stopping paying the debt and withdrawing from the euro aren't a panacea. The distributional struggle that is going on now over which class is going to pay for the crisis would continue. This doesn't alter the fact that default and leaving the eurozone would, by the break with austerity involved, create more favourable conditions to defend wages, pensions, jobs and services, in particular by fighting for the broader alternative programmes put forward by RMF and People Before Profit.

A third objection—not apparently advanced in the Greek debates—would be that these programmes resemble nothing more than the alternative economic strategy put forward by the reformist left during the 1970s. As advocated by Tony Benn and his allies and by the Communist Party, this strategy proposed a series of measures to increase state control of the economy in order to break the hold of the multinational corporations and reconstruct a more dynamic and competitive British capitalism.[21]

It is indeed true that the content of the RMF and People Before Profit programmes substantially overlaps with that of the alternative economic

20: For Keynes's shifting views on wage-cutting, see Harman, 1996, pp15-17.
21: Holland, 1975, is the most substantial case made for the alternative economic strategy; for a critique, see Sparks, 1977.

strategy. But to dismiss them on these grounds is to ignore the radically different context from that of the 1970s. After a generation of deregulation that has produced a devastating economic slump, to advocate measures increasing political control of the economy is to pursue an offensive strategy that challenges the power of capital. It is crucial here how the programme is conceived. If it is treated, as the alternative economic strategy was, as a reformist attempt to rescue capitalism, then the dangers are obvious. But, if it is seen as a set of transitional demands, in the sense in which these are understood by the early Communist International and by Trotsky, then everything changes.

Transitional demands start from the immediate needs of the struggle, but the logic of pursuing them implies a conflict with capital. As the *Theses on Tactics* adopted by the Third Congress of the Comintern in 1921 put it:

> The communist parties do not put forward any minimum programme to strengthen and improve the tottering structure of capitalism. The destruction of that structure remains their guiding aim and their immediate mission. But to carry out this mission the communist parties must put forward demands whose fulfilment is an immediate and urgent working class need, and they must fight for these demands in mass struggle, regardless of whether or not they are compatible with the profit economy of the capitalist class or not... In place of the minimum programme of the reformists and centrists, the Comintern puts the struggle for the concrete needs of the proletariat, for a system of demands which in their totality disintegrate the power of the bourgeoisie, organise the proletariat, represent stages in the struggle for the proletarian dictatorship, and each of which expresses in itself the needs of the broadest masses, even if the broadest masses are not consciously in favour of the proletarian dictatorship.[22]

This is how the programmes under discussion should be understood. Not paying the debt, nationalising the banks, introducing capital controls, programmes of public investment—all these are necessary in order to address the needs of the vast majority in economies wrecked by speculation and slump. But implementing them would involve a massive confrontation with the existing structures of economic and political power. It therefore points towards, not a reconstruction of capitalism, but a move beyond it.

It doesn't follow that these programmes are universally valid—abandoning the euro, of course, means nothing in Britain—or complete. For example, starting as they do from the consequences of the economic and financial

---

22: Degras, 1956, volume I, pp248-249. Thanks to Sam Ashman for clarifying this issue.

crisis, neither addresses the crucial question of climate change. The Campaign against Climate Change has produced, with the support of several trade unions, a report and pamphlet setting out detailed proposals to create a million jobs in alternative energy industries, in refitting homes and public buildings on a low-carbon basis, and in public transport, a programme that has now been endorsed by the TUC. These proposals would have the double benefit of cutting CO_2 emissions and addressing the unemployment crisis that even the IMF now recognises. Who after Copenhagen doubts that they could only be won over the fiercest resistance by capital?[23]

And, of course, any programme is empty without the political will and social power to translate it into reality. Whether or not these emerge will depend on the developing movements against austerity. Resistance may need a political alternative, but that alternative will remain a dream without resistance. Nevertheless, one important element of an effective response by the anti-capitalist left to the crisis is explaining what we want as well as what we're against.

AC

References

Allen, Kieran, 1990, *Is Southern Ireland a Neocolony?* (Bookmarks), www.marxists.de/ireland/neocolony/index.htm

Allen, Kieran, 2009, *Ireland's Economic Crash: A Radical Agenda for Change* (The Liffey Press).

Callinicos, Alex, 2010, *Bonfire of Illusions* (Polity).

Campaign against Climate Change, 2009, *One Million Climate Jobs NOW!*, www.pcs.org.uk/en/resources/green_workplaces/green_campaigns/one-million-climate-jobs-now.cfm

Degras, Jane, 1956 (ed), *The Communist International 1919-43* (Oxford University Press, 3 volumes).

Eckholm, Erik, "Recession Raises Poverty Rate to a 15-Year High", *New York Times* (16 September), www.nytimes.com/2010/09/17/us/17poverty.html?_r=1&ref=todayspaper

Hall, Ben, Peggy Hollinger and Tony Barber, 2010, "Fiscal Rules Face Obstacles, warns Lagarde", *Financial Times* (14 September).

Harman, Chris, 1996, "The Crisis in Bourgeois Economics", *International Socialism* 71 (summer), http://pubs.socialistreviewindex.org.uk/isj71/harman.htm

Holland, Stuart, 1975, *The Socialist Challenge* (Quartet).

ILO-IMF, 2010, "The Challenges of Growth, Employment and Social Cohesion", www.osloconference2010.org/discussionpaper.pdf

Krugman, Paul, 2010, "The Third Depression", *New York Times* (27 June), www.nytimes.com/010/06/28/opinion/28krugman.html?_r=1&ref=columnists

Lapavitsas, Costas, A Kaltenbrunner, D Lindo, J Michell, J P Painceira, E Pires, J Powell,

---

23: Campaign against Climate Change, 2009.

A Stenfors and N Teles, 2010a, "Eurozone Crisis: Beggar Thyself and Thy Neighbour", Research on Money and Finance (March 2010), www.researchonmoneyandfinance.org/media/reports/eurocrisis/fullreport.pdf

Lapavitsas, Costas, A Kaltenbrunner, G Lambrinidis, D Lindo, J Meadway, J Michell, JP Painceira, E Pires, J Powell, A Stenfors and N Teles, 2010b, "The Eurozone between Austerity and Default", Research on Money and Finance (September), www.researchonmoneyandfinance.org/media/reports/RMF-Eurozone-Austerity-and-Default.pdf

Milne, Seumas, 2010a, "If the Cuts are to be Derailed, There Must Be an Alternative", *Guardian* (8 September), www.guardian.co.uk/commentisfree/2010/sep/08/cuts-derailed-alternative-unions

Milne, Seumas, 2010b, "This Tide is Already Changing Britain's Political Landscape", *Guardian* (15 September), www.guardian.co.uk/commentisfree/2010/sep/15/cuts-weaken-coalition-ed-miliband

Oakley, David, and Kerin Hope, 2010, "Greece Rules Out Possibility of Default", *Financial Times* (15 September).

People Before Profit Alliance, 2009, "An Alternative Economic Agenda", www.peoplebeforeprofit.ie/files/PBPA%20Alternative%20Economic%20Agenda_0.pdf.

Pimlott, Daniel, 2010, "Doubt Cast on Osborne's 'Fair' Cuts Pledge", *Financial Times* (22 August).

Press Association, 2010, "Nick Clegg Defends Radical Benefit Cuts", *Guardian* (16 September), www.guardian.co.uk/politics/2010/sep/16/clegg-defends-benefits-cuts

Rawnsley, Andrew, 2010, "When Ministers Talk of Lynch Mobs, You Know They're Scared", *Observer* (12 September), www.guardian.co.uk/commentisfree/2010/sep/12/spending-cuts-minsters-coalition

Reich, Robert, 2010, "Forget a Double-Dip, We're Still in One Long Big Dipper", *The Huffington Post* (14 August), www.huffingtonpost.com/robert-reich/forget-a-double-dip-were_b_682334.html

Sparks, Colin, 1977, "The Reformist Challenge", *International Socialism* 97 (1st series) (April), www.marxists.org/history/etol/newspape/isj/1977/no097/sparks.htm

There will be blood

On Sunday 19 September 2010 engineers finally sealed the Macondo oil well in the Gulf of Mexico, which had exploded five months earlier and caused the "the world's largest accidental offshore oil spill".[1] The explosion of the Deepwater Horizon oil rig in April killed 11 workers and the subsequent spill caused enormous damage to the local environment, but the effects of the disaster were felt far more widely. In Washington, Barack Obama has come under attack from a resurgent Republican right over his mishandling of the situation. BP, the corporation which owned the well, has been hammered by public opinion and the markets. But the disaster has also brought into sharp focus the danger posed to workers and the environment by the increasingly risky strategies for extracting oil that are being pursued by the fossil fuels industry.

Anatomy of a disaster

BP had high hopes of the possible gains to be made from the Macondo oil well. As Ed Crooks of the *Financial Times* reported:

> Less than a year ago, Deepwater Horizon seemed to have set BP on a very different course. Last summer, the group drilled the deepest well ever developed for a commercial operation and struck oil. On September 2, it announced it had discovered a "giant" field, christened Tiber, which was likely to hold more than 500 million barrels of recoverable oil. BP's shares rose by 4 percent in a single day, a rare event for a company of BP's size. Moreover, it seemed that the initial reaction was, if anything, understated.

1: Crooks, 2010b. At around five million barrels, only the eight million spilled intentionally by Iraqi forces retreating from Kuwait in 1991 is greater.

Tiber was a harbinger of a new dawn for the company, in which production from the deep water of the Gulf would drive global growth.[2]

But despite BP's optimistic outlook, its cavalier attitude to safety meant that an explosion like that on the Deepwater Horizon was an accident waiting to happen. Subcontracting and cost-cutting had been central concerns of BP's operation for years. In an article examining the BP Texas City refinery disaster, which cost the lives of 15 workers in March 2005, Tomas Mac Sheoin quotes a consultant who claims that "BP's culture was designed to be the most efficient cost-cutter in the industry...out of that came too many corners cut on maintenance and safety".[3]

BP had contracted a corporation called Transocean to handle the extraction process at the Macondo oil well. The *Wall Street Journal* reported that the corporation had seen a rising tally of accidents on its operations, claiming that "nearly three of every four incidents that triggered federal investigations into safety and other problems on deepwater drilling rigs in the Gulf of Mexico since 2008 have been on rigs operated by Transocean".[4]

At the time of the disaster a group of executives were visiting the rig to celebrate its safety record. Workers were sealing an exploratory well before moving into production when a methane gas bubble rose up the drill column, causing the explosion.[5] The rig lacked an acoustic trigger, a remote controlled safety device that could have sealed the well before the explosion took place. The trigger is not legally required in either the US or Britain, unlike Norway and Brazil which demand them by law. The device would have cost $500,000—small change compared to the $560 million replacement cost of the rig, let alone the billions in liabilities BP now faces.[6]

The effect of the explosion on the local environment has been disastrous. According to the *Guardian*:

> The White House says the BP oil spill is probably the greatest environmental disaster the US has faced, but the true impact on surrounding ecosystems could take months or even years to emerge. Experts say the unprecedented depth of the spill, combined with the use of chemicals that broke the oil down before it reached the surface, poses an unknown threat.[7]

2: Crooks, 2010a.
3: Mac Sheoin, 2010.
4: *Wall Street Journal*, 10 May 2010.
5: For more on the explosion and the immediate aftermath, see Bergfeld, 2010.
6: *Wall Street Journal*, 28 April 2010.
7: *Guardian*, 31 May 2010.

The use of the chemical dispersant Corexit in the Gulf led to severe criticisms from scientists. The two versions of the chemical used by BP were "carcinogenic, mutagenic, and highly toxic", and are banned from use in Britain due to their damaging effect on sea life.[8]

"Louisiana, the nearest state to the leaking well, some 42 miles offshore, has been the most impacted. The state's governor, Bobby Jindal, said more than 100 miles of its 400-mile coast had so far been polluted." Discussing the effects on wildlife, Prosanta Chakrabarty, a Louisiana State University fish biologist, said that "every fish and invertebrate contacting the oil is probably dying. I have no doubt about that".[9]

The economic ramifications of the environmental disaster intensified the public outcry over the oil spill. The fishing industry is a major employer in the Gulf of Mexico, worth over $2.4 billion a year.[10] The *Financial Times* interviewed a local fisherman who said that "the way things are looking now, we won't be able to fish for a few months". "This is the very beginning of our peak season," he said. "This is the time we work 25 days a month." The economy also depends on services provided to the fishing industry:

> Rene Cross Junior, manager of the nearby Cypress Cove marina, said 30 to 40 boats were leaving each day to help clean up the spill. He was worried for his business, which includes a hotel used by competitive fishermen. "We were booked for fishing every weekend from June through August," he said. "But this is going to devastate the fishing.[11]

The long-term concerns about fishing in the Gulf were exacerbated by the meagre haul of shrimp and oysters when waters were reopened for fishing. Most fishermen with their own boats have been employed by BP to assist the clean-up operation, but many who depend on the fishing industry for their livelihoods have been left out of work. The knock-on effects could be disastrous for the long-term employment prospects in the region:

> Local seafood buyers bereft of supply are closing their docks to keep losses from multiplying, leaving shrimpers who couldn't get hired by BP with few outlets to sell their catch. Meanwhile, national frozen fish buyers are driving

---

8:    *Guardian*, 20 May 2010.
9:    *Guardian*, 31 May 2010.
10:   Hall, Jervis and Levin, 2010.
11:   Crooks, 2010a.

down prices, threatening to eviscerate the Gulf seafood industry's future markets by signing new contracts for Asian and Latin American shrimp.[12]

Even Barack Obama's attempts to quell fears over the safety of Gulf seafood by serving shrimp at his birthday party are unlikely to overcome what could be a generational economic and environmental shock to the region.

Obama has faced growing criticism over his failure to deal with the disaster decisively. It is a sign of how disillusioned and demobilised much of Obama's base must be that he can be outflanked on the issue by Sarah Palin, who popularised the slogan "Drill, baby, drill".[13]

When Obama visited the region in June, he told reporters he was going there to find out "whose ass to kick", while his secretary of the interior Ron Salazar promised to keep a boot "on BP's throat".[14] Despite the rhetoric, various attempts to stop the leaking oil failed before a temporary seal was established on 15 July, almost three months after the explosion.

In an effort to divert criticism, Obama took to calling BP "British Petroleum", a title the corporation had ditched in 1998. This rhetorical shift unsurprisingly elicited howls of outrage from the likes of the *Daily Mail*, complaining of "anti-British prejudice".[15] The Tory mayor of London Boris Johnson commented that there was "something slightly worrying about the anti-British rhetoric that seems to be permeating from America".[16] The revelations about BP's lobbying of the British government over a prisoner transfer deal with Libya added fuel to the fire when secretary of state Hillary Clinton sought to ratchet up the pressure on BP by suggesting an inquiry into whether or not the corporation had played a role in securing the early release of the man convicted over the Lockerbie bombing, Abdelbaset al-Megrahi.[17]

As Gary Younge observes, "For some his performance over the BP oil spill is metaphoric—an inability to articulate and reflect the public's urgency and discontent".[18] But it would be a mistake to write off the genuine concern shown by many Americans about the environmental damage caused at the

---

12: *Los Angeles Times*, 26 August 2010.
13: Palin argued that the problem was with the government's response to the accident and failure to hold BP accountable for any wrongdoing and insisted that "increased domestic oil production will make us a more secure, prosperous, and peaceful nation"—Silva, 2010.
14: Crooks, 2010a.
15: *Daily Mail*, 7 June 2010.
16: BBC News, 2010.
17: *Guardian*, 15 July 2010. For analysis of how al-Megrahi was framed for the bombing, see Basketter, 2009.
18: Younge, 2010.

height of the spill: a poll in late May showed that 50 percent of Americans believed that protecting the environment should be a higher concern than promoting economic growth against 43 percent who thought otherwise.[19]

The US administration eventually established a compensation fund for those affected by the spill which BP would fund over three and a half years to the tune of $20 billion.[20] But it seems increasingly unlikely that even this amount will be paid out by BP. The new chief executive of the corporation, Bob Dudley, told City analysts that the total was likely to be lower than previously expected and that a facility had been set up to repay money from the fund back into BP's coffers. Analysts at Citigroup predict that the corporation could resume paying out profit dividends as early as February.[21] BP also moved to shift the blame for the explosion towards its contractors Transocean and Halliburton in what was widely perceived as an attempt to further minimise the amount it would be forced to pay out in compensation.[22]

BP has already shed around $9 billion in assets in order to cover the costs of the compensation fund, and it hopes to sell over $20 billion more. Credit Suisse has argued that BP is pursuing a "shrink to grow" strategy.[23]

Yet, after all the drama and the devastation, the *Financial Times* could smugly conclude, "For the global oil industry, it looks like being no more than a bump in the road towards further exploitation of deepwater oil reserves, even in the Gulf of Mexico".[24] This reflects the entrenched power of the fossil fuel corporations and their determination to continue squeezing oil from the planet.

Beyond the horizon

As global oil reserves dwindle, the struggle to control access to them has intensified. Rigs like Deepwater Horizon, drilling down over a mile into the seabed, have become a profitable proposition as oil prices have risen. As prices are certain to rise even higher as we approach the peak of oil production, the exploitation of ever more inaccessible sources of oil will commercially become viable.

An example of the lengths oil companies are prepared to go to in order to procure oil is provided by the current attempts by firms such as Cairn Energy to drill in the Arctic. In response to Cairn's claims that the

---

19: Hall, Jervis and Levin, 2010.
20: To put that figure into some sort of context, BP made $25 billion in profits in 2008.
21: *Guardian*, 13 September 2010.
22: *Guardian*, 8 September 2010.
23: Wardell, 2010.
24: Crooks, 2010c.

process is "relatively straightforward" and that "our programme is conventional", John Sauven argues:

> This industry has lost its grip on reality. Anyone who has seen the remarkable images coming from the Arctic over the last few days will know how unusual, dangerous and extreme this business has become. While icebergs the size of football stadiums are towed out of a rig's path, ships equipped with high-pressure water cannons blast smaller chunks into submission. And all the while the clock is ticking. As the winter freeze edges nearer, this frantic exploration company rushes to finish the job before sheet-ice cuts off the region completely.[25]

The exploitation of tar sands in Alberta, Canada, is another example of the trend. Tar sands contain bitumen which can be extracted and combined with water to create a form of synthetic crude oil. According to Greenpeace:

> Extracting tar sands bitumen from the forest wilderness in Alberta, Canada has major environmental impacts—not least the significant increase in greenhouse gases (GHG) produced by extracting and processing the bitumen into a usable product. The extraction process is thought to produce on average three times the GHG of conventional oil production.[26]

Tar sand exploitation leads to massive deforestation in Canada and threatens numerous First Nation indigenous areas. Each barrel of finished oil requires two barrels of fresh water, the leftovers of which are dumped in a toxic reservoir.

Tar sand exploitation is also incredibly inefficient. In order to measure the efficiency of preparing a given fuel, one must compare the energy return on energy input (EROEI)—that is, how much energy has to be used to extract the fuel. In his book *The Party's Over*, Richard Heinberg argues that imported oil today has an EROEI of between "8.4 (that is, 8.4 units of energy returned on every unit invested in exploration, drilling, building of drill rigs, transportation, the housing of production workers, etc) and 11.1, depending on the source". This compares with an EROEI of over 100 for oil discovered before 1950, and 40 between 1950 and 1970.[27] Estimates for tar sands EROEI range from 1.5 to 5.2.[28]

25: Sauven, 2010.
26: Greenpeace, 2010.
27: Heinberg, 2003, p138.
28: Hall, 2008. The figure of 7.2 given in one estimate relates only to tar sand found on the surface that need not be mined.

The scramble for oil also lies behind much of the US policy in the Middle East. The US's attempt to occupy Iraq and control its emerging rivals' access to Iraq's oil reserves has been a failure. Iraq's first major oil deal was a $3 billion contract with the China National Petroleum Company in 2008.[29] Moreover, the failure of the US to subdue the resistance in Iraq and Afghanistan has increased the confidence of China to compete for control of oil resources elsewhere—notably in Africa.[30] In fact, the reduction of easily accessible oil reserves gives leverage to several rivals of the US:

As the world runs out of easily accessible oil reserves, international oil companies such as BP, ExxonMobil, Shell and ConocoPhillips—once classified as "supermajors" due to their dominance of the market—have found themselves sidelined by national oil companies which control the rights over the largest oil reserves.

More than three quarters of all oil reserves are now controlled by state-owned companies such as Saudi Aramco (Saudi Arabia), Gazprom (Russia), the National Iranian Oil Company and Petroleums of Venezuela.[31]

The relationship between capitalism, the state and oil is readily apparent in the case of the BP oil spill. Despite the oil corporations' attempts at greenwash, rebranding themselves as deeply concerned about the environment, they still rely on fossil fuels for the bulk of their profits. As Paul McGarr argued in this journal a number of years ago:

There is indeed no reason in abstract why capitalism has to be dependent on fossil fuels and industries linked to them. Capitalism can profit from anything it can turn into a commodity... Once patterns of production become established and with them great concentrations of wealth and power established, they are hugely resistant to change. The people who head the giant corporations, and who embody the logic they must follow to survive and expand as profit-seeking beasts, will resist with all their power anything which fundamentally threatens their current basis of profit and power—the fossil fuel based economy.[32]

Oil is the lifeblood, the lubricant of capitalism. Without it, the gears

---

29: *New York Times*, 28 August 2008.
30: Assaf, 2008.
31: Bergfeld, 2010.
32: McGarr, 2005, pp119-120.

of production would seize up. As the price of oil rises, so will tensions over access to and control over it. And, of course, the continuing burning of it and other fossil fuels is bringing about catastrophic climate change that threatens the future of life on this planet. All of this underlines the importance of fighting for programmes such as the One Million Climate Jobs Campaign that has now been endorsed by the TUC.

JJ

References

Assaf, Simon, 2008, "Multinationals' Scramble for Africa Fuels New Conflicts", *Socialist Worker* (9 August), http://www.socialistworker.co.uk/art.php?id=15663

Basketter, Simon, 2009, "Lockerbie Evidence Shows Grave Miscarriage of Justice", *Socialist Worker* (29 August), www.socialistworker.co.uk/art.php?id=18869

BBC News, 2010, "BP Oil Spill: Obama Comments 'Not anti-British'", www.bbc.co.uk/news/10303619

Bergfeld, Mark, 2010, "Not Beyond Petroleum", *Socialist Review* (July/August), www.socialistreview.org.uk/article.php?articlenumber=11333

Crooks, Ed, 2010a, "BP: The Inside Story", *Financial Times* (2 July).

Crooks, Ed, 2010b, "BP Oil Spill Well 'Effectively Dead', Says US", *Financial Times* (19 September).

Crooks, Ed, 2010c, "BP Leak just a Bump in Road for Oil Industry", *Financial Times* (19 September).

Greenpeace, 2010, "Tar Sands in Your Tank", www.greenpeace.org.uk/media/reports/tar-sands-your-tank

Hall, Charles, 2008, "Unconventional Oil: Tar Sands and Shale Oil", www.theoildrum.com/node/3839

Hall, Mimi, Rick Jervis and Alan Levin, 2010, "Is Oil Spill becoming Obama's Katrina?", *USA Today* (27 May), www.usatoday.com/news/washington/2010-05-27-Spill-poll_N.htm

Heinberg, Richard, 2003, *The Party's Over: War, Oil and the Fate of Industrial Societies* (Clairview).

Mac Sheoin, Tomas, 2010, "Chemical Catastrophe: From Bhopal to BP Texas City", *Monthly Review* (September), http://monthlyreview.org/100901macsheoin.php

McGarr, Paul, 2005, "On the Road to Catastrophe: Capitalism and Climate Change", *International Socialism* 107 (summer), www.isj.org.uk/?id=119

Sauven, John, 2010, "Weaning the World off Oil", *Guardian* (31 August), www.guardian.co.uk/commentisfree/cif-green/2010/aug/31/wean-world-off-oil-greenpeace-arctic-protest

Silva, Mark, 2010, "Gulf Oil Spill: Palin Still Wants to 'Drill Here, Drill Now'", *Los Angeles Times* (3 May), http://latimesblogs.latimes.com/dcnow/2010/05/gulf-oil-spill-sarah-palin-still-wants-to-drill-baby-drill.html

Wardell, Jane, 2010, "BP's Life on Frontiers of Energy Industry at Risk", Associated Press (29 August), www.google.com/hostednews/ap/article/ALeqM5gRUo7dMpL3LMzwiyQVN_a-R5DnQAD9HTA62Oo

Younge, Gary, 2010, "Tea Party is Creating Waves for Republicans", *Guardian* (9 June), www.guardian.co.uk/commentisfree/cifamerica/2010/jun/09/tea-party-success-us-primaries

Greece: striking back

Greece has been at the heart of the struggle over austerity in Europe. Panos Garganas is editor of the weekly paper Workers' Solidarity and a leading member of the Sosialistiko Ergatiko Komma (SEK, Socialist Workers Party), Greek sister organisation of the British SWP. He talked to Alex Callinicos in Athens on 8 September, the day that a five-hour strike by railway and public transport workers shut the city down, announcing the resumption of hostilities between the Greek working class and the social democratic government of George Papandreou after the summer break.

First of all, I want to ask you about how severe the economic crisis is in Greece. Recently there was a shocking statistic that April to June 2010 was the seventh successive quarter that Greece has experienced a contraction of output.

It is getting worse—this is clear from the latest results. The predictions at the beginning of the year were for a contraction, but they were hoping it would be anything between 1 and 2 percent. Now it's heading for between 4 and 5 percent. The tourist industry is badly hit. Construction in August was at the lowest point in 15 years. These are areas on which the Greek economy depends, so obviously the crisis is getting worse in terms of the recession.

And it may get worse also in terms of the fiscal crisis, although the government are proudly announcing that they have cut the deficit by 40 percent in the first seven months of the year. But there are doubts whether this will continue, because they've been very tough in the area of cuts, but they're doing badly in the area of state revenue. The recession is hitting their plans. They were hoping for more money through raising value added tax from 19 to 23 percent, but that's not working in the recession. So both in terms of economic activity and in terms of the fiscal crisis, things are getting worse.

Just to follow up on that, even if the fiscal measures aren't working from the government's perspective, what sort of impact are they having on people's working conditions, their income, and so on?
First of all, they're having a bad impact on unemployment because no people are getting state jobs—there's a ban. There are also short-term contract workers whose contracts are not being renewed. Government policy is pushing unemployment up directly through what's happening at the state level and indirectly because of the recession its measures are intensifying. So unemployment is heading for a figure of over one million, which is huge for a country the size of Greece. The whole population is 11 million, so one million unemployed is gigantic.

What would you say the government's strategy is? How it does hope politically to deal with the resistance and get through and satisfy the European Union and the International Monetary Fund, and how strong is its position?
Well, the government is hoping that the package of measures it voted through parliament will be the end of the story and that it will not have to go through a new round of attacks at the general level, as it has done in the past six months. In the past six months it has voted through the agreement with the IMF and a number of cuts in hospitals and so on. So it's hoping that this is out of the way and that what will follow is confrontations with particular sectors. It's hoping there will be no more general strikes, because it says it's put behind it the measures that provoke the whole of the working class, like social security "reform", pension "reform", and so on.

What it has in mind is that it will be able to isolate sectors—for example, power workers, bank workers, who are opposed to privatisations that have to be carried through. At that level the government has no choice—this portion of the plan agreed with the IMF and the EU has to be implemented in the coming months. So in political terms it is hoping it will not provoke any generalised response and it will be able to handle individual strikes in sectors that will come under the hammer in the coming months.

Some hope! The government is weaker politically as a result of what has happened in the first half of the year. It knows it has provoked the strongest response from the working class since the junta collapsed in

1974 and that is a fact that has created a lot of discontent in Pasok, the ruling party. The government has just been reshuffled and there's been an attempt to bring back into the government old hands of Pasok so that they can cool down the feelings of revolt.

But it is very doubtful whether this operation will work. There are elections coming up on 7 November. They concern local authorities but there has been a new set-up where the country has been divided into 13 regions, so the elections for the leaders of the regions are practically national elections, like general elections. The government is very worried that people's anger will be expressed in a hammering for Pasok that will weaken the government even further.

There's clearly been a formidable response by the Greek working class movement to the austerity measures—six general strikes in as many months during the first half of 2010. But how would you assess in more depth the response, both at the rank and file level where, as you've already said, there's considerable combativity, and also in terms of the trade union leadership, given that the most powerful wing of the union bureaucracy is aligned to Pasok, the ruling party?

During the summer and coming into the autumn, there has been a debate going on: did we achieve anything by having all those general strikes? Some people say the government has been able to push through what it wanted, so it was all in vain. This argument is something that is affecting people, that is pushing people back. But at the same time, there are developments in the opposite direction.

During the summer the government tried to confront truck owners and owner-drivers, who were out on strike, by imposing military discipline and ordering them back to work, to break up the strike. That didn't work. The government was forced to go into dialogue with their unions to turn them back. The strong tactic was practically destroyed. And if it didn't work for truck owners—people would say they could be easily isolated from the working class (since they are owners, they're not even working class)—the government won't be able to use it against, for example, power workers and other powerful sections of the working class.

Yes, the general strikes did not bring down the government, which would be the only way to avoid the measures being voted for in parliament, but they were not a failure in terms of creating a movement that provides the background for every sector that will fight in the coming months.

But the trade union bureaucracy is accepting this argument that the general strikes failed and suggesting that we should try other tactics. Sections of the left also accepted the argument and say we should now orient on the elections. And we have to argue that there's no other way but to fight back and build a strike movement, using the general strikes of the past six months to build this movement up.

As you just said, the stakes are very high in Greece: to defeat the austerity measures really requires bringing down the government. It seems to me clear that lots of people here understand this. But then naturally that poses the question: if you're prepared to see the government fall, what's the alternative? There's been some discussion on the Greek radical left about what the logic of resisting austerity is. Some people, including SEK, have argued that it's necessary to refuse to repay the debt, to be prepared to withdraw from the euro, indeed if necessary from the European Union as such, and other people on the left say this is a nationalist regression and that it isn't a viable strategy. So I'd be interested to know what you think about these questions.

One of the most important developments politically in Greece has been that these questions are being debated in public. This is partly because of the severity of the crisis: there was a meeting in Como a few days back where Jean-Claude Trichet, the president of the European Central Bank, had to face the question of whether Greece might get out of the euro. He replied, of course, that this is unthinkable, but the crisis itself is forcing bank governors to debate the issue.

The good development is that this debate is also happening among rank and file activists and the left. So in the last three or four months, there's been an initiative by left-wing economists posing this alternative, that we should stop paying the debt and confront the consequences—that is, nationalise the banks and go back to a national currency, because the European authorities would not accept a step like that.

In terms of the logic of this proposal, it's formidable. Greece pays €1 billion every week to service the debt at the level it is now. And the level will be increasing even if the IMF-EU plan works. They project that the level of the debt as a percentage of gross domestic product will go up, so the payments that the Greek state has to carry out in the coming years will go up, and they will be unbearable. So the idea that we will stop these payments and confront the consequences is very concrete. It's becoming very popular with people who are involved in the strikes.

Practically, everywhere where we raise these questions the response is: "Yes, it's an excellent idea, but how could we do it?" This is where the debate is heading now, I think: people will start discussing more seriously how these measures can be implemented.

Sections of the left have responded that this is isolationism. There's been criticism that this is the wrong way for the left to go, that this is the way Latin American populists have gone, that in Europe we have an alternative—building alliances inside the EU so that the left and the unions and any progressive movements will pressurise towards a reform of the Maastricht Treaty and the European Central Bank, for a change of policy at the EU level. This is an idea that is in the air. There's no sign of anyone in terms of governments or political parties at the EU level moving in that direction. So promising Greek strikers that there's going to be a reform like that is pie in the sky. People have to fight to save jobs and pensions and wages in the here and now.

And the proposal that we should stop paying the debt meets these requirements. The so-called internationalist alternative misses the boat. So this is the first thing that has to be clarified in this debate. At the second level, of course, there are political forces that think that if we stop paying the debt and withdraw from the discipline of the euro, we can have a revival of Greek capitalism. But first of all there aren't that many people who argue along these lines. And secondly to say that we are in danger of becoming Greek nationalists if we go in that direction is overstating the dangers. If a default is forced on the Greek state, and the left argues for stopping paying the debt and for nationalising the banks and going back to the drachma and so on, it will have to confront the sections of the ruling class that may have it in mind that OK, now we can have a nice devaluation and make the workers pay. It'll be a fight, but it'll be the next fight we have to face.

OK—last question: Greece has in relative terms the largest radical left in Europe and one of its key sections, namely Synaspismos (the Coalition of the Left of Movements and Ecology), is in crisis. SEK is part of another grouping, ANT.AR.SY.A (Anti-capitalist Left Cooperation—the acronym means Rebellion in Greek), which has been drawing more forces towards it. What would you say are the prospects for the radical and revolutionary left in Greece and how much influence do you think they can have over the development of the struggle in this crisis?

There's been a concerted attack on the left throughout the past few months. Pasok in government uses the argument that the left that supports the strikes is destroying the economy. Papandreou said in parliament: you think you're destroying Greek capitalism—in fact you're destroying the Greek economy. And that has been the line of attack from the government and the media, and it's putting a lot of pressure on the left.

They're putting pressure on the Communist Party (KKE), which has considerable influence in the unions. During the general strikes KKE activists were organising the picket lines stopping the ferry boats moving out of the port of Piraeus and there was hysteria that they were keeping tourists away. The same pressures are on Synaspismos, which was under attack from 2008, when it supported the youth revolt, and the then right wing government and the media were saying that effectively you're supporting the anarchists who are smashing bank windows and so on.

So one element that we have to keep in mind in these debates on the Greek left is that the whole of the Greek left is under pressure. There's a huge ideological attack and the fact that we have a social democratic government means that it can be orchestrated. Sections of the left have capitulated. The right wing of Synaspismos, who have broken away, are moving in the direction of collaboration with Pasok. So in a sense this campaign has been effective—they have produced a split in Synaspismos.

The problem is that the rest of Synaspismos are not clear about how to handle this attack, this split. Rather than say that, well, these are people who have capitulated under these pressures, we have to make sure we reply effectively, they are seeking ways of minimising the significance of the split. You remember the Velvet Revolution of 1989 in Czechoslovakia? They're thinking of a velvet divorce, which isn't the most effective tactic, because it gives a lot of leeway for the breakaway group to keep pulling them to the right. This is what's happening in Synaspismos. Then, because of that, there's polarisation. There are people who want to shift to the left and the leadership is trying to contain these centrifugal forces.

The far left and the regroupment of the anti-capitalist left, ANT.AR.SY.A, are a counterweight to these tendencies, both in terms of activity, supporting sections of workers who go on strike, plus politically and ideologically—politically by raising the question of not paying the debt, which is a very powerful weapon for the left, and ideologically by explaining that the social-democratic forces have tied their fortunes with Greek capitalism. They will go down as Greek capitalism is in such a huge crisis, but the left has to make sure that it isn't part of the shipwreck. This is what's at stake.

I think the regroupment on the left will proceed. There are people who are breaking with Pasok, people who are breaking with Synaspismos, and they are seeking an alternative. We have not reached the stage yet where ANT.AR.SY.A is a home for these people—by no means. But the hope that this will happen in the coming period is alive.

Just on the struggle immediately ahead, there's going to be a big demonstration in Salonica this Saturday, 11 September, as Papandreou launches his autumn plans, after the reshuffle and going into the elections, and the unions—even Pasok-supporting unions—have called for a demonstration. People are saying it's going to be very big. It will be the launching pad for all the things we've been discussing. Bus workers and transport workers in Athens have initiated the autumn campaign by going on strike today. Demonstrators in Salonica will give a much bigger push.

Then we'll see how it goes on from there. For example, we'll see how this coordinated campaign started by rail workers and transport workers will continue. Greek Rail is bankrupt. There's a lot of pressure from the IMF for the government to dismantle it—privatise what can be privatised and forget about the rest. Rail workers are under the hammer. So one of the confrontations of the autumn will be around rail workers and transport workers in Athens.

Power workers are also under attack, but they are much more powerful, and their union is to the left of the rail workers' union, so the government is very careful in confronting them. But it will have to confront them. And then there's the question of privatising the public banks, which produced a confrontation during the summer. Hellenic Postbank has a strong union. They went on strike and were very effective. So the idea that the government will be able to sell Postbank to one of the other banks, bolstering the banking sector, is in the plans of the government and will produce confrontation.

So there are many areas where there will be bitter strikes in the coming months. We'll see whether we'll be successful in generalising them and producing a wave of general strikes in support of these groups of workers. That's what's at stake—after the election, I would say. The election result will set the tone. If the government is hammered, it will have second thoughts about going into any of these confrontations. If it is successful, then it will go for them, and there's going to be a fight.

Postscript: There is a fight already. The demo in Salonica was big (20,000 is the official police figure) and militant. Since then, rail workers have staged a very successful 24-hour strike on 14 September in response to the government's announcement of its plans for privatisation. The rail unions plan to continue with stoppages for five days in late September. It's going to be a hot autumn in Greece.

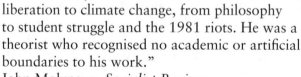

The "South Africa moment": Palestine, Israel and the boycott

Tom Hickey and Philip Marfleet

Israel faces a new challenge—one the country's leading strategists consider increasingly effective. This does not come mainly from the towns and refugee camps of the West Bank or Gaza, but from an energetic global movement of solidarity with the Palestinians. Since its launch in 2004 the campaign for boycott, divestment and sanctions (BDS) has stimulated a host of collective actions across five continents, demanding an end to military rule and to Israel's occupation, and raising important questions about the Zionist movement and imperial power in the Middle East.

The invasion of Iraq in 2003 refocused attention on imperialist interests in the region, highlighting the complex web of relationships through which the US and its allies maintain access to oil and strategic territory. With support from Egypt, Turkey and the Gulf States, the US mobilised overwhelming military force against Iraq's Ba'athist regime. At the same time it made enormous efforts to exclude Israel from the confrontation. Even the most strident neoconservatives among advisers of President George W Bush were aware of the danger to US allies of direct Israeli engagement in the Arab world.

Bush renewed his commitments to the Israeli government, therefore, supporting its policy of colonisation of the West Bank and increasing military aid that was already at historically high levels. The *quid pro quo* was an Israeli

assurance to stay out of the war zone, at least publicly.[1] It nonetheless drama-
tised the historic links between the US and Israel: one result was that protests
over the invasion worldwide made Palestine a central anti-imperialist issue.
Everywhere the keffiyeh—the Palestinian headscarf—was worn on demonstrations as a symbol of resistance and as a statement of solidarity with both
Iraqis and Palestinians.

This support was timely for Palestinian activists, who faced acute
difficulties. Successive Israeli governments had ensured there could be no
meaningful "peace" agreement in which Palestinians would control even
a fraction of the land to which they had a historic claim. At the same time
the Israeli government pursued aggressive settlement of the West Bank,
the ghettoisation of Gaza and discrimination against Israel's Arab population. It was aided by a Palestinian national leadership determined to contain
mass activism and increasingly reliant on a CIA-trained security force.[2] The
national movement was weaker than at any time since the establishment of
the Palestine Liberation Organisation (PLO) in 1964.

In 2004, aware of new possibilities on the international scene, a small
group of academics and writers launched the Palestinian Campaign for
an Academic and Cultural Boycott of Israel (Pacbi). This enjoyed immediate success and the following year a Boycott, Divestment and Sanctions
Campaign national committee (BNC) was established, calling for a
worldwide boycott of Israeli products and firms and for action against companies trading with or investing in Israel. It also called for governments and
international bodies to impose economic sanctions directly on Israel. The
new movement focused on human rights and international law, pointing to
Israel's discrimination against Arab citizens, its illegal settlements, the military regime in the West Bank and the siege of Gaza. It asked governments,
including Israel's closest allies, to require the same conduct on the part of
Israel as that expected from other states.

The BNC has called on trade unions and student unions, NGOs and
organisations of civil society to organise boycotts and campaigns for divestment, and to apply pressure for official sanctions. It encourages collective
action that can be organised in the workplace, on campuses, in trade union
branches and in communities. The movement has mushroomed, providing
Palestinian activists with an opportunity to build coalitions of solidarity

---

1:   There were many accounts of clandestine Israeli involvement: see, for example, Borger,
2003.
2:   By the late 1990s the Palestinian Authority, which administered areas under notional
PLO control, had 30,000 US-trained police at its disposal. See Hawks, 1998.

worldwide. The BNC now embraces almost 200 Palestinian organisations—marking unprecedented unity across a society in which there have been extremes of factionalism and conflict—and has won tangible support in Europe, Africa, Asia, Australia and North America. This article examines the background to these developments, the lessons from previous campaigns for boycotts and sanctions, and the implications for the Palestinian movement.

Double standards

The call for boycott, divestment and sanctions (BDS) has emerged in the context of a historic crisis of the Palestinian national movement in which the key issue is the ability of Palestinians to act as sole agents of their liberation. For decades leaders of the movement insisted that national liberation was a matter exclusively for Palestinians. They expressed scepticism about external involvement and often actively opposed the participation of those who wished to engage alongside them. While they requested solidarity in principle they opposed concrete action, especially when this involved collective activity in the Arab states. This had the effect of isolating the Palestinians and containing the radicalising impacts of Palestinian struggle, notably the intifadas of 1987 and 2000. The BDS campaign has reversed this trend, promoting collective action which links those involved both with the Palestinians and with others engaged in solidarity worldwide. One index of the effectiveness of the new approach is the furious reaction in Israel, where the campaign has engaged much media attention and where, in July 2010, members of the Knesset (parliament) introduced a bill to penalise Israelis and others deemed to have endorsed calls for BDS.[3]

According to the Reut Institute, an Israeli think tank, BDS has become an important element in what it calls the global "delegitimisation" of Israel:

> The effectiveness of Israel's delegitimisers, who represent a relatively marginal political and societal force in Europe and North America, stems from their ability to engage and mobilise others by blurring the lines with Israel's critics. They do so by branding Israel as a pariah and "apartheid" state; rallying coalitions around "outstanding issues" such as the "Gaza blockade"; making pro-Palestinian activity trendy; and promoting grassroots activities such as boycotts, divestments and sanctions as a way to "correct Israel's ways".[4]

3: See Lis, 2010.
4: See report of the Reut Institute, 2010.

For Reut, the "Delegitimisation Network tarnishes Israel's reputation, constrains its military capabilities, and advances the one-state solution".[5] It views the BDS campaign as an important part of networks with potential to pose an "existential threat" to Israel—"a systemic, systematic, and increasingly effective assault on its political and economic model".[6]

This assessment is important: Reut is a "national security" policy group close to the state that expresses the views of leading Israeli politicians and strategists. It recognises, in effect, that BDS raises issues about occupation, dispossession, racist exclusion and persecution of the Palestinians which are not only subversive of Israeli policy but of the histories that sustain it. Reut also notes, "Israel has been successfully branded by its adversaries as a violent country that violates international law and human rights".[7] The BDS campaign has highlighted Israel's double standards and those of governments which present themselves as guardians of freedom and rule of law, but ignore the judgements of their own courts in relation to Israel.[8]

"Creeping apartheid"

The Israeli writer Gershom Gorenberg, a historian of the post-1967 settlement process, sees occupation of the West Bank and Gaza in 1967 as Israel's acquisition of "an empire".[9] By the end of 2008 the West Bank (not including East Jerusalem) contained 121 settlements viewed by Israel's Interior Ministry as official "communities", plus 12 other large settlements and small settlement points on land annexed by Israel in 1967 and made part of Jerusalem. There were, in addition, some 100 unrecognised settlements usually described in the Israeli media as "outposts".[10] The number of settlers in the West Bank stood at 479,500.[11] They have been part of a long-term plan, says Gorenberg, "to create facts that would determine the final status of the land, to sculpt the political reality".[12]

5:   Reut Institute, 2010.
6:   Reut Institute, 2010.
7:   Reut Institute, 2010.
8:   For example, in July 2004 the International Court of Justice found Israel's "separation wall" and its settlements in the Occupied Territories to be contrary to international law. Western governments ignored the ruling.
9:   Gorenberg, 2007, p5.
10:   B'Tselem, no date a.
11:   According to Israel's Central Bureau of Statistics, 285,800 settlers were living in the West Bank, excluding East Jerusalem. In addition, based on growth statistics for the entire population of Jerusalem, the settler population in East Jerusalem at the end of 2008 was estimated at 193,700 (B'Tselem, no date a).
12:   Gorenberg, 2007, p364.

In one respect the project has been successful—Israel has implanted communities that are forward bases in areas many Zionist leaders long wished to annex outright. These have been integrated into Israeli territory "proper". They are connected administratively and physically to Israel's major cities, with many effectively forming suburban commuter zones. But settlement has not achieved all the aims set out by its architects, among whom expansionist zealots hoped to incorporate swathes of territory by establishing colonies which would populate "Eretz Israel" ("the Land of Israel" or "the Whole Land of Israel") and evict its existing inhabitants.[13] Jewish communities of the West Bank have remained a small minority among the wider Palestinian population, reliant upon an army of occupation to facilitate land grabs and the seizure of water resources, and to suppress local resistance.

For 20 years after Israel's invasion of the West Bank and Gaza, colonisation continued as "slow-motion annexation" supported by intensive repression: mass arrests, collective punishments, assassinations, curfews, closures, demolitions and military invasions of villages, colleges and university campuses.[14] In 1987 there was a national uprising—a remarkable movement in which every Palestinian community was involved in mass action which echoed the first intifada against British rule and Zionist settlement in the 1930s. But neither this movement nor a further intifada in 2000 slowed the pace of colonisation. Settlement of the West Bank accelerated. According to the Israeli human rights group B'Tselem, between 2000 and 2008 the number of settlers in the West Bank increased at a rate of 12,000 a year. By the end of the decade several "settlements" had populations of more than 30,000.[15] Jewish-only zones encircled East Jerusalem, while other large population centres were strategically placed to render impractical the plans of Palestinian leaders who held out hopes for a West Bank state. Israel was committed to what Israeli geographer Oren Yiftachel calls "creeping apartheid...uncompromising attempts to Judaise the entire Israel/Palestine space".[16] The Palestinians were to be confined to Gaza and to fractions of territory in the West Bank in the expectation that poverty and despair would finally exhaust their resistance.

These developments slowly produced a reassessment by Palestinian activists of how to address issues of national independence in general and

---

13: Eretz Israel has been defined in many ways, from an entire region encompassing all land from the Mediterranean to Mesopotamia, to the geographically narrower areas of today's West Bank and Gaza.

14: Gorenberg, 2007, p369.

15: For detailed figures including statistics on each settlement see B'Tselem, no date b.

16: See Yiftachel, 2005, p128.

international solidarity in particular. It necessitated a sharp move away from strategic principles that had dominated Palestinian national politics for more than 40 years. In 1964 President Nasser of Egypt prompted conservative Palestinian leaders to establish the PLO—an attempt at containment and management of those impatient with his record vis-à-vis Israel. The organisation quickly came under the influence of Palestinians who had a different agenda. Yasser Arafat and his organisation Al-Fatah had begun armed attacks on Israeli forces, attracting thousands of young activists to their guerrilla strategy. When Fatah joined the PLO it soon took control and set out to lead the movement along the lines of conventional nationalism, aiming to establish a Palestinian state that would enjoy parity with other Arab states of the post-colonial era.

The mass of PLO activists came from refugee camps and from impoverished urban areas of the Palestinian diaspora. Arafat and his colleagues, however, represented the Palestinian elite. Almost without exception they were businessmen or professionals, among whom a number had become wealthy as a result of their role in the development of the Gulf States during the 1950s and 1960s. This produced a strategic difficulty: although Palestinians were scattered across the states of the Arab east and the Gulf, where their economic and political weight was considerable, PLO leaders were determined not to alienate the region's rulers, with whom they believed they had much in common. The PLO leadership therefore resolved to maintain a policy of "non-interference", giving undertakings that Palestinian struggles would not affect politics within the states of the region. The organisation intended to use financial and military support from the Arab regimes to sustain armed struggle against Israel along the lines of the Algerian resistance, which had recently succeeded in ending French rule. Following the 1967 war, and Israel's occupation of the West Bank, Gaza and other Arab territories, key figures in Fatah proposed that they could emulate the Algerian and Chinese models of guerrilla warfare:

> The fact that there were now nearly one million Palestinians under Israeli occupation suggested that conditions were right for a popular war of liberation. Those who entertained this idea believed they could now apply Mao Zedong's thoughts about revolutionary armed struggle. The one million Palestinians under Israeli occupation would be the revolutionary sea in which Mao's fish—in this case Palestinian guerrillas—would swim.[17]

17: Assessment of Arafat's biographer Alan Hart of the views of Fatah veterans who attended the organisation's first congress in 1967. See Hart, 1984, p236.

The idea was implausible. Palestine was a tiny country in which rural warfare had little chance of success and where the Zionist movement had long been able to call on a large and efficient military machine. In 1967 Fatah attempted to lead an armed uprising in the West Bank. It was a costly failure: the guerrillas lost hundreds of fighters and Arafat barely escaped with his life. The PLO was now locked into a dual strategy certain to cause problems. It was committed both to the principle of "non-interference" in the Arab states and simultaneously to armed struggle against Israel—a conflict in which its *fedayeen* would fight against overwhelming odds.

In 1969 Fatah leaders convinced King Faisal of Saudi Arabia to provide more arms and financial support, including by means of a "liberation tax" of 5 percent on the earnings of the many Palestinians working in the kingdom. The *quid pro quo* was a renewed assurance not to intervene in domestic affairs of the Arab states. Arafat biographer Alan Hart comments, "The significance of Saudi Arabia's support for Fatah cannot be exaggerated. As time proved, with Saudi Arabia on its side, Fatah was indestructible—as long as it was pursuing policies the Saudis could endorse".[18]

Fatah was heading towards the first of several tragic confrontations, not just with Israel but with the Arab rulers. Thousands of young activists had joined Fatah or the radical "fronts" of the Palestinian left.[19] In Jordan, where some two thirds of the population consisted of displaced Palestinians, they were confronted by the forces of King Hussein. After a long standoff during which Arafat's anxiety about "interference" in Arab domestic politics in effect kept the king in power, Hussein brutally attacked the movement in 1970—an act of repression that came to be known as "Black September". The PLO as a whole retreated to Lebanon but never recovered. For the next ten years it was harassed by Lebanese forces and by the Syrian state. Israel also attacked savagely, notably during its invasions of Lebanon in 1978 and 1982.

Throughout this long period Arafat clung to "non-interference" as a key organising principle. He also insisted that national liberation was a matter for Palestinians alone: others should endorse the liberation struggle but must not engage in any action that might disturb the political agenda of their own rulers. This approach amounted to an obsession. Although the presence of Israel affected the population of the whole region, Arafat and his colleagues continually discouraged the mass of the people in Arab states from linking

18: Hart, 1984, p288.
19: Some, such as the Popular Front for the Liberation of Palestine, represented indigenous radicals opposed to Fatah's accommodation with the Arab states. Others were the latter's instruments within the PLO, armed groups implanted in the movement, and backed with arms and finance from Libya, Iraq, Syria and elsewhere.

their predicaments with those of the Palestinians. The Fatah leaders were determined to maintain relations with the region's rulers, with whom they believed they enjoyed social and political parity. They acted in effect as a bourgeoisie without a state, confining their "own" population to a strictly nationalist agenda. This was congenial to the kings, emirs and presidents of the region, who used formal backing for the PLO as part of a chorus of rhetorical opposition to Israel, the better to maintain their own privilege.

Tabitha Petran comments on the impact in Saudi Arabia, where Palestinians contributed a significant proportion of the labour force and had led historic oilfield strikes in the 1950s: "Aid to al-Fatah [was] a means of preserving social peace at home... A by-product of al-Fatah's organisation of Palestinians in the Gulf could be a 'well-behaved' labour force".[20] Determined to integrate the PLO into the state system of the Arab world, Arafat and his friends succeeded in isolating the Palestinian movement from those who identified most closely with it: the mass of people in neighbouring states and, most importantly, the workers whose struggles against their own rulers were suppressed by those calling for "national unity" in the face of Israel and imperialism.

Intifada

This policy reached a further disastrous conclusion in the late 1980s. Expelled from its base in Lebanon after the Israeli invasion of 1982, the PLO had been reduced to a shadow of the movement that galvanised young activists a generation earlier. Israel meanwhile stepped up colonisation of the territories occupied in 1967, integrating the Palestinian population into its economy. The West Bank and Gaza had become bantustans on the South African model—reservoirs of cheap labour from which workers commuted daily to Israeli factories and farms under conditions that recalled the pass laws of the apartheid system. When an uprising began in 1987 it engaged the mass of Palestinians in all manner of collective actions. There was an immediate response across the region. Millions of people identified with the youth of the intifada, contrasting their courage with the empty promises of the Arab rulers. Demonstrations were organised in the Gulf, in Turkey and in North Africa. In Sudan there was a brief general strike. The regimes took fright. In Kuwait police were ordered to attack a large march, with a local newspaper declaring such events "could be exploited by those who fish in troubled waters to create disturbances".[21]

20: Petran, 1987, p92.
21: The pro-government newspaper *Al-Ra'i Al-'Am* reported, "Such demonstrations could

In Egypt there was a national work stoppage followed by demonstrations in the key industrial city of Mahalla al-Kubra. Here workers not only backed the Palestinians but attacked the Egyptian regime and its servitude to the US and the International Monetary Fund. The interior minister accused demonstrators of "sabotage and incitement".[22] But the movement spread, with mobilisations of students and professional syndicates in Cairo and Alexandria—developing the kind of momentum regimes throughout the region feared, in which identification with the Palestinians stimulated confidence to address poverty, inequality and repression. The Egyptian government warned that its forces would "sever any foot that attempts to march in demonstrations".[23] Its reaction found support among PLO leaders, Arafat making a symbolic visit to the Gulf to embrace Kuwaiti leaders and declare local demonstrations "a tactical mistake".[24] Within weeks, an Arab summit in Algiers had backed Arafat with high rhetoric and a pledge to the PLO to provide $1 million a day.[25]

Palestinians were again at the centre of regional politics, their struggles stimulating solidarity and a desire to emulate the resistance. But PLO leaders rushed to put out the flames, protecting regimes which connived in Israel's repression or which undertook their own offensives against the movement, isolating Palestinians from those most eager to support them.

By 1994 Arafat was back in Palestine as leader of a statelet in Gaza and the West Bank. He soon concentrated power in the hands of leaders who would become a byword for corruption. Using aid from the Gulf regimes and training from the CIA, he created a security apparatus committed to the suppression of the young people who had energised and directed the intifada. Fatah succeeded in isolating and demobilising the most effective mass movement in Palestinian history, setting the scene for the emergence of Hamas as the first mass Islamist organisation in Palestine, and encouraging Israel to accelerate its policy of colonisation.

In 1998 Israeli foreign minister (soon to be prime minister) Ariel Sharon broadcast on national radio, encouraging the Jewish settler movement

---

be exploited by those who fish in troubled waters to create disturbances."—*Mideast Mirror*, 10 February 1988.

22: *Mideast Mirror*, 4 January 1988.

23: Egyptian interior minister Zaki Badr declared, "I will sever any foot that attempts to march in demonstrations…demonstrations are impermissible even if peaceful in support of the Palestinians in the occupied lands and we will meet this with all-out firmness." Reported in *Mideast Mirror*, 12 January 1988.

24: See *Middle East Report*, 1988, p51.

25: Arab states pledged some $330 million to the PLO for the year.

to seize the initiative before peace talks which might give Arafat notional authority in limited areas of the West Bank. He told them, "Grab more hills, expand the territory. Everything that is grabbed will be in our hands. Everything we don't grab will be in their hands".[26] Between 1997 and 2001 the settler population in the West Bank (excluding East Jerusalem) increased by about 50,000 people as "creeping apartheid" increased its grip.[27]

Towards BDS

This is the context in which a new generation of Palestinian activists addressed questions of international solidarity. They were encouraged by discussions at the World Conference against Racism, Racial Discrimination, Xenophobia and Related Intolerance, organised by Unesco in Durban in 2001, at which a draft statement opposed "movements based on racism and discriminatory ideas, in particular the Zionist movement, which is based on racial superiority".[28]

In debate veterans of the anti-apartheid struggle identified parallels between Israeli practice and that of the racist South African state, recommending BDS campaigns similar to those that played a key role in their international strategy. For the first time in 50 years Palestinians engaged directly with activists committed to solidarity organised from below and which could deliver concrete outcomes. The reaction from Israel gave testimony to the impact of the Durban debates. Foreign minister Shimon Peres described the conference as a "bizarre show", "a farce" and a "bomb...not made of explosives, but made of hatred, of extreme anti-Israeli expressions".[29]

For Palestinians, the new relationships were of great importance. At home the Arafat administration was disintegrating. In one sense Fatah had achieved its goal—authority over territories in which it exercised formal control. But Palestinian society was being suffocated by fresh seizures of land and water, restrictions on economic activity and comprehensive controls on movement. By 2002 hundreds of military checkpoints divided the West Bank into separate areas, making meaningless the idea of progress to a state with territorial integrity. Israel had also begun to construct its "Separation Wall", planned to run for 680 kilometres through the West Bank, involving

---

26: Gorenberg, 2007, pp371-372.

27: B'Tselem, no date b.

28: Delegates from Israel and the US immediately withdrew. A milder final statement on Palestine declared, "We are concerned about the plight of the Palestinian people under foreign occupation" and their "inalienable right...to self-determination and to the establishment of an independent state". See BBC World Service, no date.

29: Press briefing by Peres. See Israel Ministry of Foreign Affairs, 2001.

the largest single annexation of land since the 1967 occupation, and leaving less than 12 percent of historic Palestine to the indigenous population.[30] Some 95,000 people—4.5 percent of the population—were to be isolated from the West Bank, and 200,000 in East Jerusalem would be entirely separated from Palestinian territory.[31]

For South Africans, the conclusions were obvious: Palestinians were being confined to enclaves in a process familiar from the apartheid years. Following the Durban conference, Ronnie Kasrils and Max Ozinsky—leading figures in the anti-apartheid struggle—asked Jewish South Africans to join them in a declaration of support for Palestine. Their statement, "Not in My Name", made the similarity of apartheid and Israeli policies explicit. In 2002 Archbishop Desmond Tutu told a conference in the US about his visit to the Occupied Territories:

> I've been very deeply distressed in my visit to the Holy Land; it reminded me so much of what happened to us black people in South Africa. I have seen the humiliation of the Palestinians at checkpoints and roadblocks, suffering like us when young white police officers prevented us from moving about.[32]

Tutu also issued a call for an international boycott. He argued:

> The end of apartheid stands as one of the crowning accomplishments of the past century, but we would not have succeeded without the help of international pressure—in particular the divestment movement of the 1980s. Over the past six months a similar movement has taken shape, this time aiming at an end to the Israeli occupation... If apartheid ended, so can the occupation, but the moral force and international pressure will have to be just as determined. The current divestment effort is the first, though certainly not the only, necessary move in that direction.[33]

For a younger generation of Palestinians, parallels with apartheid and calls for BDS made much sense. They had been deeply affected by Israel's colonisation of the West Bank and Gaza, witnesses to the most recent phase in construction of what Israeli historian Ilan Pappé terms "Fortress Israel"—an attempt "to construct and then defend a 'white' [Western] fortress in a 'black'

30: Stop the Wall, no date.
31: Parry, 2003.
32: Tutu, 2002.
33: Tutu, 2002.

[Arab] world".[34] Encouraged by the South Africans, in 2003 Palestinian academics called for a boycott of Israeli academic institutions. In 2004 Pacbi was launched formally in Ramallah. In 2005 the BNC brought together 170 organisations in Palestine and the diaspora with commitments to raise active support for BDS worldwide, including—significantly—in the Arab states.[35]

Gaza and after

International initiatives directed at academic and consumer boycotts grew steadily. In December 2005 the regional council of Sør-Trøndelag in Norway declared for a comprehensive boycott of Israeli goods. In February 2006 an Anglican parish in Britain divested from the Church of England's Central Board of Finance over ownership of shares in Caterpillar—a company profiting from the illegal occupation. In May 2006 the conference of Natfhe, the lecturers' union in Britain (a predecessor of the University and College Union, UCU), voted for action against Israeli academic institutions, and the Ontario section of the Canadian Union of Public Employees (CUPE) condemned Israel's "apartheid wall" and announced its own BDS policy. Willie Madisha, president of the Congress of South African Trade Unions (Cosatu) applauded CUPE, declaring the issue of Palestine had finally entered the arena of workers' internationalism:

> It is time for the global workers' movement to stand firm and principled against hypocrisy and double standards. We cannot remain silent any longer. It is time to stand in word and in deed with the peoples of the Middle East and heed their call to support the struggle against occupation. There will be no peace in this region and in the world, without justice.[36]

In August 2006 the Dublin Festival of World Cultures ended its sponsorship by the Israeli embassy, Venezuela withdrew its ambassador in Israel, the Locarno International Film Festival renounced support from the Israeli Ministry of Foreign Affairs, and the Greek governing body for film pulled out of the Haifa International Film Festival. In September 2006 61 Irish academics from a variety of disciplines wrote to the *Irish Times* calling for a moratorium on European Union support for Israeli academic institutions until Israel abided by United Nations resolutions and ended occupation of Palestinian territories. In October 2006 the University of

---

34: Pappé, 2006, p253.
35: Members of the BNC are listed at BNC, no date a.
36: Cosatu, 2006.

Michigan Student Government demanded the university divest from Israel, and the Belgian hi-tech company U2U ceased cooperation with its Israeli partners because of Israeli war crimes.

In 2007 a series of British trade unions including the National Union of Journalists, Unison, the Northern Ireland Public Service Alliance and the Transport and General Workers' Union (now part of Unite) adopted policies on BDS. The Congress of UCU voted overwhelmingly to circulate its members with the Palestinian boycott call, encouraging them to examine the moral implications of links with Israeli academic institutions.[37] Weeks later the Irish Congress of Trade Unions voted for BDS.

The invasion of Gaza in December 2008 changed the pace of events. For weeks a formidable armed force pounded Palestinian towns and refugee camps, razing industrial, commercial and residential areas. The population was defenceless: already strangled by an Israeli boycott imposed when Hamas won an election victory in January 2006, it was now blitzed from the air, land and sea. The BNC issued an emergency statement:

> [We call] upon international civil society not just to protest and condemn in diverse forms Israel's massacre in Gaza, but also to join and intensify the international Boycott, Divestment and Sanctions campaign against Israel to end its impunity and to hold it accountable for its persistent violation of international law and Palestinian rights.[38]

BDS campaigns proliferated. Social workers in Mauritius; city councillors in Birmingham; the Maritime Union of Australia; the World Council of Churches; Galway City Council in Ireland; the Scottish Trades Union Congress; the Edinburgh International Film Festival; the Norwegian Government Pension Fund; the Municipal Council for Cooperation of Bilbao, Spain; Danske Bank in Denmark; the Dutch pension fund ABP; and Italian supermarket chains COOP and Conad, all adopted boycott positions or began the process of divestment.

In a significant development, the South African Transport and Allied Workers Union, part of Cosatu, resolved that its members would not unload an Israeli ship due to dock at Durban. Shortly afterwards the Western Australia branch of the Maritime Union of Australia resolved to boycott all Israeli vessels and all vessels bearing goods arriving from or going to Israel. The BNC identified a shift from "traditional, mostly symbolic,

---

37: UCU Congress report at UCU 2007.
38: BNC, 2008.

solidarity" to "a new, qualitatively advanced phase of BDS".[39] Initiatives were under way, it said, in Norway, Sweden, Britain, Ireland, Turkey, Canada, Belgium, Malaysia, Spain, the US, Brazil and New Zealand. The committee declared, "Our 'South Africa' moment has arrived".[40]

Boycott—a short history

For those engaged in building solidarity in the form of BDS, questions arise about how such campaigns have been organised and targeted, and what lessons can be learnt from their long history.

What is a boycott? The term encompasses all manner of actions in which there is collective abstention from relations with individuals or institutions: most boycotts from below are organised on such a basis but can be differentiated in respect of the nature of the target, those who are its specific focus and the operation of the campaign. Boycotts may be primary or secondary, targeting producer or consumer; they may be direct or indirect; they may target inputs, products or the whole process of production and distribution.[41] While a primary boycott targets the offending firm, organisation, institution or country, a secondary boycott attempts to ostracise or isolate those who trade or otherwise associate with the target. A direct boycott targets the offender explicitly, while an indirect boycott lists conditions for legitimate and illegitimate trade or association. A consumer boycott aims to hamper the sales of goods by the offender through dissuasion. An input or material boycott aims to impede the production process by interfering with the acquisition of inputs to the production process.

The idea of boycott first became important in the late 18th century as part of efforts by British abolitionists to discourage use of slave-produced sugar.[42] When in 1791 parliament rejected a bill to abolish slavery, abolitionists argued to abstain from use of slave-produced sugar and rum from the West Indies. The campaign involved some 300,000 people against products "soaked in the blood of slaves".[43] In 1824 the radical abolitionist Elizabeth Heyrick wrote a pamphlet addressed to the elite abolitionists of the Society for Effecting the Gradual Abolition of Slavery (the "Anti-Slavery Society"), arguing that gradualism was a hypocrisy that played into

---

39: BNC, 2009.
40: BNC, 2009.
41: Wolman, 2009 [1916].
42: Midgley, 2007; Sussman, 2000.
43: Sussman, 2000.

the hands of the planters.[44] She argued for immediate abolition and for a popular sugar boycott—a call which proved important to the momentum of the emancipation movement. Similar campaigns emerged in the US as slave-produced commodities were targeted by Quaker and Free Black abolitionists. At the same time, however, Northern merchandise was boycotted by Southern supporters of slavery—an example of retaliatory abstention that often developed in this period.

The term "boycott" emerged in rural Ireland in 1880. Captain Charles Cunningham Boycott was land agent and manager of the estate of Lord Erne in County Mayo. Taking advantage of the dearth of alternative employment, Boycott reduced the wages of tenant farmers who, organised by the Irish Land League, withdrew their labour. When he attempted to undermine the strike the local community imposed a campaign of isolation—no one spoke to him or served him in shops, and his mail was not delivered. Boycotts have since developed as a tactic deployed by a host of political parties, trade unions, pressure groups and campaigning movements.[45] Formalised as state policy, they may take the form of legal or quasi-legal embargoes sanctioned by statute and enforced by state power or international bodies. When organised from below boycotts are typically initiated by those who lack other means to secure their aims, usually because of an extreme disproportion in power between the contending parties and/or particular difficulties in implementing alternative forms of action.

Consumer boycotts

The boycott became a familiar tactic in North America in the late 19th and early 20th centuries, in part through the efforts of James Redpath, an American journalist who had observed the Mayo campaign. It was deployed widely in the US by labour movement organisations which distributed "unfair lists", identifying firms from which consumers should refuse to buy. One of the most successful consumer boycotts took place in 1902, when the price of kosher meat on the Lower East Side of New York rose sharply as wholesalers cornered the market. Fanny Levy, wife of a unionised cloth worker, and Sarah Edelson, proprietor of a small restaurant, mobilised for

44: Heyrick's arguments prefigured those developing today and which divide those for whom a boycott is aimed exclusively at the produce of illegal Israeli settlements, addressing only the issue of the Occupied Territories, and those for whom it is a tactic with a wider rationale that addresses the entirety of the oppression and dispossession that the Israeli state represents. See Heyrick, 1824.

45: For a recent literature survey from which much of this historical synopsis is drawn, see Hawkins, 2010.

a consumer "strike" targeting butchers' shops and were joined by 20,000 women. Meat already purchased was confiscated and destroyed. The *New York Times* called for the repression of this "dangerous class [of] women... [who] mostly speak a foreign language".[46] The boycott spread to Brooklyn, Harlem, Newark, Boston and Philadelphia. Small butchers joined the protest and refused to sell. Prices eventually fell. The American Jewish Historical Society notes the tactic was used in rent strikes in 1904, 1907-8, and in food boycotts in 1907, 1912 and 1917.[47] Participants formed a National Consumers' League, awarding a "white label" or "union label" to firms complying with their conditions, and campaigned over conditions in textile sweatshops, domestic manufacture and the use of child labour.[48]

During the inter-war period the tactic was adopted by opposing forces. In the 1920s the Ku Klux Klan organised boycotts of Jewish and Roman Catholic businesses.[49] At the same time labour unions and consumer boycotts targeted "over-priced" goods in "buyers' strikes". The League of Women Shoppers (LWS), founded in 1935, provided information about the wages and conditions of workers producing goods and identified stores trading with Nazi Germany, Mussolini's Italy and Imperial Japan.[50] It developed a "Don't buy where you can't work" campaign aimed at African-American consumers. The LWS and the American Federation of Hosiery Workers campaigned against Japanese and German goods and services. By 1940 their efforts were supported by prominent individuals. Albert Einstein became an enthusiastic supporter. The six largest chain stores in the US eventually undertook not to buy Japanese manufactured goods. These campaigns were supported abroad by the Indian National Congress, the CGT in France and the TUC in Britain.[51]

Similar developments were under way in Europe. In 1890 brewery workers in Berlin organised a beer boycott as part of a labour dispute. Their success led employers to form a brewers' consortium. In 1894 a further dispute erupted, with brewery workers supported by the Social Democratic Party.[52] Political tensions around use of the law to curtail boycotts led the

---

46: American Jewish Historical Society, 2010.
47: American Jewish Historical Society, 2010.
48: Hawkins, 2010.
49: Hawkins, 2010.
50: Hawkins, 2010.
51: The six were FW Woolworth, SS Kresge, McCrory, SH Kress, F&W Grand Stores and the National Dollar Stores.
52: Turk, 1982.

German Imperial Court to recognise the legitimacy of the tactic in 1906.[53] In 1901 the Amsterdam water transport leagues tried to organise an international boycott of British shipping in an attempt to end the Boer War, and to protest at British use of concentration camps in South Africa.[54]

Beyond Europe, the most dramatic use of the boycott was in the Swardeshi movement, part of the Indian movement for independence. Initiated in Bengal in 1905 in protest at partition of the province, the campaign aimed to convince consumers to use Indian products rather than British imports. It was already a popular and developing movement when the boycott was adopted by Gandhi and the Indian National Congress, which targeted British products and urged Indians not to use British schools or courts and not to work for the colonial administration or use official British titles. It was also used successfully against the colonial administration's salt tax, mobilising huge numbers of people in demonstrations.

Gandhi's strategies strongly influenced Martin Luther King, who visited India in 1959, declaring that "non-violent resistance is the most potent weapon available to oppressed people in their struggle for freedom".[55] King had already mobilised sustained campaigns in the US, notably through a bus boycott which began in Montgomery, Alabama, in 1955, and which launched the Civil Rights Movement. After almost a year, and following police intimidation and bombings by white segregationists, the Supreme Court upheld a ruling by the Federal Court that transport segregation was unconstitutional, reasserting the boycott as a key weapon of the oppressed.

Boycotts could be mobilised for other purposes, however. The rise of anti-Semitism in Europe in the late 19th century produced a series of campaigns against Jewish businesses and products. In Warsaw, Jewish businesses were boycotted in 1912 after the Jews of the city supported the election of a socialist deputy to the Russian Duma. Jewish-owned commercial operations were also targeted after German military withdrawal from Poland in 1918.[56] In 1936 a boycott of Jewish businesses was backed by both the Polish government and the Catholic Church. In 1928 the Nazis initiated regional boycotts against Jewish shops in Germany, and from 1933 they coordinated nationwide campaigns in which Jewish businesses were targeted for attacks soon sanctioned by state policy. In the US a boycott of German goods and services met a counter-boycott of Jewish-owned stores. From 1938 until

---

53: Schaffner, 1910, pp23-33.
54: Hawkins, 2010.
55: King, 2000, pp135-136.
56: Heller, 1993.

the US entered the Second World War, the pro-Nazi Christian Front, a Catholic organisation, boycotted Jewish businesses in Irish neighbourhoods of the American north east.[57]

Apartheid, boycott and sanctions

Boycotts are not ends in themselves—and they are not always the appropriate means to achieve specific objectives. The relevance of a boycott depends on the nature of the objective, the balance of forces and the feasibility of particular tactics. In addition, the effect of a boycott is typically not the attainment of the overall objective but rather a contribution to the latter. These issues are illustrated in the most important of recent boycott campaigns—that against apartheid South Africa.

After the Sharpeville massacre of 1960, when 69 people were shot dead by police, anti-apartheid campaigners called for UN sanctions against the South African regime, a demand opposed by successive British and US governments. In 1976 state-sponsored killings during the uprising in Soweto stimulated further international condemnation of apartheid, intensifying the boycott campaign. In 1977 the UN finally adopted Resolution 418, imposing a mandatory arms embargo on South Africa. Piecemeal economic sanctions followed until in 1994, following the formal end of the apartheid regime, the UN lifted its arms embargo and South Africa was readmitted to the General Assembly.

These were formal actions of states and international bodies—but the boycott campaign was driven by grassroots activism. In Britain the Anti-Apartheid Movement (AAM) initiated consumer and sports boycotts as well as pressuring the government for formal economic sanctions.[58] The AAM initiated the "secondary" boycott against British companies operating in South Africa, notably Barclays Bank and Shell/BP. It also targeted sport, with striking success: there were high-profile mobilisations against South African teams visiting Britain, with pitch invasions, destruction of cricket squares and many clashes with police.

In the trade union movement it was slower going—it was easy to pass resolutions against apartheid but more difficult to commit union branches to a ban on South African goods or contacts. Union leaders were reluctant to support formal consumer boycotts, arguing that this would affect jobs in the UK, and employment possibilities and working conditions for black South Africans. It was 15 years from the commencement of the campaign

57: Grover, 2003.
58: Fieldhouse, 2005.

to boycott and isolate South Africa before the TUC supported mandatory economic sanctions and an effective boycott of goods.

In the case of South Africa, campaigns for boycott moved gradually from consumer boycotts to producer boycotts, and from the primary boycotts of goods, artists and sporting ties to secondary boycotts of companies trading with, investing in or otherwise profiting from the apartheid system. In addition, activists encouraged campaigns calling for official government economic and financial sanctions on the South African regime. There were several outcomes:

● increased public awareness, particularly in Europe and the US, of the realities of the racist regime;
● reassurance for South Africans engaged in the struggle that their predicament and sacrifices were not invisible, together with concrete demonstrations of solidarity;
● growing sensitivity in the circles of global capital that long-term risks of association with the apartheid state might outweigh short-term financial advantages;
● growing anxiety among senior agents of apartheid that a crisis would intensify as long as the structures of their system remained in place.

Those in struggle were strengthened and emboldened industrially and politically. Millions of people worldwide embraced the South African cause through practical actions that also strengthened their own resolve to resist exploitation and oppression.

The pivotal moment in the fight against apartheid did not come until the mid-1980s. It was closely tied to risings in the townships between 1984 and 1986 and attempts at the repression of the movement that were broadcast worldwide. Internal struggle, in the form of a popular mass movement rather than armed resistance or sabotage, insistently registered not only the oppression but also the courage and dignity of those engaged in resistance. This growing international awareness transformed the boycott into a serious political issue, notably in the US where the Democratic Party organised pickets outside the South African embassy and a massive divestment campaign spread across American universities. In August 1985 South African president P W Botha made his notorious "Rubicon" speech, refusing to make reforms or to free African National Congress (ANC) leader Nelson Mandela. The result was a massive flight of capital from South Africa, partial default by the regime on its foreign loans, and a sharp fall in the value of the rand.

Renewed access to capital markets—a necessity for the South African economy—came to depend on attainment of a political settlement. Although the township risings were eventually defeated by the apartheid state, they had fundamentally altered the strategic situation. Sections of the South African ruling class, realising that the apartheid system could not survive, began to reflect on how a transition could be accomplished with the least loss of their wealth and power. It was against this background that the "Boycott Barclays" campaign finally succeeded. The most high-profile international financial partner of the apartheid system sold off its South African subsidiary in 1986.

The history of the South African struggle is not simply an inspiration or an example of the kind of contribution to liberation that can be made by international solidarity movements. It also contains important lessons about relationships between internal resistance to oppression by the oppressed and external solidarity that can be organised in support of that resistance. Whatever the differences between struggles against South African and Israeli versions of apartheid, the similarities loom large. Outright military victory was and is not a viable aim in either case, and negotiations could not take place or have any prospect of progress until those with power foresaw that the cost of stonewalling would exceed the cost of meaningful compromise. In South Africa the mutually reinforcing factors of internal mass mobilisation and external solidarity pressure for divestment and boycott produced a change in the balance of forces. Without external pressure on companies and governments internationally, the risings might now be remembered as heroic but not regime changing. Without mass struggle internally, and the repression it exposed, the external BDS movement would not have been able to develop widespread support among trade unions, students, activists and eventually growing numbers of politicians.

The boycott movement was a profound expression of international solidarity, animated from below. It began as an argument about moral responsibility comparable to the anti-slavery campaigns of the 18th and 19th centuries, but came to target those who traded and associated with the apartheid regime—campaigners arguing that such activity made participants complicit in apartheid. This was a moral argument with political intent.

A boycott of Israel

Do the campaigns against apartheid South Africa provide a model for action in solidarity with the Palestinians? Veterans of the anti-apartheid struggle maintain that they do. In December 2009 an international trade union conference on BDS, organised by the UCU in London, heard from Ronnie Kasrils, for many years a key figure in the ANC. For Kasrils, the differences between South Africa and Israel—including their contrasting colonial histories—are less important than their similarities. His recent visits to Palestine, he said, were "a surreal trip into an apartheid state of emergency". Even hardened South African activists were unprepared for what they encountered. He recalled the illegal settlements, roads reserved for the use of settlers, multiple checkpoints and a "monstrous" wall: "I can't recall anything quite as obscene in apartheid South Africa".[59]

In the same vein and at the same event Cosatu international secretary Bongani Masuko and head of campaigns George Mahlangu offered their support to the Palestinian struggle as "a global symbol of resistance against apartheid, occupation and colonialism in our age".[60] On the Cosatu website the identity and commonality of the two struggles are registered:

> Their [Palestinians'] struggle is for the same cause as that heroically waged by South Africans against apartheid not so long ago. It is in this light that South Africans have always and shall continue to support these sister peoples in their quest for justice and dignity.[61]

Can BDS be applied to Israel much as the AAM directed its strategy towards South Africa—and can it have a similar impact? A consumer boycott is unlikely to bring crisis to the Israeli economy, a socio-economic system supported by massive US aid. It will, however, bring to worldwide public attention the circumstances of the Palestinians—which have been obscured by decades of ideologically distorted reporting and by the efforts by partisans of Israel to dismiss the Palestinian case. An academic boycott will not terminate research and development within Israel, not least because of the umbilical relationship between industrial, military and political activity on the one hand and most academic research on the other.[62] It will, however, focus attention on ideological, infrastructural, technical, psychological and military support for the occupation provided by all Israeli universities, permitting scholars and scientists outside Israel to consider whether they wish

---

59: Kasrils's statement to the international trade union conference on BDS, hosted by UCU, London, December 2009.
60: Masuko, 2009.
61: Cosatu, 2009.
62: There has been a dramatic growth of compendia of evidence of the complicity of Israeli academic institutions with maintenance of the occupation and suppression of Palestinian resistance. All universities are involved in the training of military personnel, and/or military or intelligence-related research, or psychological or anthropological research that sustains the occupation and secures the founding myths of the Israeli state. See Bricup, 2007.

to make themselves complicit with oppression at second hand by collaborating with Israeli institutions.

Cultural and sporting boycotts will not promptly make Israel a no-go area for visiting celebrities. They can, however, show that some people refuse to perform in a tortured land where millions are denied not only entertainment but land, water and basic rights. The cumulative effect can not only reinforce networks of international support around the Palestinians but also project into Israeli society an awareness of how vast numbers worldwide view the occupation. It is in this context that Israeli peace activist Udi Aloni, a supporter of BDS, argues, "It is time for clarity; who is on this side and who on that side. The other side are the ambassadors of the occupation".[63]

Anti-apartheid activists point out that, in addition to mass mobilisation by the workers' movement, their struggle required an international solidarity movement that took decades to develop. Efforts began in the late 1950s but did not become effective for almost 20 years. In the case of Palestine events have recently progressed quickly, with the formation of many local BDS campaigns, the emergence of international BDS networks, and a number of high-profile successes in the cultural arena.[64] A group of Israelis has created Boycott! Supporting the Palestinian BDS Call from Within, involving "citizens of Israel, [who] join the Palestinian call for a BDS campaign against Israel, inspired by the struggle of South Africans against apartheid".[65]

Arab organisations in Israel have begun work on a boycott of 1,000 companies based on or linked with illegal settlements. In May 2010 even Palestinian president Mahmoud Abbas endorsed a law banning trade in goods produced in the settlements in areas under the Palestinian Authority—a reluctant response to mass campaigns for boycott in which Palestinian youth have called for all homes and communities to be cleared of illicit Israeli products.[66] The significant impact on Israeli businesses was described by hard-hit Israeli factory owners as "insufferable" and by the settlers' Yesha Council as "economic terrorism".[67]

Of these developments, the most important is the impact on the Palestinian movement at large. The establishment of the BNC is highly significant. Its website has been named Global BDS Movement, an initiative unthinkable in the 1990s when Palestinian society was controlled by

---

63: See Nieuwhof, 2010, for Aloni's support of BDS.
64: By the time of publication a series of musicians had refused to play in Israel. The list included Elvis Costello, Gil Scott-Heron, Carlos Santana, Faithless, Pixies and Leftfield.
65: Boycott!—Supporting the Palestinian BDS Call from Within, 2010.
66: For a critique of Abbas's involvement in BDS activity see Abunimah, 2010.
67: Frykberg, 2010.

leaders convinced that politics must remain local and not be projected onto agendas elsewhere.[68] The BNC celebrates the fact that BDS initiatives "have been multiplying all over the world", and calls for extensive engagement of Palestinians with transnational activists.[69] Formal leadership of the Palestinian national movement still lies with Fatah, which retains shaky authority in the West Bank through control of the Palestinian Authority, and with the more stable Hamas in Gaza. But local leadership has been distributed more widely and Palestinian communities, schools, colleges, universities, workplaces, trade unions and other activist groups now have complex links abroad, including through BDS networks.

Confined physically by Israel, Palestinians are emerging from the restrictive political environment associated with decades of self-imposed isolation. This goes some way to addressing the historic problem of the national movement: its inability to confront the chronic weakness of Palestinian political forces acting alone and its leadership's unwillingness to align Palestinian struggles with those of the mass of people in the region. This opening comes at an important moment when Arab politics in general has become somewhat less introverted. Military interventions in the region, world crisis, democracy activism and the strong workers' movement in Egypt have all had an impact, prompting Palestinian activists to look beyond traditional organisations. When the BNC held its Second National Congress in Nablus in May 2010, delegates addressed directly the challenge of "encouraging civil society worldwide to join the global BDS movement".[70] They face formidable problems but are moving fast, achieving a momentum which is alarming Israel's strategists. To this extent they have indeed reached a "South Africa moment".

68: www.bdsmovement.net
69: BNC, no date b.
70: BNC, 2010b.

References

Abunimah, Ali, 2010, "The PA's Disingenuous Boycott Campaign", *The Electronic Intifada* (25 May), http://electronicintifada.net/v2/article11286.shtml

American Jewish Historical Society, 2010, "Bravo, Bravo, Bravo, Jewish Women! The Kosher Meat Boycott of 1902", www.ajhs.org/scholarship/chapters/chapter.cfm?documentID=197

BBC World Service, no date, "Article 2: All people are entitled to rights without distinction based on race, colour, sex, language, religion, opinion, origin, property, birth or residency", www.bbc.co.uk/worldservice/people/features/ihavearightto/four_b/casestudy_art02.shtml

BNC, no date a, http://bdsmovement.net/?q=node/126#members

BNC, no date b, "About Us", www.bdsmovement.net/?q=node/68

BNC, 2008, "Stop the Massacre in Gaza—Boycott Israel Now!", http://bdsmovement.net/?q=node/235

BNC, 2009, "The BNC Salutes South African Dock Workers Action!", http://bdsmovement.net/?q=node/286

BNC, 2010a, www.bnc-europe@bdsmovement.net

BNC, 2010b, "The Second National Conference on Boycott, Divestment and Sanctions (BDS)", www.pacbi.org/pics/file/BNC-Second-National-BDS-Conference-31-5-2010-ENG%5B1%5D.pdf

Borger, Julian, 2003, "Israel Trains US Assassination Squads in Iraq", *Guardian* (9 December), www.guardian.co.uk/world/2003/dec/09/iraq.israel

Boycott! Supporting the Palestinian BDS Call from Within, 2010, "Palestinians, Jews, citizens of Israel, join the Palestinian call for a BDS campaign against Israel", http://boycottisrael.info/

Bricup, 2007, *Why Boycott Israeli Universities?* (Bricup), http://www.caiaweb.org/files/Why_boycott_Israeli_Universities.pdf

B'Tselem, no date a, "Land Appropriation and Settlements", www.btselem.org/english/Settlements/Statistics.asp

B'Tselem, no date b, "Population by Year in West Bank Settlements", www.btselem.org/English/Settlements/Settlement_population.xls

Cosatu, 2006, "South African Trade Union Congress Supports CUPE Boycott of Israel", www.connexions.org/CxLibrary/Docs/CX5270-COSATU.htm

Cosatu, 2009, "COSATU supports the International Week against Apartheid Israel", http://bit.ly/cosatu1

Fieldhouse, Roger, 2005, *Anti-Apartheid: A History of the Movement in Britain* (Merlin).

Foner, Philip S, 1975, *History of the Labor Movement in the United States, Volume 2: From the Founding of the AFL to the Emergence of American Imperialism* (International).

Foner, Philip S, 1977, *History of the Labor Movement in the United States, Volume 3: The Policies and Practices of the AFL, 1900-1909* (International).

Friedman, Monroe, 1999, *Consumer Boycotts: Effecting Change Through the Marketplace and the Media* (Routledge).

Frykberg, Mel, 2010, "Palestinian Economic Boycott Hits Israeli Settlers" (Inter Press Service), www.ipsnews.net/news.asp?idnews=51511

Glickman, Lawrence B, 2009, *Buying Power: A History of Consumer Activism in America* (University of Chicago).

Gorenberg, Gershom, 2007, *Occupied Territories: The Untold Story of Israel's Settlements* (IB Tauris).

Grover, Warren, 2003, *Nazis in Newark* (Transaction).

Hart, Alan, 1984, *Arafat: Terrorist or Peacemaker?* (Sidgwick & Jackson).

Hawkins, Richard A, 2010, "Boycotts, Buycotts and Consumer Activism in a Global Context: an Overview", *Management and Organisational History*, volume 2, number 2.

Hawks, F, 1998, "The Palestinian Authority and the CIA—Who Will Protect the Guards?", *Strategic Comments*, volume 4, number 10.

Heller, Celia S, 1993, *On the Edge of Destruction: Jews of Poland Between the Two World Wars* (Wayne State).

Heyrick, Elizabeth, 1824, *Immediate Not Gradual Abolition; Or An Inquiry Into The Shortest, Safest, And Most Effectual Means Of Getting Rid Of West Indian Slavery*, www.recoveredhistories.org

Hindman, Hugh D, 2002, *Child Labor: An American History* (Amonk).

Israel Ministry of Foreign Affairs, 2001, "Briefing by FM Shimon Peres and Deputy FM Michael Melchior to the Diplomatic Corps—4-Sep-2001", http://bit.ly/peresfm

King, Martin Luther Jr, 2000, *The Papers of Martin Luther King, Jr, Volume 4: Symbol of the Movement, January 1957—December 1958* (University of California Press).

Lis, Jonathan, 2010, "Israelis Calling for Anti-Israel Boycotts could Face Heavy Fine", *Haaretz* (15 July), www.haaretz.com/print-edition/news/israelis-calling-for-anti-israel-boycotts-could-face-heavy-fine-1.302013

Masuko, 2009, "Speech to BDS conference", www.youtube.com/watch?v=WFIIgDvjcVE

Middle East Report, 1988, "The Uprising", number 152.

Midgley, Clare, 2007, *Feminism and Empire: Women Activists in Imperial Britain, 1790—1865* (Routledge).

Nieuwhof, Adri, 2010, "Interview with Udi Aloni", *The Electronic Intifada*, http://electronicintifada.net/v2/article11277.shtml

Pappé, Ilan, 2006, *The Ethnic Cleansing of Palestine* (One World).

Parry, Nigel, 2003, "Is it a Fence? Is it a Wall? No, It's a Separation Barrier", *The Electronic Intifada*, http://electronicintifada.net/v2/article1775.shtml

Petran, Tabitha, 1987, *The Struggle Over Lebanon* (Monthly Review Press).

Reut Institute (2010), *The Delegitimisation Challenge: Creating a Political Firewall*, http://reut-institute.org/en/Publication.aspx?PublicationId=3769

Schaffner, Margaret A, 1910, "Effect of the Recent Boycott Decisions", *Annals of the American Academy of Political and Social Science*, volume 36, number 2.

Storrs, Landon, 2000, *Civilising Capitalism: The National Consumers' League, Women's Activism, and Labor Standards in the New Deal Era* (North Carolina Press).

Sussman, Charlotte, 2000, *Consuming Anxieties: Consumer Protest, Gender and British Slavery, 1713-1833* (Stanford).

Stop the Wall, no date, "Frequently Asked Questions about the Apartheid Wall", www.stopthewall.org/FAQs/33.shtml

Turk, Eleanor L, 1982, "The Great Berlin Beer Boycott of 1894", *Central European History*, volume 15, number 4.

Tutu, Desmond, 2002, "Apartheid in the Holy Land", *Guardian* (29 April), www.guardian.co.uk/world/2002/apr/29/comment

UCU, 2007, "Congress Business Section 5: International and European work", www.ucu.org.uk/index.cfm?articleid=2555

Wolman, Leo, 2009 (1916), *The Boycott in American Trade Unions* (Johns Hopkins).

Yiftachel, Oren, 2005, "Neither Two States Nor One: The Disengagement and 'Creeping Apartheid' in Israel/ Palestine", *The Arab World Geographer/Le Géographe du Monde Arabe*, volume 8, number 3, http://bit.ly/creepingapartheid

Hamas, Gaza and the blockade

Jamie Allinson

The Israeli commando raid on the Turkish ship the *Mavi Marmara*, part of the international "Freedom Flotilla" on a mission to break the blockade of Gaza, seemed to cross a boundary not broken even in the 2006 war against Lebanon or the 2009 war against Gaza. These three events together mark a distinct phase of what the Western press calls the "Israeli-Palestinian conflict".

A tense and frightening stasis characterises the Middle East since the second intifada. Israel, assured by its US patron of overwhelming conventional and nuclear superiority, barely even pretends to negotiate with the Palestinians any more. The basic Israeli policy is one of physical separation based on force. Yet that force is incapable of achieving its objective: to crush a resistance that is only politically strengthened by Israel's increasing belligerence. Hence the pattern of grinding oppression of the Palestinians punctuated by outbursts of extreme violence by Israel.

Israel had allowed a previous humanitarian flotilla to dock in Gaza in August 2008. The assault on the *Mavi Marmara*, unanimously approved by the Israeli cabinet despite the opposition of senior civil servants, represents a step-change in the violence the state is prepared to use.[1] The flagrancy of the attack, carried out by special forces against unarmed third-country civilians sailing further into international waters, stimulated a further revival of worldwide solidarity with the Palestinians, which rightly identified the siege

---

1:    Shulman, 2010.

of Gaza as the main issue.[2] The backlash of the Israeli attack led even US secretary of state Hillary Clinton to declare the blockade "unsustainable".[3]

Israel maintains that its blockade prevents Gaza from becoming "an Iranian port" by which the (elected) Hamas government of the territory would import weapons.[4] The blockade imposed on the territory since 2007 has, in the words of UN under-secretary-general John Holmes, "worsened conditions of life for one and a half million Palestinians, deepened poverty and food insecurity, prevented reconstruction, and increased aid dependence by destroying livelihoods and economic activity".[5] Gazans remain unable to repair the destruction visited upon them by the Israeli assault of early 2009 because Israel will not allow building materials to enter the territory.[6]

Israeli spokespeople claim they have no choice but to blockade Gaza because Hamas is an Islamic fundamentalist terrorist organisation that does not recognise Israel's right to exist. Since Israel's "right to exist" implies the denial of the right of Palestinians to return to their homeland on a basis of equality with Israeli Jews, one might wonder why Hamas—or anyone committed to the idea of racial equality—is obliged to recognise it. Nonetheless, the objection is false. For almost the two decades of its existence Hamas strategy has called for a generation-long ceasefire, a *hudna*, implying de facto recognition of the Israeli state in its 1967 borders, provided Israel withdraws to those borders and removes its settlements in the West Bank and East Jerusalem.[7] It is Hamas's insistence on the Palestinian right to resist the occupation and their refusal to negotiate terms that will perpetuate it that earns the organisation the enmity of Israel and the Western powers.

How did Hamas come to occupy this position and does the movement have the capacity to end the blockade and liberate Palestine? Is the organisation really, as one fallen British leftist claimed in response to Israel's 2009 attack on Gaza, "an anti-Semitic, misogynistic, homophobic, anti trade union, authoritarian, clericalist movement" seeking "the ultimate goal of establishing a theocratic state, where every detail of Palestinian life is governed by its hard-line misinterpretation of the Qur'an"?[8] In what follows

---

2:   Israeli spokespeople claimed that the Freedom Flotilla activists were armed Al Qaida affiliates—a contemptibly feeble piece of propaganda belied by every survivor's account. See Booth, 2010, and Ruddick, 2010.

3:   *Financial Times*, 2010.

4:   Ravid, 2010.

5:   Holmes, 2010.

6:   Reuters, 2009b.

7:   Hroub, 2000, pp86-87.

8:   Tatchell, 2009.

I argue against this view and trace Hamas's origins as a national liberation movement with Islamist characteristics, emerging from the failure of the previous generation of secular and leftist Palestinian organisations. Although its popularity has increased as those movements have waned, Hamas remains trapped in the same contradictions faced by its predecessors: contradictions brought about by a strategic perspective that divorces Palestinian liberation from the struggles for democracy and equality in the wider Arab world.

Hamas and the dilemmas of Palestinian liberation

From its foundation in 1987 the novelty of Hamas—a self-proclaimed "Palestinian national liberation movement" for which Islam is the "ideological frame of reference"—has confused many commentators.[9] Hamas is a religious movement ("the Islamic resistance movement") and its rise at the expense of secular and leftist organisations has dismayed many on the Arab and Western left. Although far from the Al Qaida affiliate it is occasionally portrayed as in the West,[10] Hamas holds deeply conservative positions on issues such as the free market and sexual liberation.[11] Hamas and Hizbollah, both Islamist organisations, are the only mass organisations in the Middle East that continue to resist Israel and the US.[12] It is important to understand how Hamas came to occupy this position, and how its politics are likely to constrain the struggle for Palestinian liberation.[13] The history of Hamas is inseparable from that of the most popular and widespread Islamist trend in the Arab world—the Muslim Brotherhood.

The Muslim Brotherhood was founded in 1928 by the Egyptian school teacher Hassan al-Banna. At this time Egypt was nominally independent but effectively under British control, British troops having suppressed a popular anti-colonial uprising in 1919. Liberal nationalists, often landowners and industrialists organised in the Wafd party, sought to win more power from Britain while discouraging any mass mobilisations that might challenge their economic position.[14] Al-Banna's organisation responded to imperial domination and social inequality by arguing for a return to the perceived principles of the early Islamic community.[15] Hamas is fundamentally a continuation of this tradition.

9: Appendix to Tamimi, 2007, p247.
10: Flimsy speculation of this kind can be found in Levitt, 2006, pp167-168.
11: Hroub, 2006, pp67-68, 77.
12: Pappé, 2006.
13: For a similar argument on Hizbollah see Harman, 2006.
14: Hourani, 2002, p329.
15: Mitchell, 1993, p233.

The idea of an Islamic community, morally reinvigorated and able to repel the colonial powers, appealed to particular social groups. Hassan al-Banna and his cadres emerged from the context of economic pressures on the old middle classes and the development of a new middle class of teachers, civil servants, engineers and so on.[16] Such groups were the mainstay of other anti-colonial movements in the Arab world and beyond. The Brotherhood differed from these by funding its petty bourgeois cadres with donations from landowners and industrialists in order to spread an Islamic revivalist message among the dispossessed of the cities, often recent arrivals from the countryside.[17] Charitable foundations and hospitals were particularly useful in this strategy. Hamas in Gaza, growing out of the Muslim Brotherhood in neighbouring Egypt, has followed the same pattern. Much of Hamas's funding comes from Palestinian businessmen, heavily supplemented by large flows of money from Gulf-based capitalists, Palestinian or otherwise.[18]

The Egyptian Muslim Brotherhood has, of course, undergone considerable evolution and generational change in the eight decades since its founding.[19] It is now the largest mass movement in Egypt (indeed, in the Arab world) with an estimated one million members, and forms the main opposition to the Mubarak regime.[20] Throughout that history the Brotherhood has played a frequently contradictory role mediating between the Egyptian ruling elite and the poverty-stricken mass of the population. On the one hand the Brotherhood must appeal to the poor; on the other its upper echelons and funders seek influence in order to bring about their vision of moral revival. In particular the regimes of Gamal Abdel Nasser and his successors have used the Brotherhood as a counterweight to the left, only then to repress the Brotherhood themselves. As a result, the Brotherhood's membership is continually embroiled in discussing the best strategic option to Islamise society, which then implies division about concrete political questions. Should the movement concentrate on *da'wa*, reviving Islamic morality from below by evangelism and social welfare work? Should it participate in the political system? Or should it consider the regime an infidel one and oppose it by terrorist means—the option of "anathema and exile"?

For the most part, the mainstream leadership of the Brotherhood have pursued the path of *da'wa* and a piecemeal search for influence.[21] They

---

16: Naguib, 2006, p16.
17: Mitchell, 1993, p329.
18: Hroub, 2006, p69.
19: Stacher, 2009.
20: Naguib, 2007.
21: Harman, 1994.

have tended to avoid direct confrontation with the state, particularly anything that would mobilise overly large numbers of workers and the poor. Hamas's politics are firmly anchored in this mainstream. The predominant influence of the Egyptian Brotherhood derives from the territorial situation between 1948 and 1967. The West Bank was annexed to Jordan but Gaza fell under Egyptian administration. Brotherhood volunteers fought against the establishment and expansion of Israel in 1948,[22] but their subsequent quietism left them unpopular among Palestinians.[23] Under Egyptian rule the Gazan Muslim Brothers—among them Sheikh Ahmed Yassin, the future leader of Hamas—were subject to the same bouts of repression and legalisation as the organisation in Egypt proper. Yassin founded the Islamic Centre, which became the Brotherhood's main base in Gaza. Although he was arrested in Nasser's renewed repression of the Brothers in 1965, Yassin, and the other members who would later form Hamas, avoided conflict with Israel.[24]

The Israeli occupation of Gaza after the 1967 Six Day War did not alter Yassin's focus on religious revivalism. Secular organisations such as Fatah, and later the avowedly Marxist Democratic Front for the Liberation of Palestine and Popular Front for the Liberation of Palestine, not the Muslim Brotherhood, took up the resistance to the occupation. The Brothers actually found their position eased by the fact that the West Bank and the Gaza Strip were under one authority—an authority more favourable to *da'wa* than Nasser had been.[25] Organisations related to the Islamic Centre offered the social welfare and healthcare services the occupation was unwilling to provide. Yassin's adherents muscled out the left in a struggle for predominance among Gazan students.[26]

The rise of an Islamist current to predominance in the Palestinian resistance was a far from inevitable development, however. An armed Islamic resistance movement emerged only after the crisis of the secular nationalist organisations after their defeat in Lebanon in 1982, which formed the backdrop to the outbreak of the first intifada in 1987. This crisis—culminating in the physical destruction and expulsion of Palestinian cadres from Lebanon in 1982, alongside the horrific Israeli-sponsored massacres of Palestinian refugees in the Sabra and Shatila camps near Beirut—resulted from their responses to the basic dilemma of the Israeli settler-colonial state and its relationship to imperialism.

22: Mitchell, 1993, p58.
23: Mishal and Sela, 2006, p16.
24: Tamimi, 2007, p17.
25: Tamimi, 2007, p19.
26: Mishal and Sela, 2006, p23.

Settler colonialism and imperialism in the Middle East

There are two basic kinds of settler colonialism, which produce different economic and political relations between the colonists and the colonised. In Australia and most of the Americas the colonists simply destroyed the indigenous population (whom they outnumbered) and took their land. In Africa (Algeria, South Africa, Zimbabwe, the Portuguese colonies) a relatively small number of settlers expropriated the indigenous population but remained economically dependent on their labour.[27] In South Africa in particular, this meant that the black working class played a crucial role in ending apartheid.

The Palestinian experience lies between these two poles. The numbers of colonists and colonised are roughly equal, the Palestinians holding a slight majority when the refugees from the Israeli ethnic cleansing of 1948 are included. Much as the more genocidally minded Israeli liberals might call for it, Israel cannot get rid of the native Palestinian population.[28] Thus the racist idea of a "demographic threat" (the "danger" posed by the relatively higher birth rate of Palestinians compared to Israeli Jews) is not just accepted in Israel: it has been bandied about by the prime minister.[29] The Israeli dilemma is how to get the land without the people. This is why the Israeli vision of a two-state solution is to render the Palestinians politically absent even if they are physically present.[30] The network of physical barriers to Palestinian life, such as the apartheid wall and checkpoints in the West Bank, has partially achieved this aim.[31]

The Palestinian dilemma, by contrast, lies in their basic weakness faced with a heavily armed settler community supported by the world's most powerful states. Palestinian labour is not economically irrelevant to Israel but, unlike US aid, it is not vital to the settler economy. The Zionist project has always sought to exclude Palestinians from the economy rather than to exploit them productively.[32] The closure of the Israeli labour market hurts the Palestinians much more than it does Israel. Although Gazan labour was becoming increasingly important to Israel prior to the signing of the Oslo accords in 1993, Israel was able to reverse this development at greater cost to the Palestinians.[33] During the first intifada Gazans lost access to 80,000 jobs on the other side of the Green Line,

---

27: Kimmerling, 2003, pp21-22.
28: Benny Morris, interviewed by Shavit, 2004.
29: Alon and Benn, 2003.
30: Kimmerling, 2003, pp3-4.
31: Weizmann, 2007, p10.
32: Hirst, 2003, pp147-148.
33: I am indebted to Anne Alexander for this point.

Israel's 1948 border.[34] The current blockade has rendered the majority of the Gazan labour force unemployed without any significant effect on the Israeli economy. The Palestinian population is also divided between the West Bank, Gaza, Israel behind the Green Line and the refugees in the Arab world and beyond. Mass mobilisation of the Palestinians always comes up against this economic limit: military resistance, on the other hand, can force withdrawals and concessions from Israel but is limited by the superiority Israel derives from US aid. Without extending the struggle to the system of imperialism in the Middle East as a whole, therefore, there can be no liberation of Palestine. Confined just to Palestinian land, the history of the Palestinian struggle repeats the same episodes of heroism and militancy leading to an exhausted accommodation to the idea of a "mini-state" on Israeli terms.

The rise of Hamas is the latest episode in this history. The exhaustion of Fatah and the Palestinian left in the early 1980s arose from their detachment of the struggle for Palestinian liberation from "internal" struggles against the surrounding Arab regimes, in particular from the potential power of the Egyptian working class. The Palestinian Liberation Organisation (PLO), under Fatah's leadership, followed a strategy of establishing bases in neighbouring Arab states while avoiding any challenge to the ruling regimes.[35] The regimes themselves observed no such restraint. Thus the PLO were driven from even the weakest frontline Arab states—Jordan in 1970 and (in the midst of civil war and Israeli invasion) Lebanon in 1982. The Palestinian left in the more left-wing "fronts" did recognise that revolution in the Arab states was a precondition for the liberation of Palestine but their idea of this revolution was Mao Zedong's "protracted people's war" or Che Guevara's guerrilla *focos*.[36] Although the revolutionary and proto-revolutionary movements inspired by the Palestinian left did reach the non-Palestinian populations, any attempt to establish liberated areas in the refugee camps was doomed: Israel, the local Arab ruling class or both would intervene to crush such areas—precisely what happened in Jordan and Lebanon.

By the early 1980s, then, the secular and leftist nationalists had hit a strategic dead end.[37] Into this crisis stepped Islamist movements, throughout the Arab world and especially in Gaza. Sheikh Yassin had carefully built up a power base in the Islamic Centre of Gaza, at new

34: Mishal and Sela, 2006, pxvi.
35: Marshall, 1989, p118.
36: Ismael, 1976, p106.
37: Balqaziz, 2006, p11.

mosques and the university, which had begun to admit more rural and conservative students.[38] Majd, a militia-like offshoot of the Islamic Centre, emerged, fighting the left and bullying people into greater religious observance.[39] An armed structure of sorts was thus already in place before the first intifada. However, it was only with the outbreak of that popular uprising in December 1987 that Hamas was officially formed.[40] The new organisation conceived of itself as primarily a national liberation movement, albeit one which proposed "Islam" as the solution to the crisis of Palestinian nationalism.

The charter of the new movement insisted upon the Palestinians' claim to all their homeland, including that part which became Israel in 1948. It also included an ample share of what Lenin called the "prejudices" of the petty bourgeoisie.[41] So, for example, the charter considers Judaism a kindred monotheism to be protected by Islamic rule but also repeats anti-Semitic claptrap found in the *Protocols of the Elders of Zion*.[42] These ideas have been abandoned by Hamas leaders and their original authors have long passed out of influence. Such passages—repugnant and counterproductive in equal measure—persist not because of any ingrained Arab or Islamic anti-Semitism but rather as a symptom of dangerous political confusion among those Palestinians who have only encountered Jews as agents of an oppressive colonial project.[43] This confusion can only be effectively challenged from a standpoint that supports resistance to that oppression. To do otherwise is to permit or encourage the identification of opposition to anti-Semitism with Zionism.

Hamas's primary appeal lay not in its charter, whatever the contents of that document. Rather Palestinians were drawn to Hamas's rejection of the PLO's proposed compromise with Israel on a two-state solution. The PLO's Tangiers Declaration of 1988 and Jordan's renunciation of any claim to the West Bank offered recognition to Israel in return for ending the intifada.[44] That compromise was particularly unpalatable to the Gazan population, the majority of them refugees who would be denied any prospect of return to their homes under a two-state deal with Israel. Hamas refused to join the PLO during the intifada but carried out essentially the same acts

---

38: Mishal and Sela, 2006, p20.
39: Mishal and Sela, 2005, pp25-26.
40: Tamimi, 2007, p55.
41: Lenin, 1916.
42: Appendix to Hroub, 2000, pp298-299.
43: Hroub, 2006, p34.
44: Hirst, 2003, p20.

of resistance.[45] The new Islamist movement denounced the manoeuvres of the PLO leadership in attempting to participate in (ultimately fruitless) negotiations at Madrid. Nonetheless, they remained financially and politically weaker than Fatah and the PLO. The balance turned in Hamas's favour as the PLO became identified with the slow surrender of Palestinian rights in the "peace process" that followed the intifada.

The peace process (also known as the Oslo process because of the role played by Norwegian mediators) comprised a series of agreements between the PLO and Israel. The first of these was the Declaration of Principles signed on the White House lawn in 1993. The main principle declared was that the Palestinians "recognise" Israel—thus legimitisng their ethnic cleansing from their homeland—in 78 percent of the land of historic Palestine. The PLO believed that this meant Israel would withdraw gradually from the remaining 22 percent occupied in 1967: the West Bank and the Gaza Strip. Israel conceived of a phased withdrawal but one in which it would retain control of settlements and roads.[46] Although Arafat and the PLO recognised Israel's right to exist, Israel merely recognised the PLO's competence to negotiate. The agreements postponed the issues of borders, refugees, Jerusalem and settlements until final talks. This manoeuvre allowed Israel not only to maintain but to expand the occupation in the form of checkpoints and settlements. The number of Israeli settlers in the West Bank and Gaza Strip increased by 50 percent in the period of the Oslo negotiations between 1993 and 2000.[47] A Palestinian Authority (PA) was established which would have an elected legislature and president. These would rule only over the most populous Palestinian areas, the rest remaining under Israeli or joint control.[48] The PA would also be tasked with policing the Palestinian population. The Israeli objective of ruling the land without the people was close to realisation.

Hamas opposed the Oslo accords from the start and throughout. They insisted on the Palestinian claim to all of historic Palestine and the right of refugees to return. They also denounced the PLO leaders who returned to run the PA and crassly enrich themselves in the manner of other Arab rulers.[49] Hamas refused to participate in elections at this time, not because they rejected democratic procedures but because they refused to legitimate Oslo.[50] It was a shrewd decision. As the Oslo process faltered the PA became

45: Mishal and Sela, 2006, p60.
46: Shlaim, 2000, p509.
47: Gresh and Vidal, 2004, pp279-280.
48: Smith, 2004, p485.
49: Chehab, 2007, p10.
50: Mishal and Sela, 2006, p138.

more and more irrelevant. Hamas did not (and does not) reject the effective principle of a two-state solution. All of its major figures have stated their willingness to sign a generation-long ceasefire provided that Israel withdraws its troops and settlers behind the 1967 border.[51] The supreme malleability of religious language allows Hamas to preserve the image of fighting for all of historic Palestine, but in practice the ceasefire means recognition of Israel. Hamas was not prepared, however, to renounce military resistance until such an agreement was achieved. Thus Hamas launched a series of suicide attacks on Israeli targets throughout the Oslo negotiations, the first of these being carried out in revenge for the Hebron massacre in 1994 when an Israeli settler reservist killed 40 worshippers at an Islamic sacred site in Hebron.[52]

Hamas's position was vindicated by the collapse of the Oslo process and the eruption of the second intifada in 2000. Israel's tactical errors—such as the botched assassination attempt on Khaled Mesh'al, a major Hamas leader in Jordan, or the exiling of hundreds of Hamas cadres to Hizbollah's Southern Lebanese stronghold—contributed to the movement's rise. The main reason was political, however. The second intifada reflected Palestinian anger at a peace process that had only made their lives worse.[53] Hamas was identified with the resistance to that process. The intifada brought Hamas and Fatah closer as their cadres fought a common enemy. Yet the continual Israeli assaults on Palestinian political and physical infrastructure, particularly the Israeli offensive on the urban centres in the spring of 2004, mostly weakened Fatah, who had embedded themselves deeply in those structures.[54] At the titular head of the Palestinian political structure stood Yasser Arafat who retained, even regained, his prestige as the leader of the Palestinian resistance. Arafat's death in November 2004 deprived Fatah of their greatest remaining claim to hegemony over the Palestinian struggle.[55] His replacement, Mahmoud Abbas, appeared keener than ever to compromise with Israel.

The contrast between this weakened Fatah and Hamas at the end of the second intifada was sharp. While Abbas scuttled after the pointless initiatives of George W Bush's successor to the Oslo process, the "road map", Hamas achieved the only withdrawal of Israeli settlements from Palestinian land when Israeli troops and colonists left Gaza in July 2005. It is true that the territory remained besieged by Israeli air, land and sea power.

51: Mishal and Sela, 2006, pxxii. See also *Economist*, 2009c, and Hroub, 2006, pp55-56.
52: Chehab, 2007, p56.
53: Shin Bet warned of this in the months prior to the Second Intifada: see Enderlin, 2004, p137.
54: Mishal and Sela, 2006, pxiv.
55: Balqaziz, 2006, p21.

It is also true that the withdrawal reflected the racial calculus of Israeli politics: ridding the state of a large and restive Arab population all the better to retain the colonies in the West Bank. Thus the Gaza withdrawal formed an integral part of "a new Israeli defence concept" of unilateral separation behind a "hard border".[56] This doctrine—what one might call "cage and ignore"—seeks to render the Palestinians' physical presence politically meaningless. The apartheid wall that physically cuts Palestinian communities off from one another is a literally concrete manifestation of this strategy. Yet Israel would not have withdrawn the settlements if the benefits of occupying Gaza outweighed the costs. It was Hamas that raised those costs. For nearly 30 years the Palestinians had been convinced that compromise with Israel was the route to regaining at least some of their land. Hamas, like Hizbollah, had shown that resistance was more effective.

The "earthquake" and the coup against Hamas

Israeli and Western media frequently refer to "the Hamas regime in Gaza" and claim that the movement came to power by coup in 2007. The precise opposite is true. Hamas has been the duly elected government of the Palestinian Territories since 2006. It was Fatah that carried out a coup with Israeli and Western backing. Hamas's success in forcing the Israeli withdrawal of 2005 opened the way to the "earthquake" of the movement's electoral victory in the Palestinian legislative council elections in January 2006.[57] Hamas decided to drop its boycott of this Oslo institution because the Oslo accords were plainly dead. Hamas also thought it could do very well in the elections. Even those expectations were exceeded. Their electoral platform, the Change and Reform list, won 60 percent of the popular vote.[58] "Change and reform" is a vacuous slogan but any Fatah candidate uttering it would have been ridiculed, so firmly were they identified with stasis and reaction. Fatah and Abbas were not only unable to mount effective resistance to Israel, but were also identified with corruption and mismanagement at every level.[59] Their campaign in the legislative elections was heavily supported by Israel and the US.[60]

Fatah and its Israeli and Western backers were incredulous at the election result. They have been trying to change it ever since by means of the blockade and extreme violence against perceived violation of that blockade.

56: Aronson, 2006, p132.
57: Balqaziz, 2006, p93.
58: Hroub, 2006, p66.
59: Mishal and Sela, 2006, pxv.
60: Rose, 2008.

The Israeli cabinet refused to recognise the new legislature and declared that it would never negotiate with "any Palestinian administration even part of which is composed of an armed terrorist organisation that calls for the destruction of the state of Israel".[61] The US and EU, who balk at any idea of sanctions on Israel for its serial violations of international law, followed in imposing a blockade on the newly elected government. Fatah stripped ministries of equipment and refused to cooperate with Hamas ministers. The Palestinian presidency was at armed odds with the legislative body and the cabinet. Fatah militias received Jordanian and US training and funds, while simultaneously engaging in "national dialogue" with Hamas under Egyptian pressure.[62] From Hamas's election in January 2006 Muhammad Dahlan, Fatah's would-be ruler of Gaza, had threatened trouble in the territory. Dahlan was recorded admitting as much by an Egyptian newspaper, saying, "I just deploy two jeeps, and people would say Gaza is on fire... Hamas is now the weakest Palestinian faction. They are whining and complaining. Well, they will have to suffer yet more until they are damned to the seventh ancestor".[63] Were two jeeps insufficient to ensure damnation, Dahlan could count on the support of the US. A senior US diplomat stated privately, "I like this violence".[64]

The notion, then, that Hamas seized power in Gaza in the summer of 2007 is a deliberately propagated myth. In the words of Dick Wurmser, then vice-president Dick Cheney's adviser on the Middle East, "what happened wasn't so much a coup by Hamas but an attempted coup by Fatah that was pre-empted before it could happen".[65] The Mecca Agreement of March 2007 was supposed to reconcile the two sides in a coalition cabinet and, in Hamas's interpretation, the subordination of the security forces to the prime minister.[66] The mini civil war between Hamas and Fatah in July 2007 essentially concerned the unwillingness of Fatah militia commanders to submit to Hamas command. Such an attitude is unsurprising but to represent the resulting conflict as a Hamas coup is a reversal of reality. "Iran Contra 2.0", the plan to get rid of Hamas in the summer of 2007, backfired badly on its perpetrators.[67] Hamas fighters were able to drive Fatah underground and out of Gaza. The opposite held true in the West Bank. Abbas simply appointed

---

61: Chehab, 2007, p8.
62: Rose, 2008.
63: Crooke, 2007.
64: Crooke, 2007.
65: Rose, 2008.
66: Al Jazeera English, 2007.
67: Rose, 2008.

a new cabinet under the former World Bank bureaucrat Salam Fayyad. The blockade and the spiralling Israeli violence required to maintain it aim at finishing the work of Dahlan in 2007 and dislodging Hamas from Gaza.

Bombing and besieging Gaza

After the assault on the Freedom Flotilla, a columnist on the Israeli daily *Haaretz* wrote, "We are no longer defending Israel. We are now defending the siege. The siege itself is becoming Israel's Vietnam".[68] The blockade of exports out of and most imports into Gaza, enforced since June 2007, is an ongoing act of slow and brutal violence punctuated by acts of intense exemplary violence to terrify the population into observing it. Israel claims to allow in "basic humanitarian supplies" but decides for itself what these are. Pasta, light bulbs, shoes and blankets have all been denied entry.[69] Canned tuna is allowed in but not canned fruit: tea but not jam.[70] Only five shipments of vehicle fuel have been allowed into Gaza under the blockade.[71] Even if very basic supplies of cooking oil and wheat are allowed in, Gazans are denied fuel to distribute them, refrigerators in which to store their products or indeed money with which to buy fresh food. As a result, according to the UN, the formal economy in Gaza has "collapsed", 70 percent of the population live on less than a dollar a day, 75 percent depend on food aid and 61 percent lack daily access to water.[72]

The total export blockade and restriction of imports—with periods of complete closure—has been Israeli policy since the failure of the attempted Fatah coup in 2007. Israel had been trying to dislodge the Hamas government since its first cabinet was formed in March 2006, however, using increased artillery fire and closure of the strip.[73] It was one such artillery attack that killed seven members of the same family on Gaza beach in June 2006, a now largely forgotten outrage that precipitated the capture of the Israeli soldier Gilad Shalit.[74] These events were the proximate trigger for the "summer war" Israel fought in Lebanon (and Gaza) in 2006. Hamas still proved impossible to dislodge and a series of inter-Palestinian talks throughout 2007 and 2008 went nowhere. It seemed that Israel was going to have to deal with Hamas. The prospect of recognising Hamas as a negotiating partner, and

---

68: *Middle East Report*, 2010.
69: BBC News, 2010.
70: BBC News, 2010.
71: BBC News, 6 July 2010.
72: Siddque, 2010.
73: Karmi, 2006.
74: Karmi, 2006.

therefore of entering a dialogue leading to the lifting of the blockade, lay behind the Israeli assault on Gaza (Operation Cast Lead) at the end of 2008.[75]

A six-month "lull" was agreed between Hamas and Israel in June 2008. Hamas held the renewal of this lull to be conditional on the lifting of the blockade: according to an Israeli think tank closely linked to the Israeli Defence Force, "Hamas was careful to maintain the ceasefire" which was only sporadically violated by "rogue" organisations, including Fatah members.[76] The head of Shin Bet, the Israeli internal intelligence force, told a cabinet meeting prior to Cast Lead that Hamas was "interested in continuing the truce, but wants to improve its terms…it wants us to lift the siege, stop attacks, and extend the truce to include [the West Bank]".[77] Israel did not lift the blockade, and had no intention of doing so, since this would leave Hamas in power. Hamas rockets were a pretext for an all-out attack to get rid of Hamas. Then foreign minister Tzipi Livni clarified this aim the week before the war on Gaza began, saying, "Israel, and a government under me, will make it a strategic objective to topple the Hamas regime in Gaza".[78] Deputy prime minister Eli Yishai reiterated the point with greater bloodlust: "[Palestinian buildings] should be razed to the ground, so thousands of houses, tunnels and industries will be demolished…the operation will continue until a total destruction of Hamas".[79]

Hamas was not destroyed despite the ferocity of the attack. The war devastated the already ramshackle infrastructure of the territory. According to the Israeli human rights group B'tselem, half of the 1,387 Palestinians killed were civilians.[80] Israel, of course, holds overwhelming military supremacy over Gaza and the Palestinians. Yet it was unable to use that military supremacy to achieve its political aim of toppling Hamas—even over a malnourished people whose territory it entirely controls from land, sea and air. Indeed, Hamas achieved recognition as the representative of the Palestinians in an Arab summit convened in Qatar during the war.[81] Israel's inability to use overwhelming firepower and air supremacy to effect political change undermines the *Dahiya* doctrine" that has come to underpin Israeli strategy. Named after the Beirut suburbs (*dahiya*) that suffered it in 2006, this doctrine applies "disproportionate force" to any area Israel considers a

---

75: Rabbani, 2009,
76: Intelligence and Terrorism Information Center, 2008, p2
77: BBC News, 22 December 2008.
78: Ravid, 2008.
79: Quoted in UN Human Rights Council, 2009, p332.
80: Al Jazeera English, 2009.
81: Reuters, 2009.

security threat.[82] The conceptual line from this doctrine to the raid on the Freedom Flotilla is not hard to trace.

What is to be done?

The use of absurdly savage force produces diminishing returns for Israel. The assault on the Freedom Flotilla only served to highlight the blockade and rendered it unsustainable even for Israel's closest allies. Turkey, traditionally Israel's strongest ally in the region, is now perceived as an enemy in the camp of Syria and Iran.[83] During the Gaza war Israel was unable to use its military superiority to get its preferred outcome. With Hamas still in power, the axis of anti-imperialist resistance linking that organisation with Hizbollah and Iran remains unbroken. The previous Gaza war constituted another blow to the project of renewed US domination in the region, already hobbled by failure in Iraq, the loss of a proxy war in Lebanon in 2006 and the unfolding prospect of defeat in Afghanistan.

Yet the very weakening of its position has led to some rhetorical change from the US and the appearance of occasional slivers of distance between the Obama administration and Binyamin Netanyahu's government. Netanyahu's coalition is committed to further settlement expansion for reasons of ideological commitment and political manoeuvre. The choice between Labour and Likud in Israel was always limited to slightly different varieties of Zionism: now that the main parties are Likud and its offshoot Kadima, the choice is between right wing Zionism, extreme right wing Zionism and genocidally right wing Zionism. At crucial points the US always backs Israel but years of intransigence have made Israeli leaders obstinate enough to embarrass even the US.

The US response to the flotilla raid was instructive. The most supportive comments came from the buffoonish vice-president, Joe Biden, long identified with most pro-Israeli section of Washington opinion and despite (or perhaps because of) this, victim of serial snubs by Binyamin Netanyahu.[84] Obama's statement could muster no more than "deep regret" for the victims of the Israeli attack.[85] Members of Netanyahu's circle see Obama as "very, very hostile" and a "strategic disaster for Israel".[86] This is partly hyperbole of the sort that describes Obama's healthcare plan as "communist". Israel can, for the time being, still count on full US support.

82: Reuters, 2008.
83: Teitelbaum, 2010.
84: McCarthy and Siddique, 2010.
85: Al Jazeera English, 2010.
86: McCarthy, 2010.

Yet the Obama administration is also eager to regain a reputation as an "honest broker" in the conflict, so that the populations of US allies such as Egypt, Saudi Arabia and Jordan can be persuaded there is something to be gained by their subservient relationship with the US. This posture is undermined by the Netanyahu coalition's obstinate attitude to continuing colonisation of East Jerusalem and its obstruction of the US-sponsored indirect talks with Abbas and the PLO-controlled parts of the PA. These talks were unlikely to go anywhere, since they did not include Hamas, but the attack on the Freedom Flotilla matches a pattern of Israeli actions to undermine them.[87] The US is not concerned with the dreadful situation in which the Palestinians find themselves. Rather the US military are concerned that the costs of supporting Israel are coming to outweigh its strategic benefits.[88]

Hamas has, since before the election of the Obama administration, been desperate to join in talks with the US.[89] The politics of the organisation, limited to the liberation of Palestine without challenging the networks of imperialist alliances in the region as a whole, will tend towards this conclusion and towards reaching an accommodation of sorts with Israel. Hamas's redline is the lifting of the blockade. This is achievable but only through a sustained campaign of popular pressure, especially in Israel's Western backers. A long term solution is unlikely because of Israel's interlocking relationship with global imperialism. The Israeli idea of security is premised on the maintenance of a "Jewish state" that excludes the Palestinians. So long as the Palestinians exist and resist, that "security" cannot be realised. Internal Israeli opposition and, especially, the increasing disquiet among diaspora Jewish communities are devoutly to be encouraged.[90] Yet, as in the case of apartheid South Africa's defeats in Mozambique and Angola, the ideology of racial supremacy is more likely to collapse if the military guarantee behind it is shown to be useless in the face of effective resistance of the kind offered by Hizbollah and Hamas.

The source of Israel's military guarantee remains the US, also the primary backer of the Arab regimes. Since the 1960s Israel has closely aligned itself with the US as a guardian of imperial interests in the region. US political and financial support is indispensable to the state. To understand the strategic dynamic between the US, Israel and the Palestinian resistance we must look to the region as a whole and its integration into the capitalist world economy.

87: *Haaretz*, 2010.
88: *Haaretz*, 2010.
89: Al-Naami, 2008.
90: Beinart, 2010.

The politics of the Middle East still revolve around the division between supporters and opponents of imperialist intervention, an intervention motivated by the vital supplies of oil in the Persian Gulf. "Radical" states confront "moderate" ones—except that radicals can become moderate (Egypt following the defeat of 1973 and the adoption of "*infitah*" neoliberal policies) and moderates radical (Iran after the revolution of 1979). The peculiar and particular importance of the resources of this region for global capitalism has produced the tendency for anti-colonial movements to confront Western hegemony, then to accept it, then to be superseded by a new movement.

Such dramatic political swings reflect waves of what Tony Cliff called "deflected permanent revolution", a concept discussed at greater length elsewhere in this journal.[91] What concerns us here is how to analyse the rise of Hamas to leadership of the Palestinian resistance and how to respond to it. Hamas, needless to say, is not a socialist or working class organisation and it certainly does not offer a vision of universal human emancipation. Like the Vietnamese NLF, Hamas has persecuted activists with whom most European socialists would feel much greater political affinity. However, the task at hand is not to pick which Palestinian faction is most ideologically acceptable—there would be few—but to understand the reasons for Hamas's rise and, from the basis of support for the resistance, search for the possibilities of a working class alternative that goes beyond the limits of Hamas's politics.[92] To do so we must again discuss the regional context, which is inextricably linked to the Palestinian struggle.

Imperialist intervention and the occupation and dictatorship that accompany it continue to dominate the Middle East. Capitalist penetration has produced a large working class but also an equally large collection of urban petty bourgeois groups resulting from the destruction of traditional artisan production and migration to the cities. These groups have produced most of the state functionaries and lesser intellectuals who have felt their continued subjugation most keenly.[93] They have sought to end that subjugation—embodied most of all in the Israeli occupation—but only in order to take what they imagine to be their rightful place within the system of capitalist states. Hamas in Palestine and the broader regional Islamic current to which it belongs represent a new generation of this phenomenon.

91: See, of course, Cliff, 1990, as well as Zeilig, 2010, and Neil Davidson's article in this issue.

92: This is not to disparage the encouraging shoots of revival on the Palestinan left, particularly among the "Sons of the Land" (*Abnaa' al balad*) group but also evident at the conference on the Palestinian left held in London on 27 and 28 February 2010.

93: An example of the general process described in Cliff, 1990, p21.

Each previous generation eventually came to accept imperialist domination because they did not base themselves on the one force with both the power and the interest to overthrow the capitalist order in the region—the working class. Hamas, and the broader Hizbollah-Syrian-Iranian axis to which it is linked is likely to follow the same path.

Why is this relevant to an understanding of the current oppression and prospects for liberation of the Palestinians? This analysis is necessary in order to approach any kind of solution to what was once called the "Palestine problem". Like the PLO before it, Hamas avoids any challenge to the Arab regimes.[94] Hamas are committed to fighting the occupation and establishing a Palestinian state but they are very concerned to ensure that this struggle does not extend to the exercise of popular power that may pass beyond these goals. Within the confines of Palestine itself they can defy Israel's military machine but not defeat it. As an alternative to Hamas's politics of limited liberation the Palestinian working class, such as it is, faces a difficult situation. The impact of nearly two generations of occupation and siege and the exclusion from the colonial economy leave the prospect of an internal South African style transition unlikely. A revival of Palestinian popular resistance would be a necessary part of challenging the colonial state but would have to pass beyond the boundaries of Palestine to be truly effective. Zionism is part of the imperialist architecture of domination in the whole of the Middle East, sustained by American money and Arab collaboration.

What are the prospects for overturning this architecture of domination? The left is always well advised to remember Gramsci's watchword, "pessimism of the intellect, optimism of the will." But one must also reckon with assessments such as that of the Washington bureau chief of the *Economist*, a magazine not noted for its ultra-leftism: "In almost any Arab country, at almost any time, political and social discontent is in danger of tipping into violence—even, some insiders and outsiders are beginning to argue, into revolution".[95] This judgement remains to be tested. What is certain is that the renewed imperialist adventures of the past decade have solidified Arab opinion against "moderate" (ie pro-Western) regimes and led to an increasing identification with the resistance forces of Hamas and Hizbollah, emboldened by their ability to stand firm against Israel.[96]

94: In 1999 Hamas accepted their expulsion from Jordan without a fight, reflecting the influence of the Jordanian Muslim Brotherhood. At the 2007 Cairo Conference Hamas representatives refrained from any criticism of the Mubarak regime, despite the raising of the slogan "Down with Mubarak" by practically every other speaker (personal recollection).
95: *Economist*, 2009a.
96: *Economist*, 2009b.

Although there are encouraging signs of struggle in Lebanon and even certain of the Gulf States, we have yet to see a large-scale working class struggle throughout the entire Arab world. However, in Egypt resistance has begun to take a working class character, involving an enormous strike wave and increasingly sharp confrontation with the Mubarak regime.[97] This is vital because Egypt is the strategic core of the Arab world. It was Egypt's separate peace with Israel in 1978 that in part precipitated the crisis of Palestinian resistance. Egypt has the most important non-oil based economy in the region. It is for these reasons that Egypt has received more US aid than any other country except Israel.[98] Both the leading Palestinian factions seek and receive influence from Egypt: Fatah through its relationship with Mubarak and Hamas through its parent organisation, the Egyptian Brotherhood.

The Egyptian opposition has opened up the horizon, if not yet the full reality, of the working class as a political subject in the Arab world.[99] Anti-imperialist, democratic and social demands have begun to meld into one another, including slogans identifying Mubarak with Israel.[100] Strike leaders from the textile workers issued a condemnation of both Israel for the flotilla attack and the Mubarak regime for its cooperation with the blockade.[101] Aid convoys and delegations to Gaza have been organised by strikers.[102] The strike wave that began in 2006 and reached a peak of confrontation with the state in the uprising in the city of Mahalla el-Kubra in April 2008 has utterly changed the Egyptian scene. In 2009, in a police state where independent workers' actions are illegal, there were "478 industrial actions by workers, including 184 sit-ins, 123 strikes, 79 demonstrations and 27 rallies".[103] For six months workers occupied the street in front of the Egyptian parliament to demand economic and political rights—including one of the first national protests by disabled people.[104]

In Egypt the poor and the workers cannot go on being ruled in the old way and the regime cannot go on ruling in the old way. The dying dictator Mubarak is trying to enforce the succession of his son Gamal as president. The situation remains open and political alternatives are presenting themselves. The workers' movement has won space for popular protest but

97: See Alexander, 2008, and Naguib, 2007.
98: Alexander, 2010, p138.
99: A full account of this is given in El-Mahdi and Marfleet, 2010. See also www.arabawy.org
100: Shenker, 2010.
101: El-Hamawaly, 2010.
102: El-Hamawaly, 2010.
103: Omar, 2010.
104: El-Hamalawy, 2010.

has not yet (since the brutal suppression of the Mahalla uprising) coalesced into a nationally organised challenge. Popular hopes may converge on Mohammed el-Baradei, the former head of the International Atomic Energy Agency, who has returned to Egypt promising political reform. The undeclared candidacy of El-Baradei has crystallised the mood for change and El-Baradei has proved adept at responding to different audiences such as in his call for combining democracy with socialism.[105] The Brotherhood is moving to support him.[106] Yet El Baradei also shows signs of an unnerving "respectability" in the eyes of the US, in particular in his attitude to Israel.[107] This is important, because it is around the issue of Egyptian cooperation with the blockade that the demands of social, national and political liberation converge.

It is here that we see the limits of Hamas's politics, linked to the intermediary role of the Muslim Brotherhood. This link can win Hamas influence but also cut it off from the potentially powerful Egyptian resistance because of the contradictory politics of the Brotherhood. One tangible example of the pitfalls of this strategy came when Hamas engineers exploded charges beneath the wall that separates the Rafah camp in Gaza from Egypt in January 2008. Palestinian women and children tore down the wall that separates Gaza from Egypt.[108] Hamas engineers had helped by laying charges at the foundations, but it was popular power and unity with poor Egyptians that broke Israel's blockade. Hundreds of thousands of people, perhaps half the population of Gaza, streamed through the wreckage to get food, water, medicine and everything else denied them. Egyptians organised convoys to the town of El-Arish to meet them, effectively shifting the national border.[109] The Mubarak regime panicked, at first claiming they authorised the movement and then repressing it viciously.[110]

The Egyptian Muslim Brotherhood, the target of much of the repression, again played a crucial intermediary role, persuading Hamas to meet Mubarak. After that meeting Mahmoud Al-Zahar, the Hamas foreign minister, declared, "Hamas will resume control over this border in cooperation with Egypt".[111] To do otherwise would have meant a full-scale challenge to the Egyptian regime—something that neither Hamas nor its allies in the Egyptian Muslim Brotherhood were willing to risk. Following the mass

---

105: Abdel Aziz, 2010.
106: *Al-Masry Al-Youm*, 010.
107: Centre for Socialist Studies, 2010.
108: Assaf, 2008.
109: Assaf, 2008.
110: Assaf, 2008.
111: Al Jazeera English, 2009.

demonstrations after the Israeli attack on the flotilla, the increasingly nervy Mubarak opened Rafah "indefinitely".[112]

Conclusion

Further confrontations, and possibly concessions, lie ahead between Hamas, Israel and the US. The assault on the *Mavi Marmara* and the popular anger it provoked have led to European diplomatic noises against the blockade.[113] A determined boycott campaign could make use of this opening to increase the pressure on Israel. Signs of distance between the US and Israeli positions have opened up but an imperial power on the back foot can ill afford to lose its one unshakably firm ally in such an important region. Hence the weakening of US language on Israeli settlements in the West Bank, from calling for an end to settlement expansion to merely asking for "restraint".[114]

The Palestinians will still have something to resist. Hamas has proven its capacity to lead that resistance but, limited to guerrilla action within the land of Palestine, it is unlikely to achieve a solution based on equality between Palestinians and Israelis. Anything less will see the leadership of the resistance pass to some other organisation. So long as the resistance continues, the attempts to crush it will continue on their brutal trajectory—save for the intervention of the Arab working class, whose potential we have at least begun to glimpse.

References

Abdel Aziz, Marwan, 2010, "El Baradei Meets with Left-Wing Opposition Leaders" *Al-Masry Al-Youm* (9 June), http://www.almasryalyoum.com/en/news/elbaradei-meets-left-wing-opposition-leaders

Alexander, Anne, 2008, "Inside Egypt's Mass Strikes", *International Socialism* 118 (spring), www.isj.org.uk/?id=428

Alexander, Anne, 2010, "Mubarak in the International Arena", in Rabab El-Mahdi and Phil Marfleet (eds), *Egypt: The Moment of Change* (Zed Books).

Al Jazeera English, 2007, "Hamas tightens control in Gaza" (14 June), http://english.aljazeera.net/news/middleeast/2007/06/2008525141145604145.html

Al Jazeera English, 2008, "Egypt-Gaza border resealed", (3 February), http://english.aljazeera.net/news/middleeast/2008/02/200852514935891560.html

---

112: Gab Allah, 2010.

113: Sherwood, 2010. For more on the Boycott, Divestment and Sanctions movement see the article by Tom Hickey and Phil Marfleet in this journal.

114: McCarthy, 2009.

Al Jazeera English, 2009, "Half of Gaza war dead civilians" (9 September), http://english.aljazeera.net/news/middleeast/2009/09/200999114019997778.html

Al Jazeera English, 2010, "Global outrage over Israeli attack" (3 June), http://english.aljazeera.net/news/middleeast/2010/05/20105316216182630.html

Al-Masry Al-Youm, 2010, "Muslim Brotherhood Throws Support behind El-Baradei" (6 June), www.almasryalyoum.com/en/news/muslim-brotherhood-throws-support-behind-elbaradei

Al-Naami, Saleh, 2008, "Last-Minute Moves", *Al-Ahram Weekly* (16 October), http://weekly.ahram.org.eg/2008/918/fr2.htm

Alon, Gideon, and Aluf Benn, 2003, "Netanyahu: Israel's Arabs are the real demographic threat", *Haaretz* (18 December), www.haaretz.com/print-edition/news/netanyahu-israel-s-arabs-are-the-real-demographic-threat-1.109045

Aronson, Geoffrey, 2006, "Evacuation of Additional Settlements on Olmert's agenda", *Journal of Palestine Studies* 35:4 (University of California Press).

Assaf, Simon, 2008, "The Week We Broke Their Prison State", *Socialist Worker* (2 February), www.socialistworker.co.uk/art.php?id=14029

Balqaziz, Abdallah, 2006, *Azmat-l-masrhu al-watanii al-falastinii: min fatah ila hamas* [Crisis of the Palestinian National Project: from Fatah to Hamas] (Centre for Studies in Arab Unity).

Bassiouny, Mustafa and Omar Said, 2008, "A new workers' movement: the strike wave of 2007", *International Socialism* 118 (spring), www.isj.org.uk/?id=429

BBC News, 2008, "Israeli leaders 'to topple Hamas'" (22 December), http://news.bbc.co.uk/1/hi/world/middle_east/7794577.stm

BBC News, 2010, "Gaza under Blockade" (6 July), http://news.bbc.co.uk/1/hi/world/middle_east/7545636.stm

Beinart, Peter, 2010, "The Failure of the American Jewish Establishment", *New York Review of Books* (10 June), www.nybooks.com/articles/archives/2010/jun/10/failure-american-jewish-establishment/

Booth, Robert, 2010, "Gaza flotilla: Sarah Colborne's account", *Guardian* (3 June), www.guardian.co.uk/world/2010/jun/03/sarah-colborne-gaza-account

Centre for Socialist Studies, 2010, "Al Barada'ii...wa halam al-taghaiir al-mafqud" [El Baradei ...and the lost dream of change], http://en.e-socialists.net/node/5604

Chehab, Zaki, 2007, *Inside Hamas: The Untold Story of Militants, Martyrs and Spies* (IB Tauris).

Cliff, Tony, 1990, *Deflected Permanent Revolution* (Bookmarks).

Crooke, Alistair, 2007, "Our Second Biggest Mistake in the Middle East", *London Review of Books* 29:13, www.lrb.co.uk/v29/n13/alastair-crooke/our-second-biggest-mistake-in-the-middle-east

Economist, 2009a, "A Special Report on the Arab World: Waking from its Sleep" (23 July), www.economist.com/node/14027698?story_id=14027698

Economist, 2009b, "A Special Report on the Arab World: Which Way will They Go?" (23 July), www.economist.com/node/14027708

Economist, 2009c, "Hamas's Foreign Policy: Acceptance versus recognition" (30 July), www.economist.com/node/14140786?story_id=14140786

El-Hamawaly, Hossam, 2010, "Egypt's Workers Take to the Streets Against Mubarak and Israel", *Socialist Worker* (12 June), www.socialistworker.co.uk/art.php?id=21455

Enderlin, Charles, 2004, *Shattered Dreams: The Failure of the Peace Process in the Middle East* (Other).

Financial Times, 2010, "The siege of Gaza must be ended" (6 June).

Gab Allah, Khalifa, 2010, "Rafah Border Opened 'Indefinitely'", *Al Masry Al Youm* (2 June) www.almasryalyoum.com/en/news/rafah-border-opened-indefinitely

Gresh, Alain, and Dominique Vidal, 2004, *The New A-Z of the Middle East* (IB Tauris).

Haaretz, 2010, "US General: Israeli-Palestinian Conflict Foments Anti-US Sentiment", (17 March), www.haaretz.com/news/u-s-general-israel-palestinian-conflict-foments-anti-u-s-sentiment-1.264910

Harman, Chris, 1994, *The Prophet and the Proletariat*, www.marxists.de/religion/harman/index.htm

Harman, Chris 2006 "Hizbollah and the War Israel Lost", *International Socialism* 112 *(autumn)*, www.isj.org.uk/?id=243

Hirst, David, 2003, *The Gun and The Olive Branch* (Faber & Faber).

Holmes, John, 2010, "Statement of John Holmes, United Nations Under-Secretary-General for Humanitarian Affairs and Emergency Relief Coordinator, on the 'Free Gaza' Flotilla Crisis", http://bit.ly/holmesgaza

Hourani, Albert, 2002, *A History of the Arab Peoples,* (Faber & Faber).

Hroub, Khalid, 2000, *Hamas:al-fikr wa-l-mumarasa al-siyaasiyya* [Hamas: Political Thought and Practice] (Institute for Palestine Studies).

Hroub, Khalid, 2006, *Hamas: A Beginner's Guide* (Pluto).

Intelligence and Terrorism Information Center, 2008, *The Six Months of the Lull Arrangement,* www.terrorism-info.org.il/malam_multimedia/English/eng_n/html/hamas_e017.htm

Ismael, Tareq, 1976, *The Arab Left* (New York University Press).

Israeli Ministry of Foreign Affairs, "Exchange of Letters between Israel and the PLO", www.israelmfa.gov.il/MFA/Peace+Process/Guide+to+the+Peace+Process/Israel-PLO+Recognition+-+Exchange+of+Letters+betwe.htm

Karmi, Omar, 2006, "Gaza in the Vise", *Middle East Report Online* (11 July), www.merip.org/mero/mero071106.html

Kimmerling, Baruch, 2003, *Politicide: Ariel Sharon's War against the Palestinians* (Verso).

Lenin, VI, 1916, "The Discussion on National Self-determination Summed Up", www.marxists.org/archive/lenin/works/1916/jul/x01.htm

Levitt, Matthew, 2006, *Hamas: Politics, Charity and Terrorism in the Service of Jihad* (Yale University Press).

Marshall, Phil, 1989, *Intifada: Zionism, Imperialism and Palestinian Resistance* (Bookmarks).

McCarthy, Rory, 2009, "Palestinian Faith in Obama 'Evaporates'", *Guardian* (13 October), www.guardian.co.uk/world/2009/oct/13/palestinians-israel-obama-abbas

McCarthy, Rory, 2010, "Netanyahu's Efforts to Heal Rift Marred as Barack Obama Branded 'Disaster' for Israel", *Guardian* (28 March), www.guardian.co.uk/world/2010/mar/28/obama-israel-us-netanyahu

McCarthy, Rory, and Haroon Siddique, 2010, "Biden Calls for 'Viable' Palestinian State", *Guardian* (10 March), www.guardian.co.uk/world/2010/mar/10/israel-homes-plan-biden-apology

Middle East Report, 2010 "Outlaws of the Mediterranean" Middle East Report Online (1 June) http://www.merip.org/mero/mero060110.html

Mishal, Saul, and Avraham Sela, 2006, *The Palestinian Hamas: Vision, Violence and Co-existence* (New York, Columbia University Press).

Mitchell, Richard, 1993, *The Society of the Muslim Brothers*, second edition (Oxford University Press).

Naguib, Sameh, 2006, *Al-Ikhwan al-Muslimun: Ru'iya ishtarakiyya* [The Muslim Brotherhood: A Socialist View] (Cairo, Centre for Socialist Studies).

Naguib, Sameh, 2007, "Interview: Egypt's Strike Wave", *International Socialism* 116 *(autumn)*, www.isj.org.uk/?id=363

Omar, Mostafa, 2010, "Egypt's brewing revolt: Part 2, The rising class struggle", *Socialist Worker* US (8 June), http://socialistworker.org/2010/06/08/rising-class-struggle

Pappé, Ilan, 2006, "The History of Israel's Destructive Role in the Middle East", *Socialist Worker* (26 July), http://www.isj.org.uk/?id=232

Rabbani, Mouin, 2009, "The birth pangs of a new Middle East", *Middle East Report Online* (7 January), www.merip.org/mero/mero071106.html

Rabab El-Mahdi & Phil Marfleet (eds), *Egypt: the moment of change* (Zed Books).

Ravid, Barak, 2008, "Livni: As Prime Minister I will topple Hamas regime in Gaza", *Haaretz* (21 December), www.haaretz.com/news/livni-as-prime-minister-i-will-topple-hamas-regime-in-gaza-1.259955

Ravid, Barak, 2010, "Netanyahu: Israel will Not Allow Establishment of Iranian Port in Gaza", *Haaretz* (5 June), www.haaretz.com/news/diplomacy-defense/netanyahu-israel-will-not-allow-establishment-of-iranian-port-in-gaza-1.294328

Reuters, 2008, "Israel warns Hezbollah war would invite destruction" (3 October), www.reuters.com/article/idUSL3251393

Reuters, 2009a, "Hamas and Jihad leaders in Qatar for Gaza meeting" (16 January), www.reuters.com/article/idUSLG112054

Reuters, 2009b, "Gaza Still Waiting for Pledged Reconstruction Aid", *Haaretz* (30 April).

Rose, David, 2008, "The Gaza Bombshell", *Vanity Fair* (April), www.vanityfair.com/politics/features/2008/04/gaza200804

Ruddick, Sian, 2010, "Eyewitness Kevin Ovenden from the Freedom Flotilla: 'I saw people shot'", *Socialist Worker* (3 June), www.socialistworker.co.uk/art.php?id=21438

Shavit, Ari, 2004, "Interwiew with Benny Morris: On Ethnic Cleansing", *New Left Review* 26 (March-April), www.newleftreview.org/?view=2497

Shenker, Jack, 2010, "Can Mubarak weather a perfect storm?", *Guardian* (5 June), www.guardian.co.uk/commentisfree/2010/jun/05/mubarak-weather-perfect-storm

Sherwood, Harriet, 2010, "White House Backs Israeli Internal Inquiry into Flotilla Deaths", *Guardian* (14 June), www.guardian.co.uk/world/2010/jun/13/eu-opposes-israel-gaza-blockade

Shlaim, Avi, 2000, *The Iron Wall: Israel and the Arab World* (Penguin).

Shulman, David, 2010, "After the Flotilla Debacle", *New York Review of Books* blog (13 June), www.nybooks.com/blogs/nyrblog/2010/jun/13/after-flotilla-debacle/

Siddique, Haroon, 2010, "Israel's Blockade Targets Hamas while Gazans Suffer", *Guardian* (31 May), www.guardian.co.uk/world/2010/may/31/gaza-blockade-israel

Smith, Charles (ed), 2004, *Palestine and the Arab-Israeli Conflict: A History with Documents* (St Martin's).

Stacher, Joshua, 2009, "The Brothers and The Wars", *Middle East Report* 249, www.merip.org/mer/mer250/stacher.html

Tamimi, Azzam, 2007, *Hamas: Unwritten Chapters* (Hurst & Company).

Tatchell, Peter, 2009, "Hamas No, Human Rights Yes", *Guardian* (18 February), www.guardian.co.uk/commentisfree/2009/feb/18/hamas-palestine-israel-human-rights

Teitelbaum, Joshua, 2010, "Turkey is Calling for a Jihad Against Israel", *Guardian* (8 June), www.guardian.co.uk/commentisfree/2010/jun/08/turkey-jihad-israel-flotilla

UN Human Rights Council, 2009, *Human Rights in Palestine and Other Occupied Arab Territories: United Nations Fact Finding Mission on the Gaza Conflict (The Goldstone Report)*, www2.ohchr.org/english/bodies/hrcouncil/specialsession/9/FactFindingMission.htm

Weizmann, Eyal, 2007, *Hollow Land: Israel's Architecture of Occupation* (Verso).

Zeilig, Leo, 2010, "Tony Cliff: Deflected Permanent Revolution in Africa", *International Socialism* 126, www.isj.org.uk/?id=641

The euro crisis and the future of European integration

Christakis Georgiou

"It is clear that since September 2008 we have been facing the most difficult situation since the Second World War—perhaps even since the First World War. We have experienced—and are experiencing—truly dramatic times... A number of markets were no longer functioning correctly; it looked somewhat like the situation in mid-September 2008 after the Lehman Brothers' bankruptcy".[1]

Jean-Claude Trichet, European Central Bank president

The crisis which hit Europe in the spring and early summer of 2010 is proof that all the talk about recovery from the crisis which broke out in September 2008 is totally off the mark. At the height of the panic in early May that gripped governments in continental Europe and investors across the world, there were many ominous signs that the situation was quite similar to that which preceded the collapse of Lehman Brothers and that precipitated the world economy into the deepest recession it has gone through since the end of the Second World War, as even such an authoritative figure as the president of the European Central Bank (ECB),

1:   Tuma and Pauly, 2010. Thanks to Alex Callinicos and Jane Hardy for reading and commenting on an earlier draft of this article.

Jean-Claude Trichet, has recognised. The risk of a wave of sovereign states in Europe defaulting on their debts forced even US president Barack Obama to step in and apply pressure on the French and German governments to agree to a solution that would avert another financial meltdown. In effect, European leaders spent three months—from mid-February to mid-May—wrangling over the exact terms on which they would provide financial assistance to the Greek state. Speculation about whether financial assistance would be provided at all and about whether the Economic and Monetary Union (EMU, the arrangement underpinning the euro) would survive the crisis was rife. And although disaster was avoided by means of a huge bailout package potentially amounting to €750 billion and the decision of the ECB to start buying sovereign debt, the debate about the future of EMU continues both among European politicians and among commentators. In the meantime, the austerity policies that accompanied throughout Europe the process culminating in the introduction of the euro in 1999 are being implemented all over again, causing pain and resistance.

European integration in historical perspective

The process of European integration was triggered by geopolitical considerations.[2] In the wake of the Second World War, the aim of France's European policy was to contain and control German resurgence.[3] The French progressively came to the conclusion that the best way, given the historical circumstances of the Cold War and the Soviet threat, of preventing German dominance would be to lock Germany into Western Europe by setting in motion a process of long-term integration of the interests of the various continental ruling classes. France would take the lead politically and Germany would provide much of the economic muscle. The first concrete form that this took was the European Coal and Steel Community (ECSC) established in 1951 after a French proposal the previous year.

The strategic aims of the French partly coincided with those of the Americans.[4] The latter were acutely aware of the necessity of rebuilding the European economies, and this for two reasons. The first was the fear of a Russian takeover of Western Europe. The Western European economies, the German in particular, had to be reconstructed and rearmed under US leadership (this found concrete expression in Nato) so as to constitute a

---

2:   Soutou, 1996, chapters 1-3, while focusing on the Franco-German relationship, provides a very detailed account of how security concerns were at the heart of diplomatic manoeuvring at the time.

3:   Van der Pijl, 2006, pp39-41.

4:   See Loriaux, 1991, pp115-132.

bulwark against the Stalinist bloc. But for reconstruction to prove effective, the Franco-German rivalries which had led to three wars in a period of 70 years had to be contained. The Marshall Plan for US aid to Europe, announced in June 1947, was conditioned on the acceptance by the Europeans of some form of cooperation.[5]

The second reason was the fear of the internal enemy, ie the European labour movements. 1947 saw insurrectionary strikes in the Renault factories in France and the fear of the Communists seizing power in France and Italy was very intense. Rebuilding Europe and bringing back some degree of economic stability would ease the pressure the labour movement was exerting.

The next step was the Treaty of Rome in 1957, which established the European Economic Community (EEC). This would progressively come into force through the elimination of tariffs by 1968.

The course of developments changed to some extent in 1958 with the demise of the French Fourth Republic and the advent of the Fifth under General Charles de Gaulle. This represented a turn to a more assertive French foreign policy based on a more centralised political system. De Gaulle had opposed the Treaty of Rome and although he did not intend to renegotiate it, he sought to steer the process of European integration towards a channel which privileged inter-state negotiations and institutional arrangements rather than the pooling of state functions in federal "supranational" institutions such as the European Commission. His aim was to exploit France's comparative advantage in the politico-military field. He thus provoked the crisis of the "empty chair" in June 1965. For six months France withdrew from the council of ministers of EEC member states. This was in protest against the fact that, as of 1966, decisions in that body would no longer be taken on the basis of unanimity but of qualified majority, something that would reduce France's influence by eliminating its power to veto decisions. The so-called "Luxembourg compromise" that was arrived at in January 1966 essentially amounted to maintaining the requirement of unanimity. It thus blocked a major move towards greater centralisation in the governance of the EEC.

De Gaulle's vision was that Europe should strive for independence from the US while at the same time remaining within the Atlantic alliance.[6] He was hostile to British entry, which he vetoed twice in the 1960s, fearing

---

5:     Van der Pijl, 2006, pp36-39; Loriaux, 1991, p120; Serfati, 2004, p196.
6:     This, too, was the vision of the main architect of the ECSC, Jean Monnet (on this, see Anderson, 2009, pp13-15). In this respect, there was continuity in French strategy and aims despite regime change in 1958. But de Gaulle's personal style and explicit defiance of US hegemony created the impression that there had been a profound break.

that this would push the EEC much more in the direction of a giant free-trade area rather than in that of the strengthening of ties between the core continental countries that could one day become the basis for the emergence of a Europe capable of balancing US power. This clash between the vision of a huge European Common Market politically subordinate to the US, a vision associated with enlargement, and that of a more restricted but much more politically independent Europe, later on associated with "deepening", is another major issue in European integration. It persists today and can explain many of the contradictions that run through the European Union.

The 1970s saw two very important changes. The first was the demise of the Bretton Woods system of fixed exchange rates and the second was the return of capitalist crisis, starting with the recession of 1974-75. Both had the potential to undo much of what had been achieved during the previous two decades. The end of fixed exchange rates led to disruptive competitive devaluations of national currencies of EEC member states and dangerous volatility in foreign exchange markets. The risk that European economies would drift apart was amplified. It could also create huge problems for all those firms that were now operating across the borders of the member states and needed stability in exchange rates to plan their operations. Similarly, the recession of 1974-75 led to a host of national uncoordinated responses. Progressively, the member states of the EEC managed to forge a common strategy. There was a first attempt at monetary coordination in 1972, called the "snake", but this foundered in following years.[7]

A second attempt followed in 1979 with the European Monetary System (EMS) and the Exchange Rate Mechanism (ERM). This time the arrangements were more favourable to weak currencies.[8] This was designed both to win the support of the Gaullists in France, now led by Jacques Chirac, who opposed the austerity needed to entrench the franc's participation in the ERM, and to protect the deutschmark from further revaluation against a rapidly depreciating dollar.[9] The failure of the snake also allowed the French to argue that the Germans had to shoulder part of the burden of adjustment if they wanted European integration to move forward. This

---

7:   Eichengreen, 2008, pp149-172, is a very good and accessible account of what follows.

8:   See the discussion in Parsons, 2003, pp164-170, for details on this. Eichengreen, 2008, p158, makes a similar point. The whole process involved a lot of manoeuvring which was not limited to exchanges between national governments but also, significantly, between the German government and the Bundesbank. The latter was extremely wary of any arrangements that might extend support to weak-currency countries and undermine its price stability policies.

9:   Callinicos, 1997, p28; Eichengreen, 2008, p158.

debate about the contours of European monetary cooperation and the balance it should achieve between the interests of weak and strong currencies is a constant feature of European integration since the 1970s. Much of the wrangling in spring 2010 had to do precisely with this.

The depreciation of the dollar was a major feature of the 1970s, and indeed, ever since it has been a major weapon for the US ruling class in its attempt to preserve its economic power. One of the post-war boom's by-products was the relative decline of the US economy compared to Germany and Japan. So the US ruling class attempted to reverse the uneven development of the previous decades through various policies and moves. These included cutting back on the level of arms expenditure,[10] protectionist measures such as a 10 percent rise in tariffs[11] and an onslaught on the living standards of US workers.[12] But equally importantly, they included the aggressive exploitation of the privileged position of the dollar as the only international reserve currency.[13]

This privilege allows the US to run huge current account deficits and effectuate significant devaluations of the dollar for relatively long periods of time without running the risk of a collapse in the value of the dollar. So in the 1970s, the US pursued the unofficial policy of allowing the value of the dollar to decline in order to boost US exports (this is sometimes referred to as the policy of "benign neglect"). The result this has had on the German and, by extension, the European economy has been to introduce a deflationary bias in the way it has been run ever since. Since German development largely depended on an export-driven strategy and since the deutschmark could not compete with the dollar as an international reserve currency—thus preventing the US from exploiting the dollar in the way it has been doing—the only strategy available to Germany has been to suppress domestic demand, speed up the rationalisation and technological upgrading of its productive apparatus, shift production abroad to locations with lower labour costs and persistently run current account surpluses.[14]

This is why the creation of the EMS was not enough for stability to return in European monetary relations. In effect, for monetary cooperation to be successful there had to be some degree of economic policy convergence,

---

10:   Harman, 2003, figure 3, p61.
11:   Van der Pijl, 2006, p96.
12:   Harman, 2007, pp127-128, figures 9 and 10.
13:   A lot has been written on this. From a Marxist perspective, probably the best known analysis is Peter Gowan's in Gowan, 1999. But see also Parboni, 1981, chapter 1, and Carchedi, 2001, chapter 5.
14:   Parboni, 1981, pp132-137.

and given the new conditions of international economic competition imposed by the US, this could only happen when the rest of Europe aligned itself on German economic policy. This did not materialise until 1983, the year of the famous tournant de la rigueur (austerity turn) in France, when President François Mitterrand decided to follow the prescriptions of the "modernising" camp within his government, led by finance minister and future architect of the new stage of European integration Jacques Delors.[15]

Delors went on to become European Commission president in 1985 and to orchestrate the Single European Act (SEA) in 1986. The act aimed to complete the internal market by removing all trade barriers by 1992. Significantly, the French also accepted the end of the Luxembourg compromise. Barriers to the mobility of capital were lifted everywhere in Europe by the end of the decade and the Treaty of Maastricht in 1991 reformed the EEC (now called the European Union—EU) and made plans for introducing a single currency by the end of the century. Underpinning the single currency, and for want of common fiscal and economic policies (the "European economic government" the French have been calling for since 1983) or a significant European budget, were five convergence criteria imposed by the Germans.[16] In 1997 these criteria became the Stability and Growth Pact.[17] The attempts made by European governments during the 1990s to fulfil these criteria led to a wave of austerity measures being implemented across Europe. This formed the background against which the revival of working class resistance and a growing scepticism in public opinion about European integration, leading to the rejection of the European constitution in 2005 by the French and Dutch electorates, have developed.[18]

15: After an attempt at Keynesian reflation and extensive social policies which caused speculation against the franc, balance of payments problems, a flight of capital and inflation, the Socialist Party government of Mitterrand, which had come to power in 1981, reverted to a very orthodox set of economic policies, including the end of industrial subsidies, severe austerity and so on.

16: These set targets for inflation and long-term interest rates, required stability in participation in the ERM and, perhaps most importantly, required that budget deficits should not exceed 3 percent and national debt 60 percent of gross domestic product (GDP).

17: The term "Growth" was added after French insistence. It has a purely symbolic role to play, namely that of creating the illusion that price stability does not take precedence over growth and employment as a policy objective. The current response to the sovereign debt crisis (whose first pillar is a more radical version of the adjustment policies of the 1990s aimed at fulfilling the convergence criteria) makes nonsense of any such assertion.

18: See Callinicos, 1994, 1997 and 1999 for accounts of the revival in class struggle as it was unfolding. Kouvelakis, 2007, is a very good study of the French case. See Wolfreys, 2005, on the French referendum and Brandon, 2005, on the Dutch one.

The introduction of the euro and the creation of a European Central Bank (ECB), paradoxically following a French initiative, strengthened the supranational and federalist features of European integration. The supranational institutions (the Commission and the ECB) send their own representatives to most of the major international forums and have exclusive authority over significant swathes of European governance, namely trade, monetary policy and regulation of the internal market.

Finally, the collapse of Stalinism in the East created new complications. On the one hand, the French and the Germans had different attitudes towards the new independent republics. Initially the French talked about a confederation of European states. But the German preference for allowing them to join as soon as possible prevailed. Running the EU already largely hinged on delicate compromises struck between 15 states. Such compromises are now much harder to arrive at in a union comprising 27 members. On the other hand, the end of the Cold War and German unification revived old fears about an all too powerful Germany dominating Europe or even being pulled too strongly to the East. The German government headed by chancellor Helmut Kohl conceded EMU—although it was much more interested in political union—partly as a gesture addressed to its European "partners" that it continued to be committed to the whole process.

Both the end of the Bretton Woods regime and of the Cold War reinforced the position of Germany within Europe. The former did so because the deutchmark, being the currency of the biggest European economy and thanks to its strength and stability, became by default the pillar on which monetary cooperation in Europe was built. The EMS was essentially a deutchmark zone.[19] This gave the Bundesbank—the German central bank—virtual control of monetary and exchange rate policy across Europe. Finally German unification added demographic and political weight to the expanded Federal Republic, something which ultimately translated into greater weight for Germany in EU institutions.[20]

Marxism and European integration

In the late 1960s and early 1970s Ernest Mandel and Chris Harman provided very sharp analyses of the process of European integration from a Marxist point of view.[21] The main points they made some 40 years ago are

---

19: Holman, 1992, pp7-8, and Parboni, 1981, chapter 5.

20: Since the revision of the treaties in 2000 in Nice, Germany sends the most MEPs to the European Parliament and the vote of its representative on the Council of Ministers weighs more than any other's. This is also the case when it comes to the governance of the ECB.

21: Mandel, 1970; Harman, 1971; see also Harman, 1991, especially pp45-48.

still relevant today and must form the basis for any understanding of the tendencies and counter-tendencies which drive the whole process forward.

The first point of fundamental importance is that European integration is a reaction to international competition and the strength of American capital. The latter's advantages in size and technological sophistication exerted strong pressure on European capital to pool its resources together so as to regain a degree of competitiveness on the world market. But the domestic markets of each of the European states on their own were not large enough to allow for the emergence of firms capable of competing with the US. This necessitated a breakdown of the barriers to trade and investment and an integration of the various markets into one single giant one—the EEC. Even before this came fully into force, it triggered a process of national consolidation of capital whose aim was to prepare each state's "national champions" for the new conditions of intensified intra-European competition that would result from the full implementation of the Treaty of Rome.[22]

Mandel argued that the strength of supranational institutions depended on the degree of interpenetration of capital in Europe. Thus the Commission's weakness at the time was a sign of the very early stage Europeanisation of capital was still at. Later on Harman identified three tendencies of capital concentration—one at the national, another at the regional and a third at the international level. Harman predicted that "if the existing state provides too narrow a base for the activities of capitals, there will necessarily be an attempt to widen that base by alliances and mergers with other states. Therefore, in the long run the trend towards regional blocs is likely to be the predominate one".[23]

Indeed, during the 1960s and 1970s "the tendency was for the concentration of capital to take place within national state structures, with the assistance of national states".[24] But this changed once the crisis of the mid-1970s hit the European economies and triggered in the long run a far reaching process of restructuring. The number of European mergers increased significantly. The figures for mergers and acquisitions concerning Europe's 1,000 largest firms show significant developments during the 1980s. In 1982-3 there were 117 mergers. The figure rose to 303 in 1986-7 and 662 in 1989-90. In the early years of the decade national deals predominated. This changed by the end of the decade. In 1983-4, 65.2 percent of the deals were national, 18.7 percent European and 16.1 percent

---

22: See, for the French case, Serfati, 2008, p13.
23: Harman, 1991, p48.
24: Harman, 1991, p45.

international. By 1988-89 only 47.4 percent were national deals, whereas 40 percent were European and 12.6 percent international.[25] These figures suggest that the net effect of the decision in 1985 to move towards completion of the internal market was both to speed up the process of restructuring through mergers and acquisitions and to promote such deals at the European level. A political decision stimulated the tendency towards the centralisation of capital at the regional level. It also seems clear that European firms sought to attain the necessary magnitude of size first by national and then by European consolidation.[26] Finally, this process was amplified in the 1990s. A study commissioned by the French Planning Commission in 2004 concluded that "through the installation of firms in other European countries and the emergence of firms established at the European level, a European economic pole has truly been constituted, in particular during the last decade, marked by the Single Market and the euro".[27]

Another indicator of the constitution of a European pole is the network of interlocking directorates at the level of multinational firms. This refers to directors simultaneously sitting on the boards of two firms. The density of these networks indicates that some sort of community of capitalists sharing a common strategy for competing on the world market exists. Kees van der Pijl studied the development of such networks at the level of the 150 largest multinationals in the 1990s. His conclusion is that "the neoliberal restructuring of capital in Europe also affected the network of interlocking directorates among large corporations. Over the first post-Maastricht decade, European capital developed into a pattern reflecting the opening up of nationally confined finance capital structures on the continent—and their transformation into a rival transnational network separate from the Atlantic one".[28] The last part of this quotation indicates something very important: a European imperialist bloc, rivalling American imperialism on the world market, is in the process of being constituted.

What emerges from this is that, over the decades, the tendency towards the concentration of capital at the regional level drove European integration forward. European institutions were reinforced once the process of Europeanisation of capital overtook in economic importance the process of national consolidation of capital. The end of the Luxembourg compromise raised the degree of centralisation of decision-making while the powers

25: Cox and Watson, 1995, pp322-324.
26: This is the conclusion that a French study of European finance networks came to in 1993. Dupuy and Morin, 1993, p15.
27: Dietsch and others, 2004, p170.
28: Van der Pijl, 2006, p283.

of the Commission in those fields where it has exclusive competence have significantly been reinforced.[29] And the power of the ECB is hardly debatable. These developments can only reinforce the pressure exerted on European states to merge further into a European super-state. It is worth pointing out here that European industrial multinationals came together after a French initiative in 1983 to form the most powerful business lobby in Europe, the European Roundtable of Industrialists (ERT). The ERT has consistently argued in favour of the deepening of European integration and, in actual fact, many of its reports and suggestions became official policy of the European Commission.[30] The Lisbon agenda of 2000 was largely inspired by a series of reports published in the course of the previous years by an Advisory Group on Competitiveness set up by the ERT to advise the European Commission on an agenda of reforms.[31]

But both Harman and Mandel also argued that the process was subject to counter-tendencies.[32] Governments were still largely influenced by national interests. This translated into attempts at protectionism and a strong preference for national consolidation rather than European partnerships and mergers.[33] This was particularly true of France. Even today, to the extent that purely national solutions can be resorted to, this temptation has not totally disappeared. Examples of this are the way in which the Berlusconi government in Italy opposed the takeover of Alitalia by Air France-KLM in 2008 and then sold off the air-carrier to an Italian financial group or the orchestration by the French government of the merger of Gaz de France and Suez aimed at protecting the latter from a hostile takeover by the Italian energy giant Enel.

29: Serfati, 2004, p200. Serfati even considers that "the Commission's power of control is greater than that of anti-trust authorities in the US".

30: For a Marxist study of the ERT, see van Apeldoorn, 2002.

31: Van der Pijl, 2006, p287.

32: There were, however, differences in the two approaches. Harman stressed much more than Mandel the resilience of the structures of the national states. He predicted that "we face a long period of hard bargaining between rival, national capitalisms, in which national ideologies will remain of key importance to the ruling classes and in which political and social struggles will by and large remain nationally based". This statement is still broadly true today given that the balance of power between the national states and the institutions of the EU still favours the national states. Mandel, however, considered that a European imperialism would emerge to challenge the US fairly rapidly. He thought that Gaullist economic nationalism was "irrational" (Mandel, 1970, p54) instead of understanding it precisely as a way of defending the interests of the capitals concentrated within the French state within the process of integration. Thanks to Alex Callinicos for pointing out the importance of the differences in the two approaches.

33: Harman, 1971, p11; Mandel, 1970, pp52-55 on Gaullism, and p105 on protectionism and economic nationalism.

But even more importantly, within the framework created by European integration, each national state seeks to defend its own interests and those of the capitals predominantly based within it. For although European multinationals operate at the regional level—apart from the very rare cases where they operate globally—they are still largely controlled by groups of capitalists which tend to have privileged relations with a particular national state.[34] So each national state seeks to bend European Union policy and strategy so as to serve the interests of the capitals based within it. The clearest example of this is the governance of the currency shared by most of these countries, the euro. It is not by chance that Germany—along with the Netherlands—has consistently favoured a strong euro. As Guglielmo Carchedi has demonstrated, Germany has the highest concentration of technologically innovative firms that benefit from a strong currency.[35] This is much less the case in countries such as France or Italy which overall depend more on a weaker euro to stimulate exports.[36] This means that quite regularly French and Italian politicians complain that the euro is too strong or that the way it is run does not take into account the needs of their industries.

So, overall, European integration is a contradictory process that tends towards the effective integration of the various national fractions of European capital while at the same time each national group of capitals attempts to fashion the process according to its own interests.[37] Moreover, weak capitals that have little chance of surviving in the open waters of the European market seek protection from the national state within which they have developed. Both of the above elements act as a powerful conservative force which holds back the full development of the tendency towards integration and that of the two constitutive parts of this tendency, namely the regional consolidation of capital and the corresponding regional organisation

---

34: Rugman and Verbeke, 2002, show that "in the overall set of 20 highly internationalized MNEs [multinational enterprises], the case of a global strategy and structure can be made for only six firms, with the additional observation that even these firms exhibit regional elements", p11.

35: Carchedi, 2001, pp129-143.

36: Hence important voices could be heard in France during the spring crisis and depreciation of the euro welcoming this development, such as Patrick Devedjian, minister for the stimulus package—*Les Echos*, 18 May 2010.

37: Alex Callinicos's account of the EU's response to the 2008 financial crash suggests a different analysis. He paints a picture of an EU paralysed under the weight of "diverging national interests" (Callinicos, 2010, p97) and predicts that "ultimate power will continue to reside in the member states" (p101). He and Jane Hardy have both criticised the analysis presented in this article for underestimating the contradictions of the EU and the power of the national states.

of state functions.[38] The only way to get rid of this obstacle once and for all would be for the most powerful state—Germany—to impose by force the political unification of the continent. The last such attempt resulted in the Second World War and during the Cold War the German ruling class were forced to accept the compromise by which their dominance in Europe would have to be peacefully agreed to by the other European states. In the face of competition from other imperialisms of continental size (the US, Stalinist Russia before 1989 and now increasingly emergent China), these states did not have any other choice but to negotiate their stake in the forthcoming European imperialist bloc under German leadership (although it is fair to say that the French are also quite influential).

Two additional points need to be made here. The first is that the whole process does not take place in a vacuum but rather in the context of a global political economy in which already constituted rival imperialisms exist. The dominant one, the US, has the capacity to act globally and to influence developments across the world, including in Europe. Its attitude towards European integration depends on whether it considers that it proceeds in a direction that challenges its interests. It has therefore favoured all those developments that would water down the EU's capacity to become strategically and politically independent by attaining a high degree of internal coherence. The US strongly supported the rapid admission of Eastern European states into the EU, vocally promoted Turkey's candidacy—a traditional and until recently very loyal US ally—and strongly opposed attempts to create an independent European military capacity and command structure outside Nato structures .[39] One of the reasons for the US offensive in the Middle East since 2001 has been the division that this would create among European states. Apart from the traditional ally of the US in Europe, Britain, other important states such as Italy, Spain and Poland lined up behind George W Bush's crusade in Iraq, despite strong opposition from France and Germany, the states that constitute the driving force behind European integration. Finally, US officials keep complaining about German economic strategy, the structural trade surpluses it generates and

---

38:   Note that something similar, albeit of much less importance, exists in the US. The 50 states of the union each have the same weight in as important an institution as the Senate. This frequently makes the centralisation of decision making rather problematic. But of course, the parallel stops there. The US has a chief of state and the armed forces elected by universal suffrage, which is the case neither for the president of the Commission nor for the president of the European Council. And the American House of Representatives, unlike the European Parliament, wields real power.

39:   On this last point, see Carchedi, 2006.

its deflationary consequences.[40] To the extent that it is German economic strategy that dominates in Europe and which tends to force other European states to adapt to it, American complaints on this front are as important as complaints about Chinese exchange rate policy.

The second point goes back to one of the predictions Mandel made in 1970. He considered that so long as institutional integration had not sufficiently advanced, there was nothing irrevocable about European economic integration. This led him to predict that "the EEC's moment of truth will arrive when Europe undergoes a general recession".[41] This proved to be true at least twice, once with the recessions of the mid-1970s and early 1980s—which ultimately resulted in the deepening of European integration through the completion of the Common Market and EMU—and a second time with the European recession of the early 1990s, one of whose results was the monetary crisis of 1992-3 which once again forced the pound, the lira and the franc to leave the Exchange Rate Mechanism (ERM). Despite this, and despite the intense speculation over whether the euro would be introduced in the end, European integration managed to move forward. According to Carchedi, "there was a recognition that further economic integration (the EMU) was needed not only for political but also for economic reasons. The crisis of the Exchange Rate Mechanism (ERM) in 1992-93 showed that this was a real concern".[42] These two sequences of events indicate a pattern where each crisis acts as a catalyst which eliminates opposition to further integration by demonstrating in practice why the dominant fractions of European capital can no longer solely rely on a single national state and why individual national states would be much weaker if left on their own.[43]

The setting up of EMU and its deficiencies

The above discussion provides the framework in which to analyse EMU, the emergence of the euro and the current crisis surrounding the single currency.

40: Bouilhet, 2009, de Vergès, 2010. Various articles in the *Financial Times* by Martin Wolf have formulated the same criticism. Wolf directs this criticism at both Germany and China. For one example, see Wolf, 2009.

41: Mandel, 1970, p102.

42: Carchedi, 2001, p13.

43: This point is also made in an opinion piece in the *Financial Times* by one of the most prominent representatives of European multinational capital, Peter Sutherland, former EU commissioner, BP and Goldman Sachs International director: "An honourable tradition of the European Union is that of turning a crisis into an opportunity. 'Eurosclerosis' and budgetary squabbles in the 1980s were the precursors of the Single European Act of 1986; and the crisis of the exchange rate mechanism in 1992-1993 accelerated the creation of the European single currency"—Sutherland, 2010.

This crisis partly stems from the deficiencies and ambiguities of the arrangements underpinning the euro, which are the reflection of the contradictory nature of the process of European integration. In that respect, its root causes stretch back to the Maastricht Treaty and its failure effectively to establish a fiscal union alongside monetary union.

As I mentioned earlier, under the EMS European monetary cooperation was organised around the deutchmark and Germany. Since the objective of strengthening the various national currencies (the exceptions being the deutchmark and the Dutch guilder—they were already strong currencies) that participated in the EMS took precedence over any other policy objective and to the extent that in practice this meant attempting to keep up with the fluctuations in the value of the deutchmark, economic policy in Europe was dictated by Germany. If, for example, after a weakening of the dollar, there was an influx of capital into the deutchmark, leading it to appreciate, then the authorities in the other European countries would be forced to raise interest rates so as to attract volumes of capital large enough to allow their currencies to follow the deutchmark. Or, in a scenario that materialised in 1992, if the Bundesbank raised interest rates to keep inflation at bay, then this would have to be generalised across the continent (and in Britain at the time, since it participated in the ERM in 1990-2). In 1992 this precipitated the European economies into a deep recession. Given that there were significant inflation differentials between Germany (and the Netherlands) and the rest of Europe, in practice this translated into the Bundesbank imposing a strategy termed "competitive disinflation" across Europe, in an effort to bring inflation down to German levels and match Germany's international competitiveness by means of the restructuring that disinflation provoked.[44] Of course, significant fractions of the ruling classes in the other European countries were only too happy to be led down that path by the Bundesbank. As Delors told an American political economist,

> Historically there has always been a minority position in France that views inflation as the most damaging for the long-term health of the economy... This minority has always sought to modernise France: to stabilise the currency, to fight inflation, and to promote healthy growth and employment. And it happened that this minority won in France during the 1980s. It was a long and difficult struggle.[45]

44: The figures cited in the previous section on mergers and acquisitions support this analysis.
45: Abdelal, 2006, pp7-8.

"Competitive disinflation" meant wage repression in order to boost profits and an end to the propping up of unprofitable firms. Its results can be seen in the graph that follows:

Figure 1: Evolution of the wage share as a percentage of GDP 1976-2006
Source: Michel Husson "Le partage de la valeur ajoutée", PowerPoint presentation, August 2009

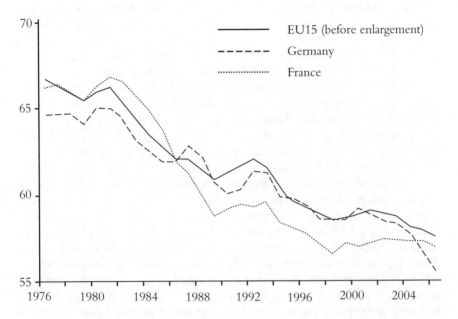

This strategy was the dominant one, despite the parallel existence of European "structural" and "cohesion" funds designed to prop up the least competitive regions of the Community by providing funds for infrastructural investment, something which essentially amounted to transfers from the richer to the poorer countries and to an embryo of a common economic policy at the European level.

But the dominance of the Bundesbank created resentment in the rest of Europe. Especially in a country like France, whose politicians like to think they have the capacity to act independently on the world market, there was a strong desire to regain control over monetary policy. In addition to this, political opposition to the strategy of "competitive disinflation" was gathering momentum, with economists, politicians and businessmen calling for alternative Keynesian policies of reflation and protectionist measures in favour of French industry. Finally, the Commission itself under the leadership of Delors was strongly in favour of a single currency. Delors presided over a committee that published a report in 1989 calling for such a development. The argument was that to solidify the European single market there had to be monetary union so as to prevent member states from pursuing disruptive monetary policies. In any case, it would be difficult to reconcile capital mobility with stable exchange rates. So eliminating them would solve the problem. Furthermore, a single currency would enhance the competitiveness and speed up the integration of the now liberalised European financial markets by making them deeper and more liquid and thus would potentially strengthen Europe's monetary weight on the world market.

All of these reasons supported the case for monetary union. Discussion and preparations for an intergovernmental conference on monetary union started in the early part of the second half of the 1980s and preceded the demise of the Soviet bloc. This point is important because the impact of the fall of the Berlin Wall on Germany's willingness to give up the deutchmark for the euro tends to be overestimated sometimes. It is certainly the case that these events did raise the stakes and put further pressure on the weak-currency countries to accept German conditions (the convergence criteria and the independence of the ECB). And the German government was eager to dispel France's reservations about German unification by making a gesture tying it to Western Europe even more firmly. But even before 1989 Germany had strong incentives to maintain monetary stability in Europe. The region's countries were now the main recipients of German exports and foreign investment and making sure their markets remained open to German capital was of paramount importance.[46] The 1970s had shown that national control of monetary policy could tempt member states to resort to competitive devaluations against the deutchmark. Finally, although this was an argument that the French were more eager to put forward than the Germans, a single currency could begin to provide sufficient monetary weight for countering the dollar's pivotal position in the world economy and the advantages that the US ruling class had been deriving from it since the early 1960s. To the extent that the German ruling class had begun emancipating themselves from the tutelage of the Americans, this was a perspective they were keen to explore.

The negotiations on monetary union were a long drawn out process that involved much bargaining and long-term calculations. On the one

---

46: Parboni, 1981, pp157-163.

hand, the French wanted to regain control over monetary policy, hoping that this would mean a less orthodox approach and an exchange rate policy that would take French interests into account as well as German ones. They also wanted industrial and economic policies at the European level similar to those that had existed in France since the 1950s and formed part of the state capitalist organisation of the post-war French political economy. On the other hand, the Germans would not give up the deutschmark unless they received serious guarantees that the new currency would be as strong. They would not settle for anything short of the independence of the new European Central Bank and strict convergence criteria to force its "partners" to imitate German economic performance, since they could not directly control fiscal policy in the rest of Europe.

The bargain that was struck was that Germany gave up its demand for greater powers for the European Parliament and more German MEPs in exchange for the independence of the future ECB and the five Maastricht criteria listed above.[47] French demands about common European industrial and economic policies were not met as Germany suspected that they would lead to hidden protectionism at the European level in the form of subsidies for ailing firms. Instead competition policy became the main instrument by which the internal market was to be regulated. This is much closer to the way the German political economy has been run in the post-war period. It was also an additional means of making sure that the necessary restructuring of the European economy would take place. Therefore, a certain strategic coherence emerged from the Maastricht negotiations: monetary and fiscal policy as well as internal market regulation would all be geared towards the speeding up of the process of restructuring, with the objective of both pushing back the labour movement and enhancing the regional consolidation of capital.

It is important to note that strategic divergences did not simply exist between national governments. They also existed within countries and between national institutions. France is probably the best illustration of this. As one of the main thinkers of the French social-liberal left has put it,

France's economic government—or, if one prefers, the economic decision-making community: the Treasury, the Bank of France, the private governing boards of the industrial and financial corporations—would not have embarked upon the EMU project if its principal aim since the March 1983 turnabout [the austerity turn] had not been to engrave in the marble of European

---

47:   Balleix-Banerjee, 1999, pp191-192.

institutions the strategy of competitive disinflation by taking away from political authorities the discretionary manipulation of monetary policy.[48]

No wonder then that the Bank of France was the only French institution, in opposition to the foreign office and the finance ministry, which was in favour of the independence of the ECB from the outset.[49] In this respect, the issue of the independence of the ECB is the clearest example of what is generally called the "democratic deficit" of the European Union, ie that decisions at the European level are taken by unelected bodies such as the European Commission and the ECB. This is no mere accident. It has to do with the fact that European capitalists wanted to shield political decision making from pressures to which it is usually subject in the sphere of bourgeois representative democracy. And it is a sign of the difficulties that the European ruling classes have in imposing their will on European workers.

But there was another very important issue, namely which countries would finally qualify for EMU. Germany would have preferred a union made up of the countries of northern Europe and, in the event that it joined the EU, Austria, as this would ensure a strong currency. But France feared that this would leave it less room for manoeuvre in the future and would make it harder to bend monetary policy towards a less orthodox direction. The French therefore defended a series of arrangements, including a looser approach to the question of budget deficits, which strengthened the probability that southern European countries such as Spain, Portugal, Italy and Greece would finally be able to join EMU.[50] These countries lagged much behind the rest of Europe in terms of competitiveness, debt problems and inflation. And they were eager to join because joining would allow them to enjoy the credibility that would flow from participation. They would, as it were, be playing in the same league as the Germans, and this would bring down the cost at which they borrowed on the international financial markets. They could then hope to use the funds saved due to lower borrowing costs to strengthen their economies and enhance their competitiveness.

The Maastricht Treaty, however, fell short of creating an economic union in one very important domain. This was fiscal policy. The Delors report that was used as the basis for negotiating the treaty did not propose a fiscal union. For the federalists, this was a step back from the previous

---

48: Cohen, 1996, pp347-348.
49: Balleix-Banerjee, 1999, pp144-148.
50: Balleix-Banerjee, 1999, pp213-240, p200.

attempt at establishing a monetary union, the Werner report of 1970.[51] This report had proposed to transfer fiscal powers (taxation, public spending and borrowing) to the European Commission. But such bold steps towards federalism had no chance of being accepted by national polities that still attached huge importance to their sovereignty, particularly in France. Fiscal powers are a defining capacity of any state. To the extent that the structures of the nation-state had not yet been sufficiently undermined by a significant degree of regional consolidation of capital, it was unimaginable to transfer fiscal powers to the European level.

The Delors committee chose to follow a more pragmatic path. The convergence criteria, especially those concerning public debt and budget deficits, were to act as a sort of straitjacket designed to push national fiscal policies towards convergence. But in terms of sovereign debt, there was no advance. No European bond, debt agency or solidarity for states facing excessive debt burdens was proposed. And the ECB was prohibited from extending credit to or buying debt instruments from national governments or Community institutions (which is precisely what it did when it started buying Greek bonds in May 2010).[52] Each state was responsible for its own debts, despite sharing a common currency. EMU was only half complete. But for a long period of time no one really seemed to notice. Not only that, but as Alex Callinicos noted in 2005, "In the run-up to the euro launch interest rates across Europe converged... This reflected the financial markets' belief that the debts of all the eurozone economies were being underwritten, in effect, by the EU", precisely the opposite of what the Maastricht Treaty laid down.[53]

Barely had European leaders left the negotiating table than the first test came. The US economy had gone into recession in 1990-1 and its effects started to be felt in Europe. And the Bundesbank raised interest rates to ward off inflation resulting from German unification. In a plot that bears some similarities to the current crisis, financial investors started doubting that European governments would follow the Bundesbank in raising interest rates and add to the already mounting unemployment that was hitting Europe. When the Danish electorate refused to ratify the Maastricht Treaty by referendum in June 1992, these doubts intensified and led to runs against the weaker currencies, including the Italian lira and the British pound. By September they had to leave the ERM.

51: Eichengreen, 2008, pp150-152.
52: This is article 21.1 of the protocol on the ECB, available online at http://eur-lex.europa.eu/en/treaties/dat/11992M/htm/11992M.html#0068000004
53: Callinicos, 2005.

The crisis seemed to prove right all those who were sceptical about EMU. It dealt a huge blow to British Europhiles who wanted to bring the pound into the euro. And, critically for what would follow, it allowed for a looser interpretation of the convergence process. As the world economy started recovering from the recession of the early 1990s, it became easier to fulfil the Maastricht criteria because of higher fiscal revenues. Still, European governments did attempt to enforce austerity measures. The result was important struggles and some victories for the labour movement, such as the 1994 general strike in Italy that broke the first Berlusconi government or the November-December 1995 public sector strikes that pushed back premier Alain Juppé's "reform" package in France.[54] So apart from austerity, which could not on its own do the job, "governments [took] one-off measures—typically in the form of additional taxes—to temporarily squeeze under the 3 percent limbo bar but abandon fiscal discipline subsequently".[55] Ten countries could therefore claim to fulfil the Maastricht criteria in 1999, and Greece joined them in 2001.

In the face of working class resistance that was too strong to break, the rules were bent so that EMU could be launched on schedule and create the illusion that it rested on strong foundations. Germany also demanded a stability pact providing for continued oversight of national budgets and penalties for countries running excessive deficits, hoping that such threats would put more pressure on governments to take on their workers. This became the Stability and Growth Pact in 1997. But when, in 2003, both France and Germany ran budget deficits exceeding 3 percent of GDP, instead of playing by the rules and fining themselves, they preferred to reform it and allow for more budgetary flexibility. Many pro-capitalist commentators complain that this set a precedent for weaker countries.

The bid to create a rival to the dollar and the current crisis

The euro was launched in 1999. Euro coins and banknotes were progressively brought into circulation in the first six months of 2002. A sense of euphoria about the prospects of European integration was quite widespread at the time. It reflected the fact that despite scepticism about the possibility to introduce the euro (in the US and among financial investors) and despite disagreements among them, the Europeans could set common goals and actually reach them. It was this enthusiasm that no doubt underpinned the Franco-German stance on the Iraq war in 2003.

54: See German, 1995, and Harman, 1996.
55: Eichengreen, 2008, p220.

The enthusiasm was reinforced by the fact that the euro's exchange rate with the dollar was moving upwards quite rapidly. During the first two years of its existence, while it was still not in circulation, the euro fell about 30 percent against the dollar. But as of spring 2002, it followed an upward course. When it reached its high point against the dollar in July 2008, its value had almost doubled when compared to its low point, in October 2000.

The strength of the euro made it a plausible candidate for becoming an international reserve currency. As I mentioned earlier, part of the rationale for adopting the euro was its potential to become a rival to the dollar. One crucial ingredient for creating such a rival to the dollar is that it will have to be trusted as a "safe haven" by investors wanting to park their money in assets that are sure to maintain their value. This is why the ECB and its president keep repeating that they have done a good job at preserving price stability since the bank was created. When asked in an interview with *Le Monde* whether the euro was in danger, the first thing Trichet responded with was the following:

> The euro is a very credible currency which maintains its value. Since its creation 11 and a half years ago, average annual inflation has been inferior to 2 percent and close to 2 percent, in accordance with our definition of price stability. This capacity of the euro to preserve its value is a crucial element for the confidence of domestic and foreign investors.[56]

But it is not enough for a rival to the dollar to be strong and stable. It also needs to be based on competitive financial markets and be widely used across the world economy (become a "world money", as this is sometimes called). Competitive financial markets must be deep, liquid and profitable. This is what the European Commission set about to create as soon as the euro was launched by eliminating the remaining fragmentation of European financial markets.[57] And this is why the eurozone keeps expanding. Slovenia joined in 2007, Cyprus and Malta in 2008 and Slovakia in 2009. Estonia will join in 2011. And the other EU member states, having accepted the treaties, are under an obligation to meet the criteria and join too.[58]

A closer look at the evidence, however, suggests that the euro has a long way to go before really being in a position to challenge the dollar's

---

56: *Le Monde*, 1 June 2010.

57: For details, see Grahl (ed), 2009, chapter 3.

58: The UK is the exception as it has opted out of the euro.

position in the world economy.[59] Some 27.3 percent of global foreign exchange reserves were held in euro-denominated instruments at the end of 2009, up from slightly above 20 percent in 1999. By comparison, the figures for the dollar were around 64 percent in 2009 and 67 percent in 1999.[60] As far as international debt securities are concerned, 31.4 percent were issued in euros and 45.8 percent in dollars in 2009.[61] But in terms of use in foreign exchange markets, which is perhaps the clearest indication of the extent to which a currency enjoys the status of world money, the dollar appeared on either side of 90 percent of such transactions with the euro lagging far behind at 40 percent.[62] The conclusion reached by the ECB itself in its latest report on the international role of the euro is that:

> The results suggest that the international role of the euro increased somewhat during the first few years of existence of the single currency. Since then, the international use of the euro has remained relatively stable relative to that of other international currencies…the use of the euro is most common in countries located in the broad geographical neighbourhood of the euro area, while the US dollar's international use is more widespread across the global economy.[63]

But parallel to the above developments, others were taking place beneath the surface that were deepening the rift between the weaker economies of the eurozone and the stronger ones. This did not become apparent because, as noted by Callinicos, interest rates tended to converge.

Starting at the beginning of the previous decade, Germany implemented a series of measures (Gerhard Schröder's Agenda 2010) that boosted its competitiveness relative to its European "partners" and returned its trade balance to surplus.[64] The measures meant that unit labour costs barely rose in Germany over the past decade, while those in the rest of Europe soared.[65]

59: For an optimistic account of the euro's prospects, see McNamara, 2008; for a pessimistic one, see Cohen, 2007. Both make the same point however: it is the institutional and political deficiencies of EMU which are the main obstacle to the euro's advance as world money.

60: ECB, 2010, p34.

61: ECB, 2010, pp15-16. This gap had almost disappeared in 2005 when the share of both currencies converged towards 40 percent. This was another sign of the enthusiasm generated by the euro soon after its introduction.

62: ECB, 2010, pp22-23.

63: ECB, 2010, p13.

64: For analysis of the measures and the political conjuncture in Germany since their implementation, see Bornost, 2005 and 2007.

65: Lapavitsas and others, figure 10, 2010, p23.

The result has been growing current account surpluses in Germany and current account deficits in the countries of southern Europe and France.[66] These surpluses and deficits became capital exports from Germany to the countries of southern Europe.[67] Germany was lending to the rest of Europe so that it could go on buying German exports, in a relationship that very much resembles that between China and the US.

All this meant that when the financial crisis erupted in 2007, and particularly after it was transformed into a deep recession in 2008 and 2009, the burden was much heavier for the southern European countries than for Germany. This had nothing to do with fiscal profligacy. As Martin Wolf has argued,

> Greece is a bad boy. But Italy, France and Germany had far more breaches [of the 3 percent budget deficit criterion] than Ireland and Spain. Yet it is the latter that are now in huge fiscal difficulties.
>
> The fiscal rules failed to pick up the risks. This is no surprise. Asset price bubbles and associated financial excesses drove the Irish and Spanish economies. The collapse of the bubble economies then left fiscal ruins behind it.
>
> It was the bubbles, stupid: in retrospect, the creation of the eurozone allowed a once-in-a-generation party. Some countries had vast asset price bubbles; many had soaring relative wages. Meanwhile, Germany and the Netherlands generated huge current account surpluses. The union encouraged a flood of capital to the surging economies, on favourable terms. When private spending imploded, fiscal deficits exploded.[68]

This left states saddled with huge budget deficits. As has been argued in this journal during the last year or so, these budget deficits were the result of the policies implemented by states with the aim of preventing the economic crisis from morphing into a depression as well as the result of the reduced fiscal revenues and increased social spending provoked by the 2008-9 recession. The overall result has been to transfer the bulk of the bad debts that were threatening the banks onto the states that bailed them out,

66: For southern Europe, see Lapavitsas and others, figure 14, 2010, p27. Jean-Marc Vittori shows how in ten years, the efficiency of the German government's attacks on its workers in comparison to the French government's inability to do the same shifted the balance in competitiveness in favour of Germany—Vittori, 2010.
67: Lapavitsas and others, figure 15 2010, p28.
68: Wolf, 2010.

thus simply displacing the problem. The euro crisis of spring 2010 was the practical demonstration of this. Speculation over whether the banks were insolvent was transformed into speculation about the solvency of sovereign entities. And while every state is subject to pressures coming from the financial markets rapidly to reduce its exposure to debt, this pressure is much stronger on small and weak states, like Greece for example. What is more, the fact that the huge deficits brought to the centre of attention the capacity of each state to pay back its debts exposed the flawed nature of EMU. Greece was on its own and everyone was aware of it now.

The result was a crisis of confidence in the Greek state that pushed up its cost of borrowing on the international financial markets, while causing the euro to depreciate. The difference in interest payments on Greek and German government bonds (German *bunds* are taken as the benchmark for European sovereign debt) widened. Something had to be done, but there was disagreement on what exactly that should be. France led a bloc of deficit countries in campaigning for a bailout orchestrated by the EU while Germany led a bloc of surplus countries (the Netherlands, Austria and Finland) which put up resistance to the idea of extensive aid to Greece.

When things threatened to get out of control in the beginning of May, with worrying signs that the crisis of confidence was spreading to Spain and Portugal and under increasing pressure from the US who were worried that a new Lehman Brothers-type collapse was in the making, the two camps found a compromise.[69] The German-led camp agreed to come up with the money and the guarantees needed to bail out Greece and potentially any other European state that would come under pressure from the markets on condition that the IMF would be involved, that strict conditionality in implementing austerity measures would apply and that making any funds available would have to be approved by national parliaments. The ECB announced it would start buying sovereign debt, a decision running counter to the Maastricht Treaty. Given that the institutions exposed to sovereign debt in the periphery were primarily German and French banks, the euro bailout can be likened to a second bank bailout, just a year and a half after the 2008 bailouts.[70]

For most commentators, the bailout represented a qualitative change in the way the eurozone was run. The French government hastened to

---

69:   See the account by Ian Traynor of the summit meeting on 9 May that decided the bailout—Traynor, 2010. A German expert is reported to have said: "This was supposed to be a German euro. It's turned into a French euro."

70:   See the figures in "Analysis", *International Socialism 127*, p6.

reinforce this impression. French minister for European affairs Pierre Lellouche told the *Financial Times* that that the bailout "amounted to a fundamental revision of the European Union's rules and a leap towards an economic government for the bloc" and likened it to Nato's Article 5 mutual defence clause.[71] And other Europhiles, feeling that the bailout had created the opportunity to overcome the deficiencies of EMU, joined in. So for example, former European Commission president Romano Prodi published an opinion piece in the same paper entitled "A Big Step towards Fiscal Federalism in Europe".[72]

Where next?

Yet a big step is not the same as having gone all the way. The European Financial Stabilisation Fund set up to administer the bailout funds is temporary. And there is disagreement between France and Germany on what exactly they need to do now. France favours tighter coordination between eurozone states and some sort of a fiscal union, either through euro-bonds or in the form of fiscal transfers between member states. Germany puts a lot more emphasis on stricter penalties and sanctions for deficit countries and coordination at the level of EU member states, where it hopes it can line up behind it Central and Eastern European states against France and the countries of southern Europe.

But probably the clearest sign of the tensions in the Franco-German axis came last March when French finance minister Christine Lagarde criticised the German trade surplus in a *Financial Times* interview.[73] According to the paper "her comments [broke] a longstanding taboo between the French and German governments about macroeconomic imbalances inside the eurozone". Although the extent to which Berlin's economic policies were accommodating or not the interests of other European states—especially those of southern Europe—had been a permanent object of disagreement between the two governments over the last two decades, Germany had been much more used to public criticism coming from the US on that front and did not find it particularly hard to ward it off. But now, in the midst of a great crisis hitting the euro, France was attempting to lay the blame at Germany's door.

Since the bailout was agreed, the two sides have been attempting to find common ground and give the impression that they want to go in the same direction. German finance minister Wolfgang Schäuble participated in

---

71:   Hall and Mallet, 2010.
72:   Prodi, 2010.
73:   Hall, 2010.

July in a French cabinet meeting and the two finance ministers have issued a joint call for the suspension of voting rights for member states that will repeatedly break rules on fiscal discipline.[74] But this is about as far as it goes for the moment. A set of tougher measures favoured by Germany—such as an orderly insolvency procedure for bankrupt European states or the setting up of a European Monetary Fund—have been rejected by France.

The divergences between France and Germany at this particular juncture are characteristic of the broader strategic disagreements that lie at the root of last spring's speculation against the euro. On the one hand, the French want the Germans to pursue more cooperative economic policies that will ease the competitive pressure that German capital is exerting on its European "partners".[75] The political rationale for this is that if Europe is to attain greater political cohesion in order to raise its game in international competition, there has to be more inter-state solidarity within the EU. There is also the fact that France finds it extremely hard to suppress the living standards of its workers to the same extent that Germany has done and that French public opinion is quite hostile to the European project—largely because it has been associated in that country with the attacks waged on workers since 1983. But France won't accept a political union along federal lines because the majority of French politicians fear that this will diminish France's political and diplomatic weight in the world. On the other hand, this is precisely Germany's strategic aim at least since the fall of the Berlin Wall. A political union will do away with Second World War memories and the inhibitions associated with them while at the same time it will institutionalise German primacy within the new federal EU. And it seems that this is the price that the Germans are putting on their eventual acceptance of more redistribution at the European level. In an interview with the *Financial Times*, Schäuble indirectly blamed France for the euro-crisis, saying that

> Europe needs leadership. Any organisation needs that. Germany cannot lead alone—that would be nonsense. France and Germany can do a great deal together... When we introduced the euro in the 1990s, Germany wanted a political union and France did not. That is why we have an economic union without a political union... Germany has a lot of experience with federalism, more than the UK or France. If you want to create a federal organisation,

---

74: Hollinger, 2010.
75: This is sometimes presented as Germany needing to assume its leadership role within Europe. I remember listening to a Greek financial analyst saying as much in a heated debate on Greek television last March as well as Costas Lapavitsas saying that Germany does not know how to rule Europe at the talk he gave at Marxism 2010 on the euro crisis.

you must be ready to have a certain amount of redistribution within it. You can dismiss that by rudely calling it a "transfer union". But strong and weaker states both have their responsibility.[76]

The problem with this stalemate is that, as proven by the crisis of spring 2010, it puts even monetary union at risk. There is now a serious discussion among bourgeois commentators and on the left over whether the euro will survive. A collapse seems highly unlikely, not least because the bailout has for the moment eased the pressure exerted on the euro. But even more importantly, there is neither a provision in the treaties for an exit procedure nor the political will to push even a small country like Greece out. For pushing Greece out would be a sign that commitment to the euro is waning. It would only reinforce the speculation over an eventual break-up. This is why, shortly after the panic was over in May, it was announced that Estonia would join in 2011. What is at stake with the euro is so important to the interests of capitalists in the core countries that they would rather come to bitter compromises than see the edifice of European integration that they have built over the last few decades crumble.

So how exactly further integration will take place is hard to tell. In any case, as in the past, it will be the result of hard bargaining and will reflect a compromise between France and Germany. But a leap to full-blown federalism seems impossible for the moment as there is no constituency for it anywhere in Europe. As Luxembourg's premier Jean-Claude Juncker put it in 2007, "We all know what to do, but we don't know how to get re-elected once we have done it".[77]

There is, however, one thing that is certain. Any solution to the eurozone's problems will have to come at the expense of Europe's workers. Soon after the euro bailout was agreed in May, the German government announced an €80 billion austerity package in a bid to force other European governments to follow in its footsteps. Austerity measures are becoming generalised across Europe. This is the second pillar of the attempt by European states to solve the euro crisis.

But there are two big unknowns surrounding the attempt at fiscal consolidation. The first has to do with the fact that the measures are partly self-defeating. Reducing budget deficits and public debts largely hinges on growing fiscal revenues. But the austerity measures will very likely push the economy back into recession and recreate the conditions that led states to

---

76: Peel, 2010.
77: Quoted in the *Economist*, 10 July, 2010, p11.

borrow heavily on financial markets. The second is the strength of working class resistance. The succession of one-day general strikes in Greece in recent months is a foretaste of what is likely to take place across Europe when the austerity measures start to bite. If the experience of the post-Maastricht period is anything to go by, we can expect working class resistance to prove a huge stumbling block for the projects of European capitalists.

Five years ago this journal argued that a new fault line had emerged in the world system and that it was in Western Europe:

> there are signs of new, widespread political dissent as the pressure on European capitalism from competition in global markets is pushing governments towards even harder versions of the neoliberal agenda, with attacks on pensions and unemployment benefits and demands for longer working hours.[78]

That pressure is now far stronger and the attacks will be far more brutal. Likewise the fault line will grow deeper and deeper. The job of the left in Europe is to both make sure it grows as deep as possible and exploit the political possibilities that will be thrown up in this situation. The instability generated by the attacks on the euro and the squabbles between the European ruling classes will only open up more spaces in which the left can intervene.

References

Abdelal, Rawi, 2006, "Writing the Rules of Global Finance: France, Europe, and Capital Liberalisation", *Review of International Political Economy*, 13:1.

Anderson, Perry, 2009, *The New Old World* (Verso).

Balleix-Banerjee, Corinne, 1999, *La France et la Banque Centrale Européenne* (Presses Universitaires de France).

Bornost, Stefan, 2005, "Germany: The Rise of the Left", *International Socialism 108* (autumn), www.isj.org.uk/?id=132

Bornost, Stefan, 2007, "Germany's Political Earthquake", *International Socialism 116* (autumn), www.isj.org.uk/?id=366

Bouilhet, Alexandrine, 2009, "L'Europe Affronte la Chine et les Etats-Unis", *Le Figaro* (25 September).

Brandon, Pepijn, 2005, "A Note on the Dutch Referendum", *International Socialism 108* (autumn), www.isj.org.uk/?id=133

Callinicos, Alex, 1994, "Crisis and Class Struggle in Europe Today", *International Socialism 63*

78:   Harman, 2005, p3.

(summer), http://pubs.socialistreviewindex.org.uk/isj63/callinicos.htm

Callinicos, Alex, 1997, "Europe: The Mounting Crisis", *International Socialism* 75 (summer), http://pubs.socialistreviewindex.org.uk/isj75/callinic.htm

Callinicos, Alex, 1999, "Reformism and Class Polarisation in Europe", *International Socialism* 85 (winter), http://pubs.socialistreviewindex.org.uk/isj85/callinicos.htm

Callinicos, Alex, 2005, "The No's Have It", *Socialist Review* (July), www.socialistreview.org.uk/article.php?articlenumber=9462

Callinicos, Alex, 2010, *Bonfire of Illusions* (Polity).

Carchedi, Guglielmo, 2001, *For Another Europe: A Class Analysis of European Integration* (Verso).

Carchedi, Guglielmo, 2006, "The Military Arm of the European Union", *Rethinking Marxism*, volume 18, number 2.

Cohen, Benjamin J, 2007, "Enlargement and the International Role of the Euro", *Review of International Political Economy*, 14:5.

Cohen, Elie, 1996, *La Tentation Hexagonale: La Souveraineté à l'Épreuve de la Mondialisation* (Fayard).

Cox, Andrew, and Glyn Watson, 1995, "The European Community and the Restructuring of Europe's National Champions", in Jack Hayward (ed), *Industrial Enterprise and European Integration: From National to International Champions in Europe* (Oxford University Press).

Dietsch, Michel, Edouard Mathieu, Moustanshire Chopra and Alain Etchegoyen, 2004, *Mondialisation et Recomposition du Capital des Entreprises Européennes* (La Documentation Française).

Dupuy, Claude, and François Morin, 1993, *Le Cœur Financier Européen* (Economica).

ECB, 2010, "The International Role of the Euro", www.ecb.europa.eu/press/pr/date/2010/html/pr100714.en.html

Eichengreen, Barry, 2008, *Globalising Capital: A History of the International Monetary System* (Princeton University Press).

German, Lindsey, 1995, "Falling Idol", *Socialist Review* (January), http://pubs.socialistreviewindex.org.uk/sr182/german.htm

Gowan, Peter, 1999, *The Global Gamble: Washington's Faustian Bid for Global Dominance* (Verso).

Grahl, John (ed), 2009, *Global Finance and Social Europe* (Edward Elgar).

Hall, Ben, 2010, "Lagarde Criticises Berlin Policy", *Financial Times* (14 March).

Hall, Ben and Victor Mallet, 2010, "EU Bailout Scheme Alters Bloc Treaties, says France", *Financial Times* (28 May).

Harman, Chris, 1971, "The Common Market", *International Socialism* 49 (first series, autumn), www.marxists.org/archive/harman/1971/xx/eec-index.html

Harman, Chris, 1991, "The State and Capitalism Today", *International Socialism* 51 (summer), www.isj.org.uk/?id=234

Harman, Chris, 1996, "France's Hot December", *International Socialism* 70 (spring), http://pubs.socialistreviewindex.org.uk/isj70/france.htm

Harman, Chris, 2003, "Analysing Imperialism", *International Socialism* 99 (spring), http://pubs.socialistreviewindex.org.uk/isj99/harman.htm

Harman, Chris, 2005, "Analysis", *International Socialism* 108 (autumn), www.isj.org.uk/?id=131

Harman, Chris, 2007, "Snapshots of Capitalism Today and Tomorrow", *International Socialism* 113 (winter), www.isj.org.uk/?id=292

Hollinger, Peggy, 2010, "Paris and Berlin Unite on Fiscal Discipline" *Financial Times* (21 July).

Holman, Otto, 1992, "Introduction: Transnational Class Strategy and the New Europe", *International Journal of Political Economy*, volume 22, number 1.

Kouvelakis, Stathis, 2007, *La France en Révolte: Mouvements sociaux et Cycles Politiques* (Textuel).

Lapavitsas, Costas, A Kaltenbrunner, D Lindo, J Michell, J P Painceira, E Pires, J Powell, A Stenfors, N Teles, 2010, "Eurozone Crisis: Beggar Thyself and Thy Neighbour", Research on Money and Finance (March), http://researchonmoneyandfinance.org/media/reports/eurocrisis/fullreport.pdf

Lauer, Stéphane, Frédéric Lemaître, Marie de Vergès, 2010, "M. Trichet: 'Nous avons besoin d'une fédération budgétaire'", *Le Monde* (1 June).

Loriaux, Michael, 1991, *France After Hegemony: International Change and Financial Reform* (Cornell University Press).

McNamara, Kathleen, 2008, "A Rivalry in the Making? The Euro and International Monetary Power", *Review of International Political Economy*, 15:3.

Mandel, Ernest, 1970, *Europe versus America: Contradictions of Imperialism* (Monthly Review Press).

Parboni, Riccardo, 1981, *The Dollar and its Rivals: Recession, Inflation and International Finance* (Verso).

Parsons, Craig, 2003, *A Certain Idea of Europe* (Cornell Univerity Press).

Peel, Quentin, 2010, "Schäuble Interview: Berlin's Strictures", *Financial Times* (19 May).

Prodi, Romano, 2010, "A Big Step Towards Fiscal Federalism in Europe", *Financial Times* (21 May).

Rugman, Alan, and Alain Verbeke, 2002, "Regional Multinationals and Triad Strategy", www.aueb.gr/deos/EIBA2002.files/PAPERS/C164.pdf

Serfati, Claude, 2004, *Impérialisme et Militarisme: L'Actualité du XXIe Siècle* (Page Deux).

Serfati, Claude, 2008, "L'insertion du Capitalisme Français dans l'Économie Mondiale", *La brèche/Carré rouge*, number 2.

Soutou, Georges-Henri, 1996, *L'Alliance Incertaine: Les Rapports Politico-Stratégiques Franco-allemands, 1954-1996* (Fayard).

Sutherland, Peter, 2010, "Radical reforms can save the euro", *Financial Times* (30 June).

Traynor, Ian, 2010, "How the euro—and the EU—teetered on the brink of collapse", *Guardian* (14 May), www.guardian.co.uk/business/2010/may/14/nicolas-sarkozy-angela-merkel-euro-crisis-summit

Tuma, Thomas, and Christoph Pauly, 2010, "Interview with Jean-Claude Trichet, ECB President", *Der Spiegel* (13 May),www.ecb.int/press/key/date/2010/html/sp100515.en.html

Van Apeldoorn, Bastiaan, 2002, *Transnational Capitalism and the Struggle Over European Integration* (Routledge).

Van der Pijl, Kees, 2006, *Global Rivalries From the Cold War to Iraq* (Pluto).

de Vergès, Marie, 2010, "Inquiet pour la Croissance, Washington Déplore la Rigueur en Allemagne", *Le Monde* (24 June).

Vittori, Jean-Marc, 2010, "France-Allemagne: 1 à 3", *Les Echos* (7 April).

Wolf, Martin, 2009, "Why G20 Leaders will Fail to Deal with the Big Challenge", *Financial Times* (1 April).

Wolf, Martin, 2010, "The Eurozone Stumbles into a Beggar-My-Neighbour Policy", *Financial Times* (19 May).

Wolfreys, Jim, 2005, "How France's Referendum Caught Fire", *International Socialism* 107 (summer), www.isj.org.uk/?id=121

Crisis and recession in Central and Eastern Europe

Jane Hardy

Despite the virtual implosion of some economies in Central and Eastern Europe (CEE)—plunging living standards in parts of the region, protests and social unrest—little attention has been paid to the crisis and recession in the ten post-Communist countries that joined the European Union (EU) in 2004 and 2006.[1] The Baltic States have gone from being dubbed the "Baltic Tigers" to suffering the effects of the crisis in the most acute form in the EU with their currencies, banking systems and economies verging on collapse. In 2010 Hungary came under speculative attack from the markets with threats to downgrade its debt to junk bonds. Only Poland and the Czech Republic look at first sight to have had a relatively soft landing.

Even before the fall of the Berlin Wall in 1990 these countries were not immune to crises in the global economy and the recessions of the mid-1970s and 1979-82 sharpened the contradictions in their economies and contributed to their eventual collapse in 1990. However, their deeper integration with and exposure to the global economy, and the EU in particular, since the fall of the Berlin Wall have meant that they are much more vulnerable to crisis and recession.

The foundations of this vulnerability were laid by the widespread adoption

---

1: In 2004 the Czech Republic, Estonia, Hungary, Latvia, Lithuania, Poland, Slovakia and Slovenia joined the EU. Romania and Bulgaria joined in 2006.

of neoliberal policies in the economies of CEE, a high dependence on foreign investment and in particular their exposure to international finance. Iván Szelényi describes this in the following way:

> Now that the crisis of global finance capitalism shakes the world in its very foundations, when we experience an economic collapse of a magnitude not experienced since 1929-1933 (a collapse that affects Hungary and in fact the entire European post-Communist region especially severely), the wisdom of the neoliberal path chosen by the post-Communist countries in 1989-90 appears highly dubious. Today, the ball got rolling from the United States, but it appears that it may trigger the greatest avalanche in this very region. Neoliberalism is in crisis in America as well, but it seems that post-Communist capitalism, which was more neoliberal than the neoliberals themselves, will have to pay twice the price for its—it appears that we have grounds to believe this today—erroneous economic and social policy.[2]

In order to understand the scale and nature of the crisis in CEE, both across the region and in individual economies, it is necessary to understand the extension of the European project to the East.

The European project goes east: 2004 onwards

Massive effort by the ruling classes of Europe and the US was put into the so-called "transformation" of CEE to ensure its integration into the global economy after the fall of the Berlin Wall. The IMF underwrote the financing of the project, while the World Bank provided funds for over-hauling the depleted infrastructure of these countries. However, there was a gap between the rhetoric and reality of the "aid" that went to CEE. The scale of resources to underpin transformation fell far short of the "Marshall Aid Plan for the East", which had been trumpeted. Various schemes such as PHARE (Poland and Hungary: Assistance for the Restructuring of the Economy) from the EU and USAID were all naked in their intention to instill a neoliberal agenda, so that these countries were open to capital for trade and investment through widespread liberalisation and privatisation.[3] There was a significant element of coercion used by the IMF through putting in stringent conditions relating to cutting public spending and rapid privatisation, but there was also extensive investment in ideologically

---

2:   Quoted in Andor, 2009, pp294-295.
3:   Between 1990 and 2001 USAID was involved in 400 activities and pumped $1 billion into Poland. See USAID 2000 and 2002.

underpinning the project. For example, USAID financed courses for trade unionists in Poland using first year economics textbooks to explain the principles of the "market economy" and the necessity for "downsizing". Leaders of the Solidarity trade union were taken on extensive trips to the US to learn about democracy and the "proper" role of trade unions.[4]

In the context of the geopolitics of the period, the fall of the Berlin Wall and collapse of the Soviet Union had opened up a window of opportunity for the US through which NATO could influence the development of CEE. These political and economic interests were reflected in a remark by assistant secretary of state Richard Holbrooke, who concluded, "The West must expand to Central Europe as fast as possible, in fact as well as in spirit, and the US is ready to lead the way".[5]

Further, changes in the organisation of finance and banking were of paramount importance and were a condition of existence for the market economy itself.[6] Moves towards establishing an independent central bank, a process which had started before 1990, underpinned the framework necessary for the neoliberal project to ensure sound money and disentangle finance from domestic capital and the political influence of the old Stalinist ruling classes. The economies of Western Europe and the US needed new markets, in which some of their largest and most profitable financial firms could operate. This was particularly true of Britain and the US, which dominate global financial services. The outcome of this scramble for assets is reflected in the large amount of foreign capital that dominates the financial sector in CEE, with about 80 percent of the banking system under foreign ownership.[7]

However, "transformation" and installing neoliberalism were not straightforward processes whereby these countries simply reflected the needs of global capitalism. The competing interests of different sections of the ruling class and struggles of organised labour made the process protracted and the outcomes a political compromise, particularly regarding privatisation and welfare. Therefore the restructuring of the state was much more complex than simply guaranteeing the conditions for the operation of transnational capital. The three Baltic States, Estonia, Latvia and Lithuania, for example, were particularly ardent in their adoption of neoliberal policies, in the case of Lithuania "even to the extent of

---

4:    Hardy, 2009.
5:    Holbrooke, 1995, p42..
6:    Grahl, 2005.
7:    HSBC, 2006.

importing a US citizen of Lithuanian origin, Valdas Adamkus, to take office as President of the Republic".[8]

The first stage of transformation after 1990 was crude and draconian and had devastating impacts on the living standards of large sections of people as these economies integrated with an increasingly liberalised global economy. In 1990 a particularly brutal version of this was the introduction of "shock therapy" in Poland, which was neoliberalism in a bullet with drastic cuts in public spending, subsidies and public sector wages. The EU strategy, however, was a much more systematic attempt to promote neoliberal reform and the influence of European transnational capital through the liberalisation and deregulation of CEE.[9] The main thrust of PHARE was to prepare countries for EU membership by demanding more and deeper measures of deregulation and liberalisation, along with a dose of social protection in case social discontent derailed reforms.

Therefore in dangling the carrot of membership, the EU managed to push Central and Eastern European economies towards adopting a specific neoliberal reform model, which was a much more radical variant than the one operating in the economies of existing members. Having to conform to EU norms, regarding state aid and rules on competition policy in particular, wedded these countries to the liberalisation of trade and investment in a way that made it difficult to accede to any demands by members of the ruling class for protection or retreat.

Two projects which consolidated the neoliberal project in Europe were extended to the post-Communist new member states. The first was the European single market, a popular symbol used to relaunch European integration in the mid-1980s and implemented in 1992, the aim of which was to restore Europe's global competitiveness with Japan and the US. In particular, this opened up previously protected sectors (for example, services, utilities and telecommunications) to trade and investment and spurred further rounds of privatisation. While the rhetoric was of innovation, competitiveness and economies of scale, the reality was that it allowed the reorganisation of European capital over a wider territory, which was manifested in an unprecedented wave of mergers and acquisitions.

The second project was that of monetary union with a central bank and single currency. This was the consolidation of the single market as it removed barriers and reduced costs for large firms by providing an undifferentiated terrain on which capital could operate. Monetary union was a

---

8:   Woolfson, 2010.
9:   Holman, 2004; Smith, 2002; Shields, 2004.

stick with which to force countries to reduce their public spending through the restrictive monetary policy in the convergence criteria of the Maastricht Treaty and Stability and Growth Pact.[10] The role of monetary policy was therefore to exert a disciplinary neoliberalism, particularly on weaker economies that would face the highest costs in terms of unemployment. [11]

Full accession to the EU in 2004 deepened and strengthened the neoliberal agenda. Earlier claims that EU enlargement provided the best way to ensure democracy in all of post-Communist Eastern Europe were immediately undermined by the inclusion of selected states and the exclusion of the remaining applicants. It was considered by the ruling classes of current EU members and representatives of capital that the costs to European capitalism of admitting the excluded states outweighed the advantages they would reap in terms of new markets for goods and new destinations for foreign investment.

The institutions of capital such as the Transatlantic Business Dialogue, the World Economic Forum, the International Chamber of Commerce and the Competitiveness Advisory Group played an active part in trying to mobilise economic interests, governments and trade unions in their desire to make CEE safe for US and European capitalism. The ERT (European Round Table of Industrialists), in particular, which consisted of the chief executives of European transnational corporations (TNCs) and represented the interests of transnational capital, played a pivotal role in trying to secure the interests of capital and exerted a strong influence on policies that were in its interests. This included most notably the implementation of the Single Market, the creation of the Trans-European Network infrastructure scheme, the restructuring of European education policy and the whittling away of social protection measures.[12] Therefore the pre-accession strategy was devised by the EU Commission with the support of the ERT.[13]

The EU Commission and the ERT therefore gave an ideological direction to the overall process of European integration including unleashing market liberalisation for candidate countries. The promise of membership ensured a restructuring of CEE in line with the EU's neoliberal trajectory and satisfied the need of European transnational capital for further expansion of capitalist accumulation. In turn, it fulfilled the objective of some sections of the ruling class to secure external pressure for

---

10: Gill, 2001.
11: Cardechi, 2001.
12: Doherty and Hoedeman, 1994.
13: Bornschier, 2000; van Apeldoorn, 2000 and 2003.

internal restructuring and therefore strengthened the hand of those who were most enthusiastic about the neoliberal model.

The crisis hits Central and Eastern Europe

The scale of the financial crisis of 2008 and subsequent recession is clearly evident in Table 1. This shows dramatic falls in GDP in the Baltic States, and with the exceptions of Poland and the Czech Republic, falls in GDP significantly above the EU average of 4.2 percent.

The crisis hit the Central and Eastern European countries in the EU through two channels. In the language of the World Bank "global deleveraging" (a massive contraction of lending) was triggered in "distressed home country financial markets" (financial institutions exposed by toxic debts), which, with the "unwinding of the real estate booms" (the crash of property prices) in some host countries, reduced the willingness of financial markets to finance sovereign debt.[14] The subsequent recession reduced demand for exports in Western Europe, having a negative impact on production and employment in small economies like the Czech and Slovak Republics, and Estonia and Hungary where exports accounted for 70 and 80 percent of GDP in 2008. To a lesser extent, this was also the case for the larger economies of Poland and Romania.

One of the impacts of integration with the EU and global economy was the domination of the banking systems of CEE by mainly Western European or US banks and finance companies. Capital inflows were larger in this part of Europe and fell more severely during the crisis. Therefore risk was transferred from Western European parent banks to affiliates in countries of CEE as cross-border loans.[15]

The growth of credit was driven by households borrowing to try and boost their living standards, and fuelled by the ability to borrow in foreign currency with a lower interest rate and longer payback period than local finance (see Table 2). 2003 to 2006 was a period of historically high global liquidity. International banks were awash with funds and there was fierce competition between them to bolster profits by lending to governments, firms and households in the post-Communist economies of the EU. Lending to ordinary people in these economies in foreign currencies was analogous to lending to poor people in the US—the so-called subprime market—where banks ratcheted up profits by lending to people irrespective of whether they could repay their debts.

14: Mitra, Selowsky and Zalduendo, 2010.
15: Pomerleano, 2010.

Table 1: Selected economic indicators 2009/2010 [16]

Country	Real GDP growth percentage (2009)	Government deficit as percentage of GDP (2009)	Unemployment (first quarter, 2010)
Average EU 27	-4.2	-3.9	8.9
Post-Communist economies			
Bulgaria	-5.0	-3.9	9.7
Czech Republic	-4.1	-5.9	7.4
Estonia	-14.1	-1.7	19.0
Latvia	-18.0	-9.0	20.0
Lithuania	-14.8	-8.9	17.3
Hungary	-6.3	-4.0	10.4
Slovakia	-4.7	-6.8	15.0
Slovenia	-7.8	-5.5	7.0
Poland	+1.7	-7.1	9.6
Romania	-7.1	-8.3	7.4
Selected comparators			
Spain	-3.6	-11.2	20.0
UK	-4.9	-11.5	7.8
Ireland	-7.1	-14.3	13.3

Although some credit went to firms, the bulk of the loans went to households, and in the majority of cases this went on financing mortgages, as can be seen from Table 3.

In general the integration of these economies with the European and global economies has shaped the nature of their vulnerability, but in the same way that the crisis has unfolded in different ways in economies of Western and Southern Europe, its scale and nature have been different in the former Communist countries of the EU.

16: Data drawn from Eurostat. See http://ec.europa.eu/eurostat

Table 2: Currency composition of loans, by country, March 2009[17]

Country	Percentage foreign currency
Bulgaria	62
Estonia	88
Hungary	72
Latvia	92
Lithuania	65
Poland	40
Romania	62

Table 3: Growth and composition of credit to the private sector from 2003 to 2008[18]

	Average growth of credit to household (percentage)	Average growth of credit to corporations (percentage)	Share of housing loans in total household spending (percentage)
Bulgaria	41	57	43
Czech Republic	26	12	65
Estonia	39	32	78
Hungary	21	7	64
Latvia	44	28	64
Lithuania	59	31	76
Poland	28	13	30
Slovak Republic	28	10	69

17: Mitra, Selowsky and Zalduendo, 2010, p109.
18: Mitra, Selowsky and Zalduendo, 2010, p50.

From economic miracle to implosion: the Baltic States

Between 2005 and 2007 the Baltic States had the highest growth rates in the EU. In these three years GDP in Latvia increased by an average of 10.8 percent year on year, while in Estonia and Lithuania in the corresponding period the year on year average was 8.8 percent. The governments of these countries had pursued the most extreme form of neoliberalism with no progressive taxes (flat tax on income), no inheritance tax and no tax on property.

However, the seemingly endless growth in the Baltic States, which drew accolades from the World Bank for being in the top 30 most "business friendly" economies, was illusory. In fact these economies were hosts to the world's fastest growing real estate bubbles. Rising living standards were the result of property speculation fuelled by cheap foreign credits as Scandinavian and other foreign banks extended mortgage credit to Latvia, Lithuania and Estonia, mostly denominated in foreign currencies (dollars, sterling, Swiss francs and euros—see Table 2). Michael Hudson describes the way in which this enabled the old nomenklatura and apparatus of the Communist Paries to obtain and sell off assets in the public domain or collateralise them for foreign loans:

> The effect has been to jump out of the frying pan of Soviet bureaucracy into the fire of "wild capitalism" and "grabitisation" by giving away or selling off public enterprises and real estate...what has emerged is a symbiosis combining the worst vestiges of the old Stalinist bureaucracy with new predatory finance.[19]

While a small number of people enriched themselves, the experience of ordinary people was dismal. The Baltic States are the worst places to work in the EU. Eurostat reports that they have Europe's lowest standards of living and the longest working hours per week. Spending on social protection per head is a quarter of the European average and income inequality is the most polarised.[20] The pace of the crisis has been swift, with unemployment in Estonia rising from 10 percent to 19 percent between the first quarters of 2009 and 2010, and in the same period unemployment increasing in Latvia from 13 percent to 20 percent (Eurostat). By 2010 this had resulted in a second wave of outward migration as people attempted to escape poverty.

19: Hudson, 2008, pp75-76.
20: Hudson, 2008.

"Good pupil to basket case": Hungary

Hungary was also deemed a shining example of market reform and model pupil of neoliberalism. Therefore it came as a surprise to those who proselytised the connection between free markets and growth and stability that Hungary was the first country in the region to be affected by the financial crisis. However, problems in Hungary predate the crisis of 2008. By 2005/2006 the budget deficit of 10 percent of GDP was deemed too high for Maastricht criteria, which stipulated a target of 3 percent. The government embarked on a series of austerity packages by increasing taxes and reducing benefits and subsidies. In September 2006 riots broke out, unprecedented in the post-1990 period, when people found out that the government had lied to them about the state of the economy in order to get elected.

The political background of high spending was a history of competition between the main parties over public spending. Parliamentary elections led to the defeat of the government in power every time until 2006—usually a protest against their austerity measures. Due to bids for popularity before each election the budget deficit would peak, creating a cyclical pattern not seen elsewhere in Europe. GDP only caught up with its 1989 level in 1999, so successive Hungarian governments had been forced to use high levels of public spending to bolster the economy.

When the crisis hit in 2008 the Hungarian economy, reeling from two years of austerity, was doubly exposed. First, credits had been taken in foreign currencies by the government, firms and households (Tables 2 and 3), which was disastrous when the value of the forint fell. In 2010 1.7 million people out of a population of 10 million had loans in foreign currency. The government estimated that 10 to 15 percent of these were "endangered"—a euphemism for liable to default. Some people have had to sell their homes and others have faced a 33 percent increase in mortgage payments.[21] The second source of Hungary's vulnerability was its dependence on the demand from Western European economies for goods, which nosedived as the crisis unfolded.

Further as the crisis morphed into a sovereign debt crisis, international finance speculatively attacked Hungarian government debt. Even though public sector debt had been dramatically cut from 10 to 3.5 percent of GDP, and was significantly lower than that of other countries (Table 1), this was deemed insufficient misery for the IMF.

21: Bryant, 2010a.

Table 4: Exports as a share of GDP in selected economies[22]

	Total	Machinery and complex products	Motor vehicles and components
Czech Republic	66.8	36.5	11.2
Hungary	65.5	42.3	6.2
Poland	34.4	13.3	4.3
Slovakia	75.7	30.8	12.4

Poland and the Czech Republic: A "velvet" crisis?

The governments of Poland and the Czech Republic attempted to avert speculative attacks on their economies by trying to distance themselves from the catastrophes elsewhere in CEE. The supervisory authorities of the Czech Republic, Slovakia, Poland, Romania and Bulgaria issued a joint statement asking that investors differentiate between the stronger and weaker economies in the region. They did not want to be seen as the subprime of Europe along with the Baltic States and Hungary.

Poland and the Czech Republic are the economies least scathed by the economic crisis. The fall in GDP in the Czech Republic puts it at just below the EU average. In 2009 Poland had a 1.7 percent increase in GDP, though this was meagre when compared with 6.8 percent in 2007 and 5 percent in 2008. Although it had the best growth in the OECD, this was not difficult given the dramatic falls elsewhere in CEE. The daily newspaper *Gazeta Wyborcza* described the country as having a "velvet crisis".[23] There are a number of factors which have cushioned Poland, to some extent, from the economic crisis and recession. A floating exchange rate meant that the zloty fell against the euro by 30 percent between August 2008 and 2009, which meant that it could steal an advantage over competitors whose currencies was not floating.[24]

Poland and the Czech Republic, unlike the Baltic States and Hungary, did not have huge property bubbles fed by foreign banks. Their exposure to foreign currencies was much lower: 8 percent in the Czech Republic and

---

22: Myant and Drahkoupil, 2011 (forthcoming).
23: *Gazeta Wyborcza*, 2009.
24: Most notably the Baltic States and Slovakia.

30 percent in Poland. Although both countries were vulnerable to the fallout from the recession elsewhere in Europe, Poland was much less exposed than the Czech Republic with a lower dependence on exports (see Table 4).

However, Poland's "success" in riding the storm of the current crisis should be treated with caution. This modest growth masks high levels of poverty with 44 percent of people earning less than 75 percent of the average wage and growing inequalities in wealth. The high average rate of unemployment of 9.8 percent only tells a partial story with youth unemployment running at 23 percent in 2010. Furthermore, 27 percent of people are on fixed term contracts—the highest number in Europe.[25] The struggle to survive is reflected in falls in savings and increasing levels of indebtedness. In the future demand will be buoyed by the fact that Poland will be the largest recipient of EU Cohesion Funds, which between 2009 and 2015 will amount to an average of 3.3 percent of GDP per year. Poland's Achilles heel is a high public sector deficit which leaves it exposed to speculative attacks on its sovereign debt. This has risen fast from 2 percent of GDP in 2007 and 3.6 percent of GDP in 2008 to 7.1 percent by 2010 (Eurostat).

Slovakia, with 15 percent unemployment by 2010, did not have a soft landing. It did not have the option of devaluing in the way that Poland did, as it had adopted the euro, and further it was particularly exposed to the recession, with exports forming 75.7 percent of GDP (see Table 4).

Different symptoms, same medicine

The broad pattern of parliamentary politics across the region has been similar. After 1990, alongside the emergence of right wing Christian Democrat political parties, the old Stalinists reconstituted themselves as social democratic parties. In post-Communist economies disillusion with parliamentary parties has been even deeper than in Western Europe as parties of the "right" and "left" have pursued privatisation and market reforms which have enriched a very small proportion of the population, leaving the vast majority with no gains from transformation. Scepticism about politics and politicians has been bolstered by widespread corruption.

The depth of the crisis has varied between the countries of CEE depending on the scale of property bubbles, the level of dependence on exports, the size of public sector deficits and whether they have had a floating exchange rate with which to steal an advantage on competitor countries. The response of governments, however, has been universally the same—to make working class people pay for the crisis. The raft of austerity packages across the

25: http://www.solidarnosc.org.pl/en/main-page/polish-labour-2010-html

region has been simply made up of variations on the theme of reducing wages and benefits, attacking pensions, cutting spending on health and welfare, and raising (regressive) taxes. Despite rising unemployment and falling GDP the IMF and EU urged even greater cuts and tax increases to reduce public sector deficits to the punitive Maastricht target of 3 percent of national income.

The crisis hit the Baltic States first and huge cuts were made to spending and wages in January 2009 that provoked street riots in Lithuania and Latvia.[26] These countries along with Hungary were seen as "exceptional" cases by some sections of the financial press, but as the recession deepened and spread, all EU post-Communist countries have been affected. In elections in the Czech Republic (May 2010) and Slovakia (June 2010), despite social democratic parties gaining the largest number of votes, right wing coalitions, committed to budget cuts and slashing public spending, have formed the new governments.[27] In return for borrowing from the IMF the Romanian government introduced draconian austerity measures in June 2010, which included cutting public sector wages by 25 percent and increasing sales tax from 19 to 24 percent.[28]

Despite Poland's supposed "velvet" landing in the recession, the right wing Civic Platform government is committed to reducing the public sector deficit from 7.9 to the 3 percent, which will mean ferocious cuts in public spending and in welfare—already in the process of being dismantled after 20 years of neoliberal reforms.[29] The government announced an increase in VAT from the beginning of 2011 and was planning more privatisation with the aim of generating 25 billion zloty to plug the gap in government spending.

The spat in July 2010 between the Hungarian government and the IMF and the "markets" is instructive. The Hungarian government had already imposed four years of austerity measures and reduced its public sector debt from 10 percent to 4 percent of GDP at the cost of the living standards of ordinary people. In July 2010 the government, afraid of losing electoral support, refused to make the further cuts that the IMF was demanding. The IMF and its acolytes balked at the fact that the "maverick" and "populist" prime minister Viktor Orban had said that implementing further austerity measures was "out of the question".[30]

There was further squealing when the Hungarian government

26: Woolfson, 2010.
27: *Slovak Spectator*, 2010b.
28: Matthews, 2010.
29: Buckley, 2010.
30: Bryant, 2010c.

decided to reduce the budget deficit by imposing a levy on banks and financial institutions (mainly foreign) for three years. This levy was described by the *Financial Times* as "the most punitive considered anywhere in the world", but was hugely popular with the electorate.[31] Taxing the banks and refusing to implement further austerity measures has caused huge consternation in the "markets". Timothy Ash (Head of Emerging Market Research at the Royal Bank of Scotland) wrote: "The new government has not learnt its lesson from the previous gaffe, while the market is in no mood to overlook fiscal laxity".[32] Another analyst, Gyula Toth (UniCredit SpA, Vienna), added: "We believe that market reality will finally force the government to take the necessary measures".[33]

The lesson of Hungary, as of southern Ireland, seems to be that those ruling classes that have been supine in agreeing cuts urged on them by the IMF then face even more demands for austerity.

Social unrest and resistance

In January 2009 Latvia had the worst riots since the collapse of the Soviet Union as 10,000 people protested in Riga. At the same time in Lithuania, for the first time since 1990, the three trade union confederations united around a set of demands.[34] A massive demonstration took place outside of parliament as well as in half a dozen cities and was followed by a cross-border protest simultaneously in Riga and Vilnius. Slogans appealed to class solidarity: "Our power is in being united! For workers' rights!"[35]

There have been further sporadic protests such as the one in Lithuania in February 2010 against a fourfold rise in electricity prices. This was initiated by Fronto Partija (the Front Party or Frontas)—a new left wing party formed in 2009, previously unknown in Lithuania. Its stated objectives include "to create a socially just Lithuania, where there is no gap between the rich minority and the poor majority, between the large owners of capital and the rest of society". The leader of Frontas admitted that his party had only omitted the word socialism from its name because it has "heavy negative connotations".[36]

In May 2009, 30,000 trade unionists protested in Prague against the way companies were using the recession as a pretext for reducing wages,

---

31: Bryant, 2010c.
32: *Bloomberg Businessweek*, 19 July 2010.
33: *Bloomberg Businessweek*, 19 July 2010.
34: Woolfson, 2010.
35: Woolfson, 2010.
36: Woolfson, 2010, p11.

salaries and other benefits. At the demonstration the Chair of the Czech Metalworkers' Federation, KOVO, Josef Stredula, read out the following statement:

> Don't allow those who did not cause the crisis to be harmed most harshly. Don't make the crisis a pretext for changes to the Labour Code, which would bring about an unprecedented curtailment of employees' rights, including groundless dismissals from work. Don't allow any hazard with the pension fund. Don't approve the new risky bill on savings. Don't allow a devaluation of saved pensions and further weakening of public finance. Act, make decisions and rule for the benefit of citizens, not in the interest of speculative profit of financial groups and lobbies and tax havens.[37]

In Romania in May 2010 tens of thousands of public sector workers protested in Bucharest against plans to cut wages and pensions. It was one of the biggest gatherings on the street since the Romanian Revolution. Marian Gruia, head of the police union, called on Romanians to unite "as we did on 1989, when we overthrew the dictatorship" of Ceausescu.[38]

In Poland protests have been rumbling. The most significant is that miners at the state-owned Kompania Weglowa (the biggest mine in Poland and one of the biggest in Europe) are balloting for strike action in opposition to plans to cut jobs from 62,000 to 45,000.[39]

The darker side of the crisis and recession is that the uneven impacts of market-led policies and their failure to benefit large sections of the population alongside the neoliberal policies of political parties, have provided the fuel for the rise of neo-Nazi parties which are overtly anti-Semitic and anti-gay. In particular, there has been an increase in the scapegoating of the minority Roma community. In Hungary in 2009 at least eight Roma were murdered by Nazis.[40] There has also been a marked increase in homophobia. In Slovakia the first gay pride event was cancelled in May 2010 when it was attacked by a neo-Nazi group, Slovenska Pospolitost.[41]

In Hungary members of the neo-fascist Jobbik party have made electoral gains. They got 17 percent of the votes in the first round of the Hungarian general election in April 2010 and came third with 842,306 votes—only just behind the leading socialist party. By the second round

---

37: EIROnline, 2009.
38: BBC News, 2010.
39: Polish Press Office, 2010.
40: Fabry, 2010.
41: *Slovak Spectator*, 2010a.

of the parliamentary elections they had won 47 out of 386 seats. Earlier in April 2010 they held a 50,000-strong rally. Walter Mayr writing in *Der Spiegel* reported: "Members of citizens' militia and neo-Nazi groups have taken over patrolling the streets on this day. In combat boots, camouflage or black military uniforms they form human chains and divide the crowd".[42] They have built on the despair of ordinary people and are strongest in poorer parts of the country where unemployment is highest.

Conclusion

The degree of support for the post-1990 market reforms has varied between post-Communist countries depending on the strength of trade unions and the organised working class and what the ruling class has been able to deliver materially. However, the level of support for neoliberalism has often been exaggerated, and what support did exist in the early days of transformation quickly dissipated as small groups, often from the previous regime, enriched themselves through privatisation. What could not be clearer is that the crisis has laid bare the class nature of the transformation. For the foreign banks, which have reaped huge profits in the region, it is business as usual. The indignation that they have displayed at the levy imposed on them by the Hungarian government is quite breathtaking.

Huge levels of anger have been manifest in the biggest demonstrations since 1990 across the whole region, underpinned by much clearer class politics than have been evident before. However, these initial explosive protests have not translated into more concerted action, and certainly have not been on the scale of Greece. The dark side of the misery and despair caused by the crisis is the growth of neo-Nazism and rise of nationalism. There are also seeds of hope in the responses of trade unions, the class politics that have underpinned the protests and the presence of new radical parties and campaigns.

42: Mayr, 2010.

References

Andor, László, 2009, "Hungary in the Financial Crisis", *Debatte*, volume 17, number 3.

BBC News, 2010, "Thousands Protest over Romania Austerity Measures", 19 May 2010, www.bbc.co.uk/news10127366

Bloomberg Businessweek, 2010, "Hungary Refuses Further Austerity after IMF Talks End", http://businessweek.com/news/2010-07-19/hungary-refuses-further-austerity-aft

Bornschier, Volker (ed), 2000, *State Building in Europe: The Revitalisation of Western European Integration* (Cambridge University Press).

Buckley, Neil, 2010, "Poland Posed for Vital Reforms", *Financial Times*, (6 July).

Bryant, Chris, 2010a, "Hungarians in Debt to Swiss Franc", *Financial Times*, (16 July).

Bryant, Chris, 2010b, "Hungarian PM Rejects Fresh Deal with IMF and Austerity", *Financial Times*, (20 July).

Bryant, Chris, 2010c, "Budapest's Mixed Messages Sow Confusion", *Financial Times*, (23 July).

Burke, Jason, 2009, "Downturn Shatters East's Dream of a Prosperous post-Soviet Future", *Observer* (8 February), www.guardian.co.uk/business/2009/feb/08/lithuania-credit-crunch-economic -crisis

Carchedi, Guglielmo, 2001, *For Another Europe: A Class Analysis of European Integration* (Verso).

Doherty, Ann, and Olivier Hoedeman, 1994, "Misshaping Europe: The European Round Table of Industrialists", *The Ecologist* 24 (July/August), www.itk.ntnu.no/ansatte/Andresen_Trond/finans/others/EU-ecologist-24-4

EIROnline, 2009, "Trade Unions Protest Against Abuse by Companies of Recession" (7 June), www.eurofound.europa.eu/eiro/2009/05/articles/CZ0905019I.htm

European Commission, 1995, *Technical Assistance for Central and Eastern European Countries and the Newly Independent State PHARE and TACIS Programmes: Background Report* (European Commission MEMO/95/78 04.05.95).

Fabry, Adam, 2010, "Hungary's Fascists on the Move", *Socialist Worker* (24 April), www.socialistworker.co.uk/art.php?id=20950

Gazeta Wyborcza, 2009, "Velvet Crisis is Tempting Foreign Investors" (17 June).

Gill, Stephen, 2001, "Constitutionalising Capital: EMU and Disciplinary Neo-liberalism", in Andreas Bieler and Adam D Morton, *Social Forces in the Making of the New Europe* (Palgrave).

Grahl, John, 2005, "The European Union and Europe", in L Panitch and C Leys (eds), *Socialist Register 2005: The Empire Reloaded* (Merlin Press).

Hardy, Jane, 2009, *Poland's New Capitalism* (Pluto).

Holbrooke, Richard, 1995, "America, A European Power", *Foreign Affairs*, volume 74, number 2.

Holman, Otto, 2001, "The Enlargement of the European Union Towards Central and Eastern Europe: The role of supranational and transnational actors", in Andreas Bieler and Adam D Morton (eds), *Social Forces in the Making of the New Europe* (Palgrave).

Holman, Otto, 2004, "Integrating Peripheral Europe: the Different Roads to 'Security and Stability' in Southern and Central Europe", *Journal of International Relations and Development*, volume 7, number 2.

HSBC, 2006, *Poland Report*, www.hsbcnet.com/transaction/attachments/pcm/pdf/poland.pdf

Hudson, Michael, 2008, "The Fading Baltic Miracle", *International Economy* (winter).

Matthews, K, 2010, "Street Level Implications of Romania's Austerity Program", www.digitaljournal.com/article/294785

Mayr, Walter, 2010, "Hungary Prepares for Shift in Power", *Der Spiegel*, (9 April), www.spiegel.de/international/europe/0,1518687921,00.html

Mitra, Pradeep, Marcelo Selowsky and Juan Zalduendo, 2010, *Turmoil at Twenty: Recession, Recovery and Reform in Central and Eastern Europe and the Former Soviet Union* (World Bank).

Myant, Martin, and Jan Drahokoupil, 2011 (forthcoming), *Transition Economies: Political Economy in Russia, Eastern Europe and Central Asia* (Wiley).

Polish Press Office, 2010, "August 13 2010", http://wiadomosci.onet.pl/2209940,10,item.htm

Pomerleano, Michael, 2010, "The Risks of a Crisis in Central and Eastern Europe are Bigger than You Think", www.voxeu.org.index.php?q=node/5226

Shields, Stuart, 2004, "Global Restructuring and the Polish State: Transition, Transformation, or Transnationalization", *Review of International Political Economy*, volume 11, number 1.

Slovak Spectator, 2010a, "Neo-Nazis Attack Slovakia's First Gay Pride Event" (22 May), http://spectator.sme.sk/articles/view/38949/2/neo_nazis_attack_slovakias_first_gay_pride_event.html

Slovak Spectator, 2010b. "Right Wing Prevails in Election" (13 June), www.spectator.sme.sk/articles/view/39196/2/right_wing_prevails_hzda.out.html

Smith, Adrian, 2002, "Imagining Geographies of the 'New Europe': Geo-economic Power and the New European Architecture of integration", *Political Geography*, volume 21, number 5.

USAID, 2000, http://usaid.gov/press/releases/2000/fs000711 5.html

USAID, 2002, "USAID Mission to Poland: List of Projects", http://usaid.gov/pl/listof1.htm

van Apeldoorn, Bastiaan, 2000, "Transnational Class Agency and European governance: the case of the European Round Table of Industrialists", *New Political Economy*, volume 5, number 2.

van Apeldoorn, Bastiaan, 2003, "The Struggle over European Order: Transnational Class Agency in the Making of 'Embedded Neoliberalism'", in Neil Brenner, Bob Jessop, Martin Jones and Gordon MacLeod, *State/Space: A Reader* (Blackwell).

Wedel, J R, 2000, "US assistance for market reforms", *Independent Review*, volume 4, number 3.

Woolfson, Charles, 2010, "'Hard Times' in Lithuania: Crisis and 'Discourses of Discontent' in post-Communist Society", *Ethnography*, volume 11, number 4.

The ironies of Indian Maoism

Jairus Banaji

Editor's introduction

"A spectre is haunting South Asia—the spectre of Maoism," the *Financial Times* rather melodramatically announced in April 2006, reporting that the Indian prime minister, Manmohan Singh, had described Maoist guerrillas as "the single greatest threat to Indian national security".[1] The scale of the Maoist-led insurgency in rural India has surprised and alarmed ruling classes for whom Marxism-Leninism was supposed to have been safely confined to the dustbin of history after 1989. The Indian Maoists have also become a subject of discussion on the left both in India and internationally. In particular, a recent article by the writer and campaigner Arundhati Roy describing her visit to a Maoist-controlled area attracted much controversy.[2]

In the following piece, the Indian Marxist scholar and activist Jairus Banaji offers a much more critical analysis of Indian Maoism than Roy provided. But first here is a little background to help the reader unfamiliar with Indian politics and society (see also the glossary).

India is by far the most important country in the world where Communism remains a powerful political force. Reflecting the twists and turns of Moscow's foreign policy, the Communist Party of India (CPI) during the struggle for national liberation from Britain had an ambivalent relationship to the dominant nationalist party, the Indian National

---

1:    Johnson, 2006.
2:    Roy, 2010a. In a later piece, which appeared after this article was completed, Roy provided a more nuanced analysis—Roy, 2010b.

Congress. But its role in different social movements gave it a significant popular base. After independence was won in 1947, Congress-ruled India pursued a policy of neutrality in the Cold War that led to a strategic partnership with the Soviet Union. Moscow's demands that the CPI moderate its opposition to Congress caused increasing tensions within the party.

These were exacerbated by the split in 1960 between the USSR and China under Mao Zedong, who denounced the Soviet leader Nikita Khrushchev's policy of "peaceful coexistence" with the West. The rise of Maoism, purporting to offer a more radical version of Marxism-Leninism than Moscow, divided the international Communist movement. Nowhere was this more true than in India. The 1962 border war between India and China deepened the divisions within the CPI, and in 1964 the pro-China faction broke away to form the Communist Party of India (Marxist,) or CPI(M).

The new party's rhetoric was more radical than the CPI's, and indeed it remains strongly "Marxist-Leninist", not to say Stalinist. But in practice the CPI(M) has pursued the same kind of parliamentary strategy that the pro-Moscow CPI also continues to follow. This has brought the CPI(M) a significant degree of success in bourgeois politics, particularly at the level of state governments (India has a quasi-federal political system in which the states have significant powers). Today the CPI(M) is the largest left party in India, dominating the state governments of West Bengal, Kerala, and Tripura. But the gap between rhetoric and practice has grown, as these governments implement neoliberal policies that have caused internal conflicts within the party as well as clashes with popular movements.[3]

It was the same gap that gave rise to Indian Maoism proper in the late 1960s. At a time when the Chinese Cultural Revolution was inspiring young radicals everywhere, the CPI(M) itself split as Charu Mazumdar and other local leaders in West Bengal placed themselves at the head of a rising in the Naxalbari district. Banaji's article traces the subsequent development of the Indian Maoists. It is worth underlining that, as he notes, they continue to operate within an ideological framework that, in common with the more mainstream Communist parties, treats India as a "feudal" or "semi-feudal" society, but that follows Mao in treating the peasantry as the key revolutionary force.

In fact, India is a thoroughly capitalist society, though one shaped by the process of uneven and combined development that Neil Davidson discusses elsewhere in this issue. A large proportion of the rural poor in India consists of workers drawn from the so-called "Scheduled Castes"

3:    Sarkar, 2007.

and "Scheduled Tribes", that is, those who have traditionally been at the bottom of the caste hierarchy or beyond its pale and subject to centuries of domination. Today the Scheduled Castes are generally referred to as "Dalits", with the general sense of the crushed or oppressed, and the tribals known as "Adivasis", a term that highlights their character as the original inhabitants of the subcontinent.

The bulk of the Scheduled Castes are agricultural labourers. They have worked, traditionally, as farm servants and casual labourers for a substantial peasantry drawn from the upper castes and so-called OBCs (Other Backward Classes). In Andhra Pradesh where the Naxalites sank deep roots in the 1970s, over 70 percent of Dalits are landless labourers. With the great awakening that swept through these masses for much of the 20th century, large parts of rural and small-town India saw a pro-slavery rebellion of sorts by the late 1970s and a dramatic increase in the number of caste atrocities, that is, murderous assaults on Dalits, their families and their settlements.

For their part, Adivasis make up a little under 10 percent of the country's population (some 84 million at the last count), with the bulk of them concentrated in the central Indian states of Chhattisgarh, Madhya Pradesh, Orissa and Andhra Pradesh. The Santals in eastern India and the Gonds of central India are among the largest groups numerically, and both have figured prominently in the Maoist movement. The Adivasis are mostly forest dwellers and migrant workers, the vast majority of them sunk in an abject poverty whose chief causes have been expanding state control of the forests and the encroachment of non-tribals.

But the last two decades have seen strong tribal resistance to the expansion of mining capital as the reopening of India to the world economy increased competition among both Indian states and industrial capitals and encouraged a quite scandalous exploitation of non-renewable resources in the resource-rich tribal belts of Orissa, Chhattisgarh and Jharkhand that remain among the most impoverished parts of the country. The picture is one of unabated ecological depletion (which includes a rampant growth of illegal mining and the widespread use of open cast mining techniques) and a continuing displacement of tribals. Elsewhere in the countryside millions of agricultural labourers from the Dalit and other communities face the grim prospect of growing joblessness and land hunger, because the central government is unwilling to risk the kind of confrontation with state legislatures that any substantial tackling of these issues will inevitably bring.

AC

Glossary

Adivasis: the term for tribals (Scheduled Tribes in official parlance), signifying their character as the original inhabitants of the subcontinent; called girijans ("hill people") in Andhra Pradesh; the majority are forest dwellers.

BJP: Bharatiya Janata Party, currently the main opposition party and the parliamentary face of a network of organisations whose stated aim is the replacement of India's democracy by a Hindu state. This conglomerate, controlled by the RSS (Rashtriya Swayamsevak Sangh), is India's closest parallel to a fascist movement, seeking to win support among Hindus by targeting minorities. The BJP was behind the horrific communal violence in Gujarat in 2002.

CRPF: Central Reserve Police Force, the chief paramilitary force involved in counterinsurgency operations

Dalits: the name (self-description) now generally used for the Scheduled Castes; it has the general sense of "the crushed" or "the oppressed"; the bulk of them are landless and many have converted to Buddhism or Christianity.

podu: the term used throughout Andhra Pradesh for shifting cultivation.

zamindars: landowners; used loosely of the dominant group in village society.

A rough periodisation of the Maoist movement in India might read as follows: (1) The seminal years of "Naxalism" from the late 1960s to the end of 1972 were defined by a split from the Communist Party of India (Marxist) (CPI(M)) in 1967 when a large-scale exodus began, and by mass upsurges in various parts of West Bengal, in largely tribal-dominated districts, and in Srikakulam along the Andhra coast, construed by the split-away "Marxist-Leninists" as uprisings of the peasantry and struggles for state power. (2) A period from the main part of the 1970s to the 1980s, when the movement reassembled itself outside Bengal, chiefly in central and southern Bihar and in the Telangana region of Andhra Pradesh. Here two major "armed-struggle" tendencies survived with substantial continuity through the whole of the 1970s: the Chandra Pulla Reddy group and a group around Kondapalli Seetharamaiah. (3) A dramatic escalation of conflict from 1985 that would lead eventually to a wholesale militarisation of the movement in the 1990s and to the civil war that is currently raging in the tribal heartlands of the formerly undivided district of Bastar in the state of Chhattisgarh.

If the party launched by Charu Mazumdar in April 1969 had disintegrated by 1971 and fragmentation remained a characteristic of the Maoist groups throughout the 1970s and 1980s, the most recent phase has seen a series of mergers and a more consolidated Maoist movement. Today the two major currents of Indian Naxalism are the CPI (Marxist-Leninist) (from here on, Liberation) which is a more or less open party that has contested elections since the late 1970s, and the CPI (Maoist), which is waging the guerrilla war in Bastar and parts of Orissa. When the Indian government describes Maoism as the country's biggest "internal security threat", it is referring not to all the various Maoist parties, which are still numerous, but specifically to the CPI (Maoist) which emerged in 2004 as a merger between People's War (PW) and the Maoist Communist Centre of India (MCCI). PW was itself the outcome of a merger between the People's War Group (PWG) founded by Seetharamaiah and a Bihar-based party, Party Unity. Unlike Liberation, the PWG had been banned (on and off) for most of its history, and so of course is its avatar, the CPI (Maoist).

Andhra Pradesh has always been the true backbone of Indian Maoism. It was the only state in the country where the Maoists were in a majority in mid-1967, when a series of state-level coordination committees revolted against the CPI(M) leadership, egged on by the Chinese Communist Party's (CCP) call for a fight against "revisionism". "The party lost 60 percent of its membership in the state," with Nagi Reddy carrying 11 of the 14 district committees with him.[1] But the Andhra Maoists stayed out of the All India Co-ordination Committee of Revolutionaries in November 1967.[2] When the dissidents either left or were forced out of the CPI(M) and the coordination of state committees renamed itself the All India Coordination Committee of Communist Revolutionaries (AICCCR) by the middle of 1968, it had more or less committed itself to forming a separate party.

Yet, as Mohan Ram wrote, "there was intense confusion in the AICCCR about the priorities towards building a party and about the kind of party to be built".[3] For Charu Mazumdar "the primary condition for building such a party was to organise armed struggle in the countryside".[4] "The major task of revolutionaries was to plunge into work among the peasant masses and set up revolutionary bases".[5] Mazumdar "had nothing to say about the role of mass organisations and the accent was on a secret party".[6]

The divisions within the AICCCR were essentially on the issue of mass work and whether a party formed in this way, with middle class youth being sent out to "rouse the peasant masses in the countryside" to "wage guerrilla war" and "build rural base areas",[7] would be in a position to sustain armed struggle. Brushing these differences aside, the Communist Party of India (Marxist-Leninist), or CPI(M-L), was formed on 22 April 1969 and launched at a May Day gathering that year, and had more or less disintegrated by 1971, with a section led by Bihar's Satya Narayan Singh dissociating itself from

---

1:   Ram, 1971, p81.
2:   I shall use the term "Andhra" as shorthand for the state of Andhra Pradesh; Andhra otherwise refers to the largely coastal region within the state.
3:   Ram, 1971, p84.
4:   Ram, 1971, p83.
5:   Ram, 1971, p86.
6:   Ram, 1971, p87.
7:   Duyker, 1987, p79, citing the CPI(M-L)'s "Resolution on Party Organisation" dated 22 April 1969.

Mazumdar.[8] Singh (or "SNS", as he was called) had described Mazumdar's line as "individual terrorism" as early as July 1970.[9] By November that year "a majority of the CPI(M-L)'s 21-member Central Committee withdrew support from Mazumdar", and he was *expelled from the party in 1971.*[10]

The CCP had come down heavily on Mazumdar, denouncing his conception of annihilation as "secret assassination", claiming he had no agrarian programme, and describing his "policy" as "wrong". Most substantially, it argued, "Without mass struggle and mass organisation, the peasants' armed struggle cannot be sustained." "Regarding the formulation that if a revolutionary does not make his hands red with the blood of class enemies, then he is not a Communist; if this be the yardstick of a Communist, then that Communist Party cannot remain a Communist Party".[11] Top leaders like Kanu Sanyal, in jail by 1972, referred to their "great disappointment, regret and disgust" at the fact that Mazumdar had refused to learn any lessons from the "valuable suggestions" of the CCP.

Class roots of revolt

Naxalbari in the north of West Bengal became a template for the Indian revolution and gave the Naxalites their name. But there was no serious attempt by the Maoist leadership to look at the nature of the struggles there or in Midnapore (Medinipur) or Srikakulam or Kondamodalu. For example, Duyker notes that in the Santal-inhabited areas of Debra and Gopiballavpur (in Midnapore) the Naxalites succeeded in "mobilising large numbers of landless labourers and sharecroppers".[12] There was widespread landlessness among the Santals of districts like Midnapore and Birbhum,[13] and it was essentially these landless tribals who formed the backbone of the mass agitations that the new party led in 1969, in harvesting campaigns that Mazumdar himself was opposed to![14] The rural upsurges in Midnapore and Birbhum coincided with the monsoons when "the landless could least expect to gain work".[15]

In Naxalbari, in the Siliguri subdivision of Darjeeling in the north, the

---

8:    Mohanty, 1977, pxx.
9:    Mohanty, 1977, p121.
10:   Mohanty, 1977, p122.
11:   Sanyal, 1972, p15, citing excerpts from a letter received from the CCP in November 1970.
12:   Duyker, 1987, p81.
13:   Duyker, 1987, pp44–46.
14:   Duyker, 1987, p85, citing the testimony of Santosh Rana who led the movement in Gopiballavpur, with his wife and brother.
15:   Duyker, 1987, p101.

land occupations that mushroomed between March and May 1967 involved Santal tea garden labourers who worked as sharecroppers on the excess land of the estates.[16] The local leadership here, Kanu Sanyal and Jangal Santhal, did not subscribe to the strategy of small squad actions and concentrated on mass agitation.[17] The agitation (on issues like eviction of sharecroppers and recovery of excess land) was given the character of a nascent insurgency because the Santals were armed with bows and arrows and remained "poised for attacks on police parties",[18] as the CPI(M)-led United Front government decided to break the movement with large-scale arrests and hundreds of tribals fled to the forest where they formed ill-armed and inexperienced guerrilla units besieged by a massive police force.[19] By August wholesale surrenders began to take place—the government had succeeded in breaking the movement by force.

In the Srikakulam Agency Area the bulk of Adivasis (or Girijans, as they were called here) were agricultural labourers.[20] Andhra Pradesh accounts for the highest incidence of tribal land alienation in the country, with non-tribals owning more than half the land in the scheduled areas. Thus here landlessness stemmed from a widespread process of dispossession that had occurred on a larger scale in the coastal tracts of Andhra where primitive accumulation by the state and by moneylenders involved the suppression of customary rights like *podu* and the appropriation of large tracts of land either as "state forests" or land seized by non-tribals.[21] In Srikakulam the Communists had built a broad-based organisation of tribals by the late 1950s, and the land occupations and crop seizures that exploded in 1968 were directed as much against those forces as against any abstract "feudalism".[22] In Kondamodalu in East Godavari "the first demand that was taken up [by the party] concerned the indebtedness of the tribals and their exploitation by the moneylenders", but "the issue on which the movement really picked up was farm wages".[23] Here the land seizures of 1969 targeted land that had been alienated to the non-tribals or mortgaged to moneylenders and did *not* include "the 'self-cultivated lands' of the landlords over which the tribals as yet felt they had no claim".[24]

16: Samanta, 1984, pp64, 77.
17: Samanta, 1984, p79.
18: Duyker, 1987, p71, citing the *Times of India*, 25 May 1967.
19: Duyker, 1987, pp74-75.
20: Mohanty, 1977, p49.
21: See the study of this by Rao, Deshingkar and Farrington, 2006.
22: Ram, 1971, p89.
23: Sinha, 1989, p192.
24: Sinha, 1989, pp192–193.

The movement in Srikakulam was crushed by the middle of 1970 and a period of decline set in.[25] Mazumdar died in custody in July 1972. On one estimate, by March 1973 there were some 17,787 Naxalite prisoners in West Bengal alone.[26] Shock attacks on the class enemy had had disastrous results. In Andhra, Nagi Reddy's group, the Andhra Pradesh Revolutionary Communist Committee (APRCC), argued, "Some persons, forming themselves into groups and without any relation to the mass movement, attack the landlords and other exploiters. We want to make it clear that these attacks carried on without any relation to a mass revolutionary movement cannot enable us to dissolve feudalism".[27] Annihilations would not "annihilate the system or the forms of exploitation".[28] The CPI(M-L)'s "methodology made the people feel that someone else and not they were the liberators".[29]

The setback was so severe that the CPI(M-L) fragmented rapidly and was badly divided in the months leading up to the state of emergency declared by prime minister Indira Gandhi in June 1975. During the emergency of 1975-7 some ten Maoist groups were banned and an estimated 40,000 cadres were in jail.[30] But within the Maoist mainstream the disintegration of the Central Committee spawned repeated attempts at reunification. Nagi Reddy, who had been opposed to the formation of a centralised party[31] and had repeatedly emphasised the need for a longish period of mass work, teamed up with Parimal Das Gupta (one of Mazumdar's earliest critics) and others nationally to form the Unity Centre of Communist Revolutionaries of India (Marxist-Leninist). This more or less disintegrated when Nagi Reddy died in 1975. In Andhra itself Nagi Reddy's group was the weakest of the three groups that existed there in the 1970s. The Andhra Pradesh Revolutionary Communist Party led by Chandra Pulla Reddy, the strongest group in the state in the 1970s, defended the armed defence of the cadres in the face of repression,[32] but combined this with mass struggles or at least the need for an active mobilisation of masses in struggle.

Despite this, CP Reddy supported SNS's drive to regroup the CPI(M-L)

25: Mohanty, 1977, p78: "When the period of decline of the CPI(M-L) started in the middle of 1970".
26: Duyker, 1987, p151.
27: Cited in Ram, 1971, p146.
28: Sinha, 1989, p179, summarising the APRCC position.
29: Ram, 1971, p149.
30: Mohanty, 1977, pxxi.
31: Dubey, 1991, p164.
32: Sinha, 1989, p218.

and was part of the "Provisional Central Committee", till he split in 1980. Thus the C P Reddy group absorbed very different sorts of influences. It would abandon the boycottism of the CPI(M-L) and start contesting elections from 1978, even winning a seat in the Andhra Assembly elections. It was also the C P Reddy group that was first active in forming the Ryothu Coolie Sanghams or agricultural labour unions. These spread rapidly in the late 1970s and were a key factor in creating substantial popular support for the Naxals in Andhra.[33] The third Maoist group in Andhra was in some ways the most orthodox, since its leader, Kondapalli Seetharamaiah, had joined the AICCCR early in 1969, and when the Central Committee disintegrated Seetharamaiah was the Andhra face of the "pro-Charu" Central Organising Committee (COC). These coordinations meant little in practice, since the Andhra Maoists were largely independent in their evolution.

In the general retreat and disintegration of the CPI(M-L) that dominated the early 1970s, both C P Reddy and the Andhra COC retained the elements of a squad organisation in north Telangana, and again the issues were less those of a peasantry than of the purely landless and Scheduled Caste labourers and farm servants in districts like Karimnagar and of tribals and other working people in the Godavari valley region.[34] Unlike the insane putschism that had controlled and destroyed the party under Mazumdar's leadership, Telangana in the late 1970s and early 1980s saw major developments that laid the groundwork for the "people's war" of the 1990s and 2000s. The PWG, formed in 1980, had substantial control of Telangana by the end of the 1980s, and it is crucial to see why.[35]

The reason, as the late human rights acivist K Balagopal explained, was that "unlike the rest of [Andhra] where the Naxalites spread through the armed squads, in northern Telangana there was a clear period in the late 1970s and early 1980s…when it was the mass organisations, mainly the agricultural labourers' associations and the student and youth fronts, that were the instrument for the spread of Maoism as an ideology and a political practice".[36] That phase "was soon to pass and the people would start depending on the armed squads for justice".[37] But Seetharamaiah, who attracted the younger generation to his group in large numbers,[38] saw no conflict between mass organisation and

---

33: Balagopal and Reddy, 1982, p1897 onwards.
34: The best account of these struggles is Balagopal and Reddy, 1982.
35: Singh, 1995, p109, citing the editor of *Andhra Prabha*: "The PWG practically runs a 'parallel government' in Karimnagar, Warangal and Adilabad districts."
36: Balagopal, 2006a, p3183.
37: Balagopal, 2006a, p3183.
38: Sinha, 1989, p281.

armed struggle,[39] and their combined impact was to strike "fatally at the power relations of rural Telangana society" and endow "the poor, the Dalits and the tribals with a voice of their own and the courage to speak out".[40] For all the violence they unleashed, their own and the even worse, more widely spread violence of the state in Andhra, it was possible for Balagopal to maintain that "there is this fear that if the Naxalites go away, 'the poor cannot survive'."[41]

If the PWG emerged as the dominant group in Andhra, even more so when the CP Reddy group split in 1984, in Bihar the field was equally divided between Liberation, Party Unity and the Maoist Communist Centre (MCC). A key factor in the survival of the PWG was its expansion into the largely tribal districts of Telangana, where the cadre encouraged tribals to cut down and cultivate reserved forests,[42] forced a substantial increase in the wages paid by tendu leaf contractors,[43] and put an end to the harassment Adivasis suffered at the hands of forest officials and the police. In Bihar the oppression of the rural poor took a different form. Though called "zamindars" by the labourers, the Bhumihars of districts like Bhojpur were in fact a substantial peasantry (kisans) and the suppression of the rural poor was as much a struggle for dignity (izzat), that is, for freedom from violence and caste oppression, as a struggle over wages and land rights. The violent colonial repression of the military labour markets of North India[44] had done little to modify the warrior ethos of zamindars and peasants alike in states like Bihar, and the Dalits who formed the bulk of labourers (mazdoors) knew that "any open challenge to upper and middle caste domination would eventually and inevitably result in armed violence".[45]

One student claimed that in the village he studied most Dalits "wanted the Maoist armed squads to remain in the area as they feared that the landlords would re-establish their dominance" if the Maoists withdrew.[46] Another was told, "Because we have arms, the zamindars have shrunk with fear".[47] Thus all of the main Bihar groups were committed

---

39: Sinha, 1989, p282, citing a PWG document: "the armed form of struggle is not the only form of struggle."
40: Balagopal, 1997, p2255.
41: Balagopal, 2006a, p3183.
42: Balagopal, 1990b, pp1884-1885.
43: Tendu is the leaf from which beedis (cigarettes) are made.
44: Richards, 2004, pp398-399.
45: Kunnath, 2009, p319.
46: Kunnath, 2009, p320; see Bhatia, 2005, p1545, for a similar narrative about the origins of Party Unity in Jehanabad district.
47: Bhatia, 2005, p1546.

to "armed struggle" to one degree or another. The Naxalites who were brought into Bhojpur in the late 1960s would later split from the CPI(M-L) (pro-Mazumdar, pro-Lin Piao faction) led by Mahadeb Mukherjee without gravitating to S N Singh's Central Committee at the other end of the pro/anti-Mazumdar spectrum.[48] Liberation was the outcome of the new Central Committee formed in July 1974 by Subroto Datta alias Jowhar, the young leader of this "third" tendency, and of the three Bihar parties was the one that showed the most substantial evolution in terms of seeking strategies for both survival and growth.[49]

In an extraordinary combination of legal and illegal work, Liberation floated a front organisation, the Indian People's Front (IPF), that contested 50 seats in the Bihar Assembly elections of 1985,[50] even as its armed squads pulled off over 60 "annihilations" between 1980 and 1984![51] Much of this violence was part of the titanic struggle the Bihar groups were engaged in against the caste-based private militias formed by the Bhumihars, Kurmis and other landed castes in their drive to exterminate Naxalism from the plains of Bihar. This warfare dominated the whole of the 1980s and much of the 1990s, and while the CPI(M-L) was successful in fighting the smaller militias, it was drawn inexorably into a caste dynamic that shaped the nature of the movement and its struggles.

Party Unity, formed in 1982, successfully fought the Bhoomi Sena in Jehanabad,[52] but by the 1990s it drew much of its support from the Kurmis, and its Dalit supporters (all of them workers) felt deserted and betrayed.[53] The MCC, which had evolved from Dakshin Desh, one of the Maoist groups that had stayed out of the AICCCR and eventually built its base in Jharkhand (then south Bihar) had a large following among Yadavs,[54] and became deeply embroiled in caste vendettas that involved horrific massacres on all sides.[55] The MCC had no interest in open organisations of any sort;[56] Party Unity's style of politics effectively drove its one open front, the Mazdoor Kisan

---

48: Dubey, 1991, p179.
49: Dubey, 1991, pp185-186. He was killed in November 1975 and Vinod Mishra became the leader.
50: Dubey, 1991, p235.
51: Dubey, 1991, p223.
52: Dubey, 1991, p251.
53: Kunnath, 2009, pp321 onwards.
54: Mohanty, 2006, p3164.
55: See, for example, Liberation's description of the MCC as "practitioners of caste war" (*jati sangharsh chalanewala*)—Dubey, 1991, p227.
56: Dubey, 1991, p254.

Sangram Samiti, underground (it was banned in 1986);[57] and Liberation had to disband the IPF in 1994, worried that its popularity was actually a threat to the "identity of the party"![58] Finally, not the least of the problems with this total absorption in left wing militarism (less true of Liberation which seems to have dismantled its squads by the late 1990s) has been the armed clashes between the various Naxal groups, involving the liquidation of each other's cadre.[59]

Militarisation of the struggle

The late 1980s saw a dramatic escalation of conflict once the PWG took the fateful decision to target the state directly by mounting attacks on the police, inaugurating a spiral of violence that has not abated till today. "It was in July 1985 that the first incident of deliberate murder of a policeman by the Naxalites took place; that was in Jagtial, a 'disturbed area' of Karimnagar, where the police in collusion with armed BJP landlords had been subjecting Naxalite youth to repeated and savage torture".[60] Balagopal himself referred to these escalating levels of violence as a "new" phase. They would transform the conflict into a full-scale war, with sizeable para-military forces converting Telangana and the adjoining forest areas into a "vast police camp" and with a profound militarisation of the PWG itself.[61] By the end of the 1980s "whole tribal hamlets were set on fire to teach them a lesson not to harbour Naxalites".[62] By 1997 Balagopal could write that "the 1990s have seen an unprecedented escalation in the magnitude of the killings. More than 60 percent of the encounter killings of the [last] three decades have taken place in the last six years".[63]

57: Dubey, 1991, pp252–253.

58: Bhatia, 2005, p1546: "IPF had to be disbanded in 1994 because it had become so popular that the identity of the party itself was at stake."

59: Dubey, 1991, p226, describes armed clashes emerging between Party Unity and Liberation by the late 1980s; they continued to slaughter each other in the 1990s. Balagopal, 1990b, p1884, refers to the "murderous assaults the Naxalite groups have been making upon each other", meaning mainly PWG attacks on CP Reddy cadre which left 30 dead on both sides in a period of just five months in 1990. Finally, see Kumar, 2003, p4982: " In a booklet brought out in August 2002, the CPI (M-L) Liberation claims that the People's War killed 52 [of its] supporters between 1998 and 2002."

60: Balagopal, 1990a, p591.

61: Singh, 1995, p111, a phrase penned, ironically, by a retired police officer, one time director general of the Border Security Force!

62: Balagopal, 1990a, p592; see Balagopal, 1987, p1171, for the burning of tribal hamlets, of the Koyas in east Godavari and the Konds in Visakhapatnam.

63: Balagopal, 1997, p2257.

Since then, over the period 1997 to 2007, the Andhra Pradesh Civil Liberties Committee has recorded roughly 1,800 "encounter" killings by the police.[64] It is crucial to note that the vast majority of the victims of these extra-judicial killings are Dalits and tribals, many of them with no direct connection to the Naxalites. The culture of impunity extended to the police establishment by the two dominant parties in the state has left a pall of fear hanging over large parts of Telangana,[65] and though it has driven the PWG into the forests of Bastar and the border districts of Orissa, spawning the delusion that Andhra has solved its Naxalite problem, the sheer incoherence of the state's strategies (repeated banning of the PWG, repeated legalisation and unmitigated repression) has left a legacy of substantial underlying support for the CPI (Maoist) (or former PWG) leaders in Andhra itself.[66] For the radical left, the key issue is whether the armed struggle that has now been displaced to the adjoining districts in Chhattisgarh and Orissa is truly the form of a movement for socialist emancipation and the kind of political culture it wants and sees as viable in a country as vast and complex as India. Before coming to this, we should look briefly at the latest phase of the conflict.

Bastar is today the frontline of the "explosive Naxal battle" that is retailed to millions of households in India through the news channels. PWG's expansion into Bastar and Gadchiroli began in the early 1980s, fleeing early waves of repression in Andhra, and by 1989 the party felt strong enough to form a mass "peasant" front called the Dandakaranya Adivasi Kisan Mazdoor Sanghatana,[67] backed by a series of armed squads that contained something under 200 cadres.[68] These expanded rapidly in the early 1990s, a period when Seetharamaiah was hounded out of the party and a new, younger leadership consolidated its hold. In fact, the 1990s threw up an explosive conjuncture. As state governments began dreaming of the fabulous sums of money to be made from the mineral-rich tribal districts they had abandoned to decades of oppression and misery, the PWG rapidly militarised itself, with major increases in lethality (vastly more sophisticated weaponry including the extensive use of landmines), an elaborate organisation of platoons, battalions and military commands, and new expansion into the tribal districts of southern Orissa. By 2001 the party (now called People's War) decided to intensify the war in ten states,[69] and in 2004 PW and the MCCI merged to form the CPI (Maoist).

64: *Economic and Political Weekly* editorial, 2009, p6.
65: Balagopal, 2003, p517.
66: See Kannabiran, 2005.
67: Navlakha, 2010, pp42–43.
68: People's Union of Civil Liberties, 1989, p2239.
69: Dash, 2006, p59.

With police forces too demoralised to handle the insurgency, in Chhattisgarh the BJP government secretly funded and armed a "private" lynch mob called Salwa Judum ("Purification Hunt" in Gondi) that has since emptied hundreds of villages by forcing inhabitants into internally displaced persons camps where they can be easily controlled. "Large swaths of Dantewara are now abandoned. Villages in Salwa Judum-controlled areas that refuse to cooperate are deemed 'Maoist' villages, and are then attacked".[70] On one count, some 40,000 tribals have been herded into these camps and others have fled deep into the forest or across the border into Khammam. Meanwhile, in the last year the Maoists have inflicted major losses on the CRPF (the official military operation in Chhattisgarh), forcing the central government to take control of counterinsurgency operations. The wholesale militarisation of the movement since the 1990s has culminated in a vanguard war trapped in an expanding culture of counterinsurgency, with tens of thousands of civilians caught between them.[71]

The critique of arms

In 2006 K Balagopal wrote, "Nothing justifies the tendency in democratic circles to talk as if all that is relevant for understanding the role of the Maoists in the area (Bastar region and Dantewara in particular) is the poverty and general backwardness of the tribes living there".[72] What he meant by this was that ultimately the kind of militarised Maoism that has emerged in India would have to stand or fall in terms of a critique from the left itself. The dispossession and oppression of tribals and the redoubled drive to open their districts to exploitation by large industrial capital, with the displacement and impoverishment this causes, have been major sources of the tenacity of Maoism in India, a movement to which tribal support has always been crucial.[73] But it is pure naivety to reduce one to the other or identify the tribals and the Maoists as if their agendas were the same or the victory of one would mean the emancipation of the other.

Responses, critical or otherwise, from the left can be classified broadly into four categories. Maoists and Maoist sympathisers abstract from

---

70: Miklian, 2009, p452; by far the best account.

71: Balagopal, 2003, p515: "Inevitably, the common people have got caught between the two parties." For "vanguard war", see Debray, 1977, chapter 2 (fundamental).

72: Balagopal, 2006b, p2183.

73: Duyker, 1987, p109, underlines the voluntary nature of tribal support for the Naxalites in Bengal: "The vast majority of Santals extended their support voluntarily. In the final analysis, the Naxalite mass-base began to crumble because this support was voluntarily withdrawn, in the face of severe police and army operations."

the profound deformities of the movement to engage in solidarity with it at any cost. They posit an almost mystical identity between the Maoists and "the people" and do precisely what Balagopal advised democratic circles not to do, namely use the poverty and general backwardness of the tribal areas as an excuse for not engaging with the CPI (Maoist) politically.[74]

A second line of response has been the CPI (Marxist)'s savage repression of all popular movements that challenge their own agendas for the state of West Bengal, using the machinery of the state to crush both the Maoists and much wider layers of the population (again largely tribal) they see as sympathising with them or opposing their own policies. Thus, whereas the CPI (Maoist) sabotaged a struggle like the one in Lalgarh by infiltrating the People's Committee Against Police Atrocities and eliminating all political rivals, the CPI (Marxist) fell back on its own vigilante groups and on state counterinsurgency forces to quell the movement there.[75] Both parties (and large parts of the state apparatus, of course) have an interest in branding what began as and was for months a democratic popular upsurge as "Maoist". And, of course, the two "Marxist" parties have been slaughtering each other's cadre.

Sharply different from both the above has been the civil liberties critique that was largely represented in the writings of the late Balagopal through most of the 1990s down to his death in 2009. Balagopal's critique recorded features that displayed an unmitigated authoritarianism on the part of a movement he had been closely associated with, features he saw as undermining its sources of support. He referred to the "ruthlessness" of the party (the PWG) that had evolved by the early 1990s,[76] to the calculated use of terror as a political instrument,[77] the "medieval forms of violence" that characterised the so-called People's Courts,[78] the lack of possibility of any opposition to the party "so long as the police are taken care of",[79] the "new" culture that had "permeated the Naxalite organisations" as they recruited large numbers of new cadres "more attracted by its weapons than its politics", and the "recognisable

---

74: Navlakha, 2010, especially p23; Roy, 2010a. Roy, 2010b is more critical of the Maoists.
75: The best accounts of their role in Lalgarh are Sarkar and Sarkar, 2009, and Rana, 2009.
76: Balagopal, 1990a, p591, about the PWG, "whose reputation for ruthlessness is as real as it is disquieting".
77: Balagopal, 1997, p2254: "That the Naxalites, in particular the CPI(M-L) (People's War), employ terror as a political instrument is a fact..."
78: Balagopal, 1990b, p1885.
79: Balagopal, 2006a, p3185.

deterioration of quality" this had brought with it.[80] More substantially, he saw the movement in Andhra culminating in "stagnation" by the 2000s and forced to sidestep the crisis by expanding into new territory, failing to consolidate a second generation of support.[81] And finally, there were clear elements of a critique of the substitutionism of a vanguard struggle where most decisions were "taken and implemented over the heads of the people but justified in the name of the people",[82] a politics that had simply "corrupted the masses into receivers of justice rather than fighters for it".[83]

These are among the most political criticisms that have been made of the obsessively violent forms Maoism has come to take and they are profoundly more significant for any future left movement in India than the uncritical solidarity of fellow travellers. The indiscriminate killing of village headmen, the widespread laying of landmines, the recruitment of minors, the sabotage of all means of communication, the ban on employment-generating public works have all started to drive a wedge between the party and its tribal sympathisers precisely in the "liberated" zones.[84]

A fourth sort of response would have to come from Marxists who have never identified with any of the Stalinist political traditions in India and do not see revolutionary movements developing in a class vacuum, in complete isolation from industrial workers and the more organised groups of wage earners and employees in the economy at large. The bulk of the Indian labour force remains unorganised into unions, and it is stupefying to imagine that a revolution against capitalism can succeed while the mass of the workers are in a state of near-complete atomisation. The impoverished notions of democracy that either reduce it to a battle for electoral supremacy or dismiss it as a fraud, the failure to encourage and develop a culture of working class organisation and debate, to encourage forms of intervention that contest capitalism in concrete ways, and build a movement that can address the widest possible range of issues starting from the desperate struggle for survival of the millions of landless in India, are all

80: Balagopal, 2003, p515.
81: Balagopal, 2006a, p3186; 2003, p515: "While expansion into new areas...is taking place steadily, they are not able to recover lost ground in Telangana and in their earlier tribal strongholds."
82: Balagopal, 1997, p2254.
83: Balagopal, 2006a, p3185.
84: Independent Citizens' Initiative, 2006, pp2978–2979; Sundar 2006; Balagopal, 2006b, pp2185–2186. To the point about the training of minors in the use of arms, the general secretary of the CPI (Maoist) responded with this flash of brilliance: "Making a fuss over age has no relevance in a situation where the enemies of the people are targeting children too, without any mercy"—Ganapathi, 2007, p69.

part of the legacy of a left that was moribund intellectually and deeply conservative in its culture.

Shankar Guha Neogi (murdered in 1991) and A K Roy of the Marxist Coordination Committee (expelled from the CPI(M) in 1973), both charismatic union leaders, stood in sharp contrast to that political tradition. They drew their popular support precisely from the landless tribals employed in the iron ore and coal mines of Chhattisgarh and Jharkhand. The CPI (Maoist)'s conception of the working class is a rhetorical one, since it is the party that embodies the "leadership" of the class and conducts the class struggle on its behalf, unelected, unaccountable and never subject to recall. This has been a consistent feature of the Naxalite groups since the late 1960s.

Secondly, the Maoist grasp of theory is unbelievably primitive, a collage of abstractions that bear little relation to reality at any level (analysis or strategy). "Semi-feudalism", "comprador bourgeoisie", "four-class alliance", "protracted people's war", etc are all slavishly copied from Mao's theorisations for China that will soon be almost a century old! For example, a leader of Liberation defends the label "comprador bourgeoisie" by saying it refers to the "increasing organic integration between Indian big business and imperialist capital".[85] But "organic integration" between capitals across national boundaries is precisely what defines capitalism, unless one is going to see the latter as an aggregation of national economies.

Third, even the mass organisations fail to be truly democratic as long as they are "controlled by a secretive and hierarchical party".[86] Yet "parties like the CPI (Maoist) require secrecy not just from the state, but also to penetrate democratic mass movements" to gain control of them, as Santosh Rana showed for Lalgarh.[87] And finally, of course, the Marxist critique will have to be able to absorb the civil liberties one, not simply ignore it. As Balagopal's colleague, Andhra's most distinguished civil rights lawyer, noted years ago, no political movement working for the overthrow of an exploitative order "has any right to reproduce the brutalities practised" by that order.[88]

85: Bhattacharya, 2006, p5191.
86: Bhatia, 2005, p1546, who goes on to say, "The 'vanguard' party lets the people bear the brunt" of actions undertaken on their behalf "without their knowledge and consent."
87: Menon, 2009, p18.
88: Kannabiran, 1993, p498.

References

Balagopal, K, and M Kodandarama Reddy, 1982, "Forever 'Disturbed': Peasant Struggle of Sircilla-Vemulawada", *Economic and Political Weekly* 17 (48) (27 November).

Balagopal, K, 1987, "A Tale of Arson", *Economic and Political Weekly* 22 (29) (18 July).

Balagopal, K, 1990a, "Chenna Reddy's Spring", *Economic and Political Weekly* 25 (12) (24 March).

Balagopal, K, 1990b, "Andhra Pradesh: The End of Spring?", *Economic and Political Weekly* 25 (34) (25 August).

Balagopal, K, 1997, "Naxalite Terrorists and Benign Policemen", *Economic and Political Weekly* 32 (36) (6 September).

Balagopal, K, 2003, "People's War and the Government: Did the Police Have the Last Laugh?", *Economic and Political Weekly* 38 (6) (8 February).

Balagopal, K, 2006a, "Maoist Movement in Andhra Pradesh", *Economic and Political Weekly* 41 (29) (22 July).

Balagopal, K, 2006b, "Chhattisgarh: Physiognomy of Violence", *Economic and Political Weekly* 41 (22) (3 June).

Banerjee, Sumanta, 2003, "Naxalites: Time for Introspection", *Economic and Political Weekly* 38 (44) (1 November).

Bhatia, Bela, 2005, "The Naxalite Movement in Central Bihar", *Economic and Political Weekly* 40 (15) (9 April)

Bhattacharya, Dipankar, 2006, "Trail Blazed by Naxalbari Uprising", *Economic and Political Weekly* 41 (50) (16 December).

Dash, Satya Prakash, 2006, *Naxal Movement and State Power (with Special Reference of Orissa)* (Sarup & Sons).

Debray, Régis, 1977, *A Critique of Arms, Volume 1* (Penguin Books).

Dubey, Abhay Kumar, 1991, *Kranti ka Aatmasangharsh: Naxalvadi andolan ke badalte chere ka adhyayan* (Vinay Prakashan).

Duyker, Edward, 1987, *Tribal Guerrillas: The Santals of West Bengal and the Naxalite Movement* (Oxford University Press).

Economic and Political Weekly editorial, 2009, "Encounters are Murders", 44 (37) (12 September).

Ganapathi, 2007, "Open Reply to Independent Citizens' Initiative on Dantewada", *Economic and Political Weekly* 42 (1) (6 January).

Independent Citizens' Initiative, 2006, "Open Letters to Government and Maoists", *Economic and Political Weekly* 41 (27-28) (8 July).

Johnson, Jo, 2006, "Insurgency in India—How the Maoist Threat Reaches beyond Nepal", *Financial Times* (26 April).

Kannabiran, KG, 1993, "Koyyuru: Reflections on a Kidnap", *Economic and Political Weekly* 28 (12–13) (20 March).

Kannabiran, Kalpana, and others, 2005, "Reflections on the Peace Process in Andhra Pradesh", *Economic and Political Weekly* 40 (7) (12 February).

Kumar, Arun, 2003, "Violence and Political Culture: Politics of the Ultra Left in Bihar", *Economic and Political Weekly* 38 (47) (22 November).

Kunnath, George J, 2009, "Smouldering Dalit Fires in Bihar, India", *Dialectical Anthropology* 33.

Menon, Nivedita, 2009, "Radical Resistance and Political Violence Today", *Economic and Political Weekly* 44 (50) (12 December).

Miklian, Jason, 2009, "The Purification Hunt: the Salwa Judum Counterinsurgency in Chhattisgarh, India", *Dialectical Anthropology* 33.

Mohanty, Manoranjan, 1977, *Revolutionary Violence: A Study of the Maoist Movement in India* (Sterling).

Mohanty, Manoranjan, 2006, "Challenges of Revolutionary Violence: The Naxalite Movement in Perspective", *Economic and Political Weekly* 41 (29) (22 July).

Navlakha, Gautam, 2010, "Days and Nights in the Maoist Heartland", *Economic and Political Weekly* 45 (16) (17 April).

People's Union of Civil Liberties, 1989, "Bastar: Development and Democracy (part 2)", *Economic and Political Weekly* 24 (40) (7 October).

Ram, Mohan, 1971, *Maoism in India* (Vikas).

Rana, Santosh, 2009, "A People's Uprising Destroyed by the Maoists", *Kafila* (23 August), http://kafila.org/2009/08/23/a-peoples-uprising-destroyed-by-the-maoists-santosh-rana/

Rao, S Laxman, Priya Deshingkar and John Farrington, 2006, "Tribal Land Alienation in Andhra Pradesh", *Economic and Political Weekly* 41 (52).

Richards, John F, 2004, "Warriors and the State in Early Modern India", *Journal of the Economic and Social History of the Orient* 47 (3).

Roy, Arundhati, 2010a, "Walking with the Comrades", *Outlook* (29 March), www.outlookindia.com/article.aspx?264738

Roy, Arundhati, 2010b, "The Trickledown Revolution", *Outlook India* (20 September), www.outlookindia.com/article.aspx?267040

Samanta, Amiya K, 1984, *Left Extremist Movement in West Bengal: An Experiment in Armed Agrarian Struggle* (Firma KLM).

Sanyal, Kanu, and others, 1972, "Peking and CP (ML)", *Frontier* 5 (4 November),

Sarkar, Aditya, 2007, "Nandigram and the deformations of the Indian left", *International Socialism* 115 (summer), www.isj.org.uk/?id=333

Sarkar, Sumit, and Tanika Sarkar, 2009, "Notes on a Dying People", *Economic and Political Weekly* 44 (26–27) (27 June).

Sinha, Shantha, 1989, *Maoists in Andhra Pradesh* (Gian Publishing House).

Singh, Prakash, 1995, *The Naxalite Movement in India* (Rupa & Co).

Sundar, Nandini, 2006, "Bastar, Maoism and Salwa Judum", *Economic and Political Weekly* 41 (29) (22 July).

Michelangelo and human emancipation

John Molyneux

M ichelangelo stands at the very summit of human fame, or celebrity as we now call it. His position is secure among that very small band of individuals—Aristotle, Shakespeare, Goethe, Mozart, da Vinci and so on—who seem to tower over history, much as one imagines the Colossus of Rhodes, and whose status is commonly given a universal, transcendental character.[1] Remarkably, he attained this pinnacle within his own lifetime, as a glance at Giorgio Vasari's contemporary *Lives of the Artists* testifies, when he was ranked even higher than da Vinci in the genius stakes (though I think it is fair to say that da Vinci has subsequently outdistanced him a little, thanks to helicopters, the *Mona Lisa* and Dan Brown) and it is probably now close to unassailable as far as the wider culture is concerned, as opposed to the specialism of art history.

Such a reputation is, of course, a decidedly mixed blessing. One downside of it, becoming the object of endless banality, has been fixed forever in a single line by T S Eliot in *The Love Song of J Alfred Prufrock*: "In the room the women come and go talking of Michelangelo." And it is almost enough to deter one from even attempting to write on the man. Another is the indignity, shared with Van Gogh, of being Irving Stoned (in *The Agony and the Ecstasy*) and then being played in the film of the same

---

1:   Images of all the works referenced in this article can be found online at www.abcgallery.com/ M/michelangelo/michelangelo.html

name by Charlton Heston (a fate Van Gogh was mercifully spared) opposite Pope Rex Harrison. Naturally such appropriation by the world of capitalist kitsch has brought with it a corresponding rejection from the avant garde. An elderly and very austere artist friend of mine, a systems painter from the 60s, tells me he detests Michelangelo's grandiloquence and much prefers Verrocchio. According to Robert Hughes, Barnett Newman once said, "I thought our quarrel was with Michelangelo," prompting Hughes's riposte: "Well, bad luck, Barney. You lost".[2]

Nevertheless, despite Eliot's implied warning and despite the vast amount of guff written on the subject, it is precisely this question of Michelangelo's exalted standing that I wish to investigate in this article, not in order to challenge or undermine it, for as we shall see I basically think it is justified, but in order to help explain it and place it on a less transcendental, more solid, more earthly, more historical foundation. The investigation will focus on, and move between, several related questions: (1) What explanations can be offered as to the causes and nature of Michelangelo's reputation and his artistic achievement? (2) What is the relation between Michelangelo's art and history? (3) What is the nature of Michelangelo's response to that history as seen in his art? Which amounts to offering a certain "interpretation" or way of looking at that art. Obviously no attempt or claim is made to offer complete or definitive answers to any of these questions—one of them alone would require a book—but it is hoped that these tentative and rather speculative observations can nonetheless move the discussion onto more fruitful ground.

The dead end of "genius"

The existing ground is not very fertile. The story begins, of course, in Renaissance Florence with the widely expressed view that Michelangelo's achievements were attributable to, and explicable in terms of, divine inspiration. How literally this was believed is hard to tell but Vasari spells it out in some detail:

> While industrious and choice spirits, aided by the light afforded by Giotto and his followers, strove to show the world the talent with which their happy stars and well-balanced humours had endowed them, and endeavoured to attain to the height of knowledge by imitating the greatness of Nature in all things, the great Ruler of Heaven looked down and, seeing these vain and fruitless efforts and the presumptuous opinion of

---

2:    For what Newman actually wrote on the subject see Newman, 1992.

man more removed from truth than light from darkness, resolved, in order to rid him of these errors, to send to earth a genius universal in each art, to show single-handed the perfection of line and shadow, and who should give relief to his paintings, show a sound judgment in sculpture, and in architecture should render habitations convenient, safe, healthy, pleasant, well-proportioned, and enriched with various ornaments. He further endowed him with true moral philosophy and a sweet poetic spirit, so that the world should marvel at the singular eminence of his life and works and all his actions, seeming rather divine than earthy.[3]

But unless one believes in this kind of personally interventionist god, this is not very helpful (and if one does, further explanation, certainly of the kind I shall attempt, seems superfluous). Three hundred and fifty years later and the level of analysis had not advanced:

Each supreme artist whom God hath sent into the world with inspiration and a particle of the imperishable fire, is a law unto himself... Michelangelo belongs to the genus of deep, violent, colossal, passionately striving natures; not to like Raffaello...to the smooth...calmly perfect tribe.[4]

In the second half of the 20th century Ernst Gombrich, unable or unwilling to invoke god, simply substitutes genius and throws up his hands:

The beginning of the sixteenth century, the Cinquecento, is the most famous period of Italian art, one of the greatest periods of all time. This was the time of Leonardo da Vinci and Michelangelo, of Raphael and Titian, of Correggio and Giorgione, of Dürer and Holbein in the north, and of many other famous masters. One may well ask why it was that all these great masters were born in the same period, but such questions are more easily asked than answered. One cannot explain the existence of genius. It is better to enjoy it.[5]

If we are not getting very far in terms of explaining Michelangelo's existence, maybe we can do better when it comes to establishing the nature of his achievement. We can again go back to Vasari and this time we find not religious mysticism but fairly clearly defined technical criteria:

3:    Vasari, 1991, p414.
4:    Symonds, 1911, voume 2, p174
5:    Gombrich, 1978, pp217-218.

Design is the imitation of the most beautiful things in Nature in all forms, both in sculpture and in painting, and this quality depends on having the hand and the skill to transfer with great accuracy and precision everything the eye sees to a plan or drawing...and the same is true for relief in sculpture. And then the most beautiful style comes from constantly copying the most beautiful things...

Neither Giotto nor those early artisans did this...But the man who wins the palm among artists both living and dead, who transcends and surpasses them all, is the divine Michelangelo Buonarroti, who reigns supreme not merely in one of these arts but in all three at once.[6]

Unpick this statement and we find three definite claims: (1) Michelangelo is supreme by virtue of his technical skill. (2) Technical skill consists in the classical notion of "mimesis", accurately copying nature. (3) The key thing is to copy, "imitate" beautiful things. That Gombrich, essentially, follows this view can be seen from the fact that he entitles the chapter of *The Story of Art* dealing with the early 15th century (Brunelleschi, Masaccio, Donatello, Van Eyck, etc) "The Conquest of Reality" and that on the early 16th (da Vinci, Michelangelo, Raphael) "Harmony Attained", and we must remember that Gombrich spoke for whole generations of art historians in this.

Moreover it is clear that in these claims and in this narrative there is an important element of truth, both about the development of art as a whole at this time and specifically about Michelangelo. I for one would think it close to impossible to stand before the *David* in the Academia or the *Moses* in San Pietro in Vincoli—these giant statues carved from single blocks of marble—and not be awestruck at the level of sheer technical skill involved in their creation. Has any human ever lived more adept than Michelangelo in the carving of stone? However, it is equally necessary to question aspects of this account and to reject the notion that it is anywhere near the whole story.

First of all it is necessary to question whether Michelangelo's prodigious skill in shaping stone (and paint) according to his will was in fact skill in "imitating" nature or representing "reality". So hegemonic, in Western culture, has been the Renaissance view of these matters and so accustomed have we become to the element of truth in its claims to naturalism (for example, single point perspective and plastic shading) that we generally "miss" or leave unsaid the numerous really obvious ways in which

---

6:    Vasari, 1991, pp277-278, 280.

this art is not naturalistic at all. For instance the *David* is an 18 foot high stone object which does not and cannot resemble in any way—dimensions, colour, texture, mobility—a 6th century BC shepherd boy, of whose actual appearance we have no knowledge whatsoever, and whose very existence is likely mythical. Likewise *The Creation of Adam*: of what could this possibly be a "naturalistic" or "realistic" representation? Even Adam's muscles and God's beard are idealised. When it comes to Jean Baudrillard's hyper-reality, his simulacrum of a simulacrum with no underlying referent, Michelangelo beats CNN and the Gulf War any day.

But even if we set those sorts of consideration aside, and adopt the conventional usage of naturalism, neither Michelangelo's own artistic trajectory nor his standing can satisfactorily be accounted for in these terms. On his death bed, aged 88, Michelangelo is reputed to have said, "I am dying just as I am beginning to learn the alphabet of my profession." Yet clearly, as he got older he moved further and further away from "technique" in the naturalist sense and more and more towards a "freer" and more "expressionist" handling of the stone. Compare an early and late work on a similar subject—the *Pietà* (or Deposition) in St Peter's, Rome, made in his early twenties, with the *Pietà* in the Florentine Duomo, made in his eighties.

The first is a technical virtuoso piece, staggering in its ability to render the folds in Mary's raiment and the veins on the back of Christ's hand. The second is rough-hewn and "unfinished" and Christ is strangely missing his right leg. Yet to my eyes the later work has an artistic power and merit that far exceeds that of the earlier one. If Michelangelo's artistic achievement rested primarily on technique and so-called naturalism he would stand with Holbein or Hals not, as he does, with Rembrandt, Shakespeare and Bach.

Thus we are compelled to leave the supposedly safe and objective waters of technical skill for the apparently subjective and dangerous waters of "interpretation". We have to attempt to confront and deal with what Michelangelo or rather his work is actually saying. For understandable reasons many art historians and critics shy away from this in relation both to Michelangelo and art in general, but some fools rush in where angels fear to tread and there is no doubt some wonderful nonsense has been written on this score. For example, Rolf Schott in the Thames and Hudson monograph on Michelangelo writes:

The pressure of everyday existence has dimmed, for our generation, the memory of mankind's divine origin. Michelangelo's work is a visual statement of what the world has lost—the sense of wonder aroused by the mystery of human existence and human form.

> As an artist, Michelangelo is impersonal. His visual work tells us nothing
> about the man himself or his environment.[7]

These lines make no sense even in their own terms, never mind as an interpretation of Michelangelo. Assuming "the world" once had a "sense of wonder aroused by the mystery of human existence and human form", when did it have it and when was it lost? Was it around in the High Renaissance for Michelangelo to make a visual statement of it? Is it only our generation that has mislaid it and was this really due to "the pressure of everyday existence"? How can it possibly be true that "his visual work tells us nothing about the man himself or his environment"? If the only thing Michelangelo's work told us, and it is not, was that the artist was very interested in the male body, that would be of some considerable significance.

The only reason for quoting Schott here (and Gombrich and Symonds) is that it seems to me that such writing, often high-flown but vacuous, sets the tone for how Michelangelo is perceived and received in our culture. Apart from seeing Michelangelo as primarily a "naturalist" the other major difficulty has been caused by seeing him as primarily a religious artist. Obviously he was a "believer", a sincere Christian, and obviously much of the work was commissioned by the church and had overtly religious themes or subject matter—all of that went with the territory and the time. But it does not follow from this that the driving force of Michelangelo's art was some pure and lofty spirituality, any more than piety was the dominant quality of Chaucer's *Canterbury Tales*. In my opinion there are few artists for whom Marx's insights that "man makes religion, religion does not make man" and that "the earthly family is…the secret of the holy family" are more apposite and more essential.

Take, for example, the *David*. This is based on a Bible story but its motivation was thoroughly secular and "political". It was commissioned in 1501 by the Operai of Santa Maria del Fiore (a sort of committee of public works) on behalf of the new republican government of Florence to celebrate the recent ousting of its Medici rulers and its independence from Sforza Milan and the Roman Papacy. The symbolism is obvious. In that the work also has a "deeper", more universal reference and resonance this is because it is a humanist statement about "man". (Clearly any such claim needs to be unpacked and this will be—a little later.)

Then there is the so-called *Dying Captive* or *Dying Slave* which now stands in the Louvre. The titles are posthumous attributions, not

---

7:    Schott, 1975, p7.

Michelangelo's, and the work itself contains no indication that the young man is a slave or captive, except in some metaphorical sexual sense—a "love slave"—or that he is dying except in the sense of an orgasmic *petit mort*. Charles de Tolnay, an esteemed Michelangelo expert, says he is "a dreaming adolescent shaking off the bonds of sleep" and Charles Sala, following him, but edging a little further, says, "In fact this figure is not dying at all, but rather absorbed in a dreamlike state…somewhere between the languorous sensuality of an adolescent ephebe and the wistfulness of a captive restrained none too convincingly".[8]

These are degrees of evasion. The capacity of art historians not to see what is literally in their faces never ceases to amaze me, for this is blatantly a work of homoeroticism. I do not say that homoeroticism is all that it is about, but it is manifestly its driving force. And indeed the moment one casts aside the taboo and the four centuries old veil of hypocrisy it is manifest that homoeroticism is a major driver of Michelangelo's art as a whole. Not only is the naked male body overwhelmingly the predominant motif, but there are several works which are not far off being mass orgies of male flesh (eg *The Battle of the Centaurs*, parts of *The Last Judgement*) and there are others, ostensibly religious in theme, where male nudes appear, in numbers, with no conceivable narrative or theological justification—there are four frontal male nudes in the background to *The Holy Family*, and more than 20 in the interstices of the Sistine Chapel ceiling. This short piece cannot possibly do justice to the role of homoeroticism in Michelangelo's work but I raise the issue simply to reinforce the point that religious subject matter does not guarantee or correspond to religious content. And no matter how pious the artist it does not preclude the art serving as a means to express thoroughly earthly concerns.

The revolution of the Renaissance
At this point I need to move swiftly from the negative to the positive, from what Michelangelo's work was not to what it was. To do so I believe it is essential to see Michelangelo in relation to his times. By his times I do not mean, principally, events but the broader and deeper social forces at work in the society in which he lived. Some major works are occasioned by specific events—Picasso's *Guernica* is the obvious example—but Picasso's cubism and his whole way of painting and representing the world were conditioned by the social relations of capitalism in its imperialist phase, as was demonstrated by John Berger in his book *The Success and Failure of Picasso*

8:    Charles de Tolnay, cited in Sala, 1995, p170.

and his article "The Moment of Cubism". When Hyacinth Rigaud painted Louis XIV, he was painting not just the features or personality of the Sun King but the whole social institution of absolute monarchy. Moreover it is necessary to understand those times, those social forces, in a Marxist, ie historical materialist, way. Only the Marxist theory of history, that is a theory that sets out from the development of the forces and relations of production and their expression in class struggle, is able to identify correctly the underlying forces at work in a society and to which artists in general, but especially great artists, respond.

It is, I suppose, necessary to insist at this point that this methodology is not a reductionist or economic determinist one. The artist—Michelangelo or whoever—is not denied their creativity, originality or personal vision, based on their unique experience. Least of all are they seen as simple vehicles or ciphers for class interests or class ideologies. (It is true that the Althusserian Nicos Hadjinicolaou propounded a view close to this in his *Art History and Class Struggle*, but this not the kind of Marxism or the kind of art history I propose.) The artist is an individual human being who not only reflects the wider society but actively responds to it, often critically, but what the artist responds to has to be part of the analysis and, generally speaking, the greater the artist the more profoundly they will engage with the deep social forces, rather than just superficial appearances, of their moment in history.

In the case of Michelangelo the best starting point for grasping his situation is a quotation from Frederick Engels in what may seem an unlikely location, namely the Introduction to *The Dialectics of Nature*. Engels is discussing the birth of modern science, not art, but it remains extraordinarily relevant:

> Modern natural science dates, like all more recent history, from that mighty epoch which we Germans term the Reformation, from the national misfortune that overtook us at that time, and which the French term the Renaissance and the Italians the Cinquecento, although it is not fully expressed by any of these names. It is the epoch which had its rise in the last half of the 15th century. Royalty, with the support of the burghers of the towns, broke the power of the feudal nobility and established the great monarchies, based essentially on nationality, within which the modern European nations and modern bourgeois society came to development.
>
> In the manuscripts saved from the fall of Byzantium, in the antique statues dug out of the ruins of Rome, a new world was revealed to the astonished West, that of ancient Greece: the ghosts of the Middle Ages vanished before its

shining forms; Italy rose to an undreamt-of flowering of art, which seemed like a reflection of classical antiquity and was never attained again. In Italy, France, and Germany a new literature arose, the first, modern literature; shortly afterwards came the classical epochs of English and Spanish literature...

The dictatorship of the Church over men's minds was shattered; it was directly cast off by the majority of the Germanic peoples, who adopted Protestantism, while among the Latins a cheerful spirit of free thought, taken over from the Arabs and nourished by the newly-discovered Greek philosophy, took root more and more and prepared the way for the materialism of the 18th century.

It was the greatest progressive revolution that mankind has so far experienced, a time which called for giants and produced giants—giants in power of thought, passion, and character, in universality and learning. The men who founded the modern rule of the bourgeoisie had anything but bourgeois limitations. On the contrary, the adventurous character of the time inspired them to a greater or less degree. There was hardly any man of importance then living who had not travelled extensively, who did not command four or five languages, who did not shine in a number of fields. Leonardo da Vinci was not only a great painter but also a great mathematician, mechanician, and engineer.... Albrecht Dürer was painter, engraver, sculptor, and architect, and in addition invented a system of fortification... Machiavelli was statesman, historian, poet, and at the same time the first notable military author of modern times. Luther not only cleaned the Augean stable of the Church but also that of the German language... The heroes of that time had not yet come under the servitude of the division of labour, the restricting effects of which, with its production of onesidedness, we so often notice in their successors. But what is especially characteristic of them is that they almost all pursue their lives and activities in the midst of the contemporary movements, in the practical struggle; they take sides and join in the fight, one by speaking and writing, another with the sword, many with both. Hence the fullness and force of character that makes them complete men.[9]

This passage, without mentioning Michelangelo's name, nonetheless fits him like glove, even down to the building of fortifications which he did for Florence in 1529. The key points are: (1) that the Renaissance is part of the birth of capitalism, or more precisely an episode in the transition from feudalism to capitalism; (2) that the transition from feudalism

---

9:    Engels, 1883.

to capitalism is a lengthy and complex international process (not a series of separate national processes).

Capitalist production and capitalist social relations develop, at first slowly, within feudalism—in its interstices, as Marx put it, primarily in the medieval towns—and its social bearers, the bourgeoisie (originally the burghers or "townsmen"), are literally the middle class, subordinate to the feudal nobility, who are the dominant class, but superior to the peasants, artisans and fledgling proletarians or wage labourers. The bourgeoisie develops economically and culturally before it achieves political, ie, state power. The fairly prolonged period in which bourgeois power more or less rivals that of the aristocracy sees the rise of the absolute monarchs who raise themselves above the contending classes, playing them off against each other but ultimately preserving the old feudal regime. The bourgeoisie's conquest of state power and establishment of full-blown capitalist states involves a series of struggles, revolutions and wars, in which there are victories and defeats, steps forward and steps back, over several centuries. The most important victories are the Dutch Revolt of 1568-1609 (and establishment of the Dutch Republic at the end of the 16th century), the English Revolution of 1642-7, the American Revolution of 1774-6 and the French Revolution of 1789-93. The French Revolution, together with the contemporaneous Industrial Revolution in Britain, is decisive. The bourgeoisie will now rule the world though mopping up operations continue well into the 20th century.

The place of Florence in the early part of this story has been extensively documented by Frederick Antal in the first chapter of his classic study *Florentine Painting and its Social Background*:

> The great economic power of Florence…grew up chiefly in the 12th century and expanded during the 13th and 14th centuries to dimensions unparalleled elsewhere in Italy or indeed Europe. Its foundations were threefold: the textile industry, the trade in textiles and other products, and banking… In all these industries it was no longer the master-craftsman but the capitalist entrepreneur, who disposed of the wares to the customer… The industry of Florence, particularly the cloth industry and the international trade connected with it, was undoubtedly the most important enterprise of an early capitalist character in the whole of the later Middle Ages… The same Florentine citizens who were the world's greatest industrialists and merchants were also its chief bankers.[10]

10: Antal, 1948, pp11-13.

This was the economic foundation of the Renaissance, Early and High, and it should be noted that the association of artistic "golden ages" with periods of spectacular wealth is common in the history of art—Venice just after Florence, Antwerp and then Amsterdam in the late 16th and 17th centuries, Paris in the 19th and early 20th, New York after the Second World War and even, in a small way, London in the 1980s and 1990s, are all examples. Arnold Hauser puts it thus:

> The new artistic culture first appears on the scene in Italy because this country also had a lead over the West in economic and social matters, because the revival of economic life starts here, the financial and transport facilities of the crusades are organised from here, free competition first develops here, in opposition to the guild ideal of the Middle Ages, and the first European banking system arises here, because the emancipation of the urban middle class takes place here earlier than in the rest of Europe.[11]

Properly to outline the interconnections between this economic development and the specific art of Cimabue, Giotto, Masaccio, Ucello, Donatello, Piero della Francesca, Botticelli and so on is beyond the scope of this article, but certain general features can be outlined. The most fundamental thing is that this art of the 14th and 15th centuries achieves—I'm tempted to say wins or forges for you can see it developing painting by painting, artist by artist—the three-dimensional space, within and behind the picture frame, within which can be depicted urban and rural spaces, solid objects and, above all, human actions and human personalities. This is an optimistic art characterised by "freedom and effortlessness of expression…grace and elegance" which serves as a visual accompaniment to the rise of humanist philosophy.[12] The sense in which the work of Leonardo, Raphael and the younger Michelangelo constitutes the culmination of this process is clear.

Overall the birth of capitalism in its early stages (and this is true in Italy, in the Netherlands, in England, in America and in France) is experienced by the mass of people, and especially the middle and lower middle classes, from which most artists and intellectuals spring, as a massive expansion in human freedom, a liberation from the restrictions, bonds and superstitions imposed by the church and the feudal aristocracy who were, of course, close ideological and practical allies, and thus a huge emancipation of the human personality. Two works by Michelangelo, the *David* and

---

11:   Hauser, 1999, volume 2, pp9-10.
12:   Hauser, 1999, volume 2, p7.

The Creation of Adam, express this more clearly, more powerfully and more beautifully than, perhaps, any others in European history.

As we have already noted the *David* was commissioned as a work celebrating political liberty in a quite definite sense, but just as Picasso's *Guernica* was painted in response to a particular war crime but has emerged as a statement about the crime of war in general, so the *David* has been pretty generally read as a statement about "man". The "perfection" of the body and its sheer scale guarantee that is seen as a celebration, but there is more to it than that. Unlike his predecessors in sculpting this subject, Donatello and Verocchio, who show David after the defeat of Goliath with the giant's head at his feet, Michelangelo shows David before the battle, thus providing a basis in the narrative for David's frowning forehead and making it a work which looks to the future in anticipation of the decisive struggle.

Moreover the *David* is not in fact in "perfect" proportion; the head and hands, especially the right hand holding the stone, are slightly too large and this has the effect of making David a brain as well as a body and a doer and maker as well as an object of desire. Thus what the *David* celebrates is not "man" as he is, but a vision of the whole man that he has the potential to become. As Gramsci says, "in putting the question 'what is man?' what we mean is: what can man become? That is, can man dominate his own destiny, can he 'make himself', can he create his own life?".[13]

The Creation of Adam depicts the moment god brings Adam to life but visually it is Adam, not god, who is the "star" of the painting and indeed of the whole Sistine ceiling. This is very much a humanist creation. The predominance of this panel over all the others, visually as well as in historical reputation, is both because of its content (the "moment" of creation) and because it is the panel with most sky and therefore most light, and because of the clarity of its forms in their semi-symmetrical composition. This semi-symmetry also hints at the potential always latent in the biblical notion of god creating man in his own image, namely the materialist (Feuerbachian, then Marxist) reversal whereby man creates god in his own image. But "man" who creates god is "man who has either not yet won through to himself, or has already lost himself again" (Marx) and the god he creates is a dream, an idealised fantasy of what he might become. When god (Michelangelo) creates man he creates him as a young man in his prime, and when man (Michelangelo) creates god he creates him as a wise and benevolent old man.

The possibility of a homoerotic reading of this scene is, or should be,

---

13: Gramsci, 1971, p351.

obvious. God and Adam yearn for each other. But this homoerotic element actually contributes to the "universality" of the image. In Michelangelo (and up to now I have simply reflected this without comment) the male figure/"man" represents or "stands for" humanity. This could hardly be otherwise in such a male-dominated society, and was indeed general practice, at least linguistically, until well into the 1970s. However, when I look at Adam (and this also applies, though less strongly, to the *David*) I think Michelangelo's homoeroticism has "softened" his depiction. He is a beautiful, but not a macho, man. There is Hegel's profound dialectic of master and slave at work here. The slave is freer than the slave owner. Mankind is represented by the despised gay man.

History's door slams shut

However, as we move from the Sistine ceiling to the wall behind the altar, ie *The Last Judgement*, we enter a different emotional world. The frescos on the ceiling participate in the same humanist optimism as Leonardo or even Giotto before them. *The Last Judgement* is a work of extreme anguish. Only a quarter to a third of the fresco, the top least visible part, shows those raised up by Christ to heaven and no particular attempt is made to depict their eternal joy. Two thirds of it focuses on the torments, mainly mental, of the damned. Hauser writes:

> It is no longer a monument of beauty and perfection, of power and youth, that arises here, but a picture of bewilderment and despair, a cry for redemption from the chaos which suddenly threatens to swallow up the world of the Renaissance...

> *The Last Judgement*...is the first important artistic creation which is no longer "beautiful" and which refers back to those medieval works of art which were not yet beautiful but merely expressive.[14]

Nor is *The Last Judgement* a one-off. All Michelangelo's major artworks that follow it—the *Conversion of St Paul* and the *Crucifixion of St Peter* frescos, the Florentine *Pietà*, and his last work, the Rondanini *Pietà*, share a similar gloomy, perhaps tragic, atmosphere. By Renaissance standards these pieces might be judged wanting—they are not beautiful depictions of beautiful things, and they certainly lack "perfection" or "harmony"—but I think they are among his finest art. I see affinities here

---

14:   Hauser, 1999, volume 2, p105.

with the Shakespeare of *King Lear* and *The Tempest*, and the Rembrandt of *The Jewish Bride* and the late self-portraits.

The question, however, is what produced the profound change in mood. For those disposed to the biographical approach to art history there is an obvious answer: the onset of old age and the approach of death. And there is clearly some truth in this, especially in the case of the Rondanini *Pietà*, on which he was working to within days of his death. It cannot, however, be anything like the whole story because, as Hauser has shown, Michelangelo's shift in style is part of a much wider shift in style in Italian and to some extent, European art—the move to Mannerism. We need therefore to look again to the wider society, to history.[15]

What happened between the ceiling (1508-12) and the wall (1535-41)? Lots of "events" certainly. Many great artists died: Botticelli, da Vinci, del Sarto, Giorgione, Giovanni Bellini, Raphael, Corregio, as well as Holbein, Durer, Grünewald and Bosch outside Italy. In 1512 Cardinal Giovanni de Medici with the aid of papal troops restored Medici rule in Florence, ending a period of republican democracy under Piero Soderini (and Niccolò Machiavelli). In 1527 the forces of the Habsburg Holy Roman Emperor Charles V defeated Rome and sacked the city, after executing one thousand of its defenders.

Faced with this development, the citizens of Florence seized the opportunity to overthrow their Medici rulers for the second time (the first was in 1494) and to re-establish their republic. Michelangelo rallied to their support and in 1529 accepted a commission to design the city's fortifications. But Pope Clement VII made a deal with Charles V to use the emperor's troops to recapture Florence and return it to Medici hands. In 1533 Alessandro de Medici was created Duke of Florence, bringing an end to the republic and inaugurating 200 years of hereditary Medici rule. The sacking of Rome and the defeat of Florence effectively bring the Renaissance to an end (except for the late Titian in Venice).

While all this is happening in Italy, Luther has launched the Reformation in Wittemburg in 1517 and this has led to the German Peasant War of 1525, in which Luther sided with the aristocracy in ferociously crushing the peasant revolt he had himself called forth. In response to the Reformation came the Counter-Reformation: humanism was eclipsed, and Pope Paul III revived the Holy Inquisition (1542) and convened the Council of Trent (1545) to repel the Protestant threat. And, most importantly in the long run, the opening up of the Americas, following Columbus, combined

---

15: Hauser, 1965, especially pp4-16.

with the Ottoman threat in the eastern Mediterranean, following the fall of Byzantium, moved the economic centre of gravity of Europe from the Mediterranean to the north west and the Atlantic Seaboard.

But it is not so much the events as their wider import that is crucial here. Let us recall that it was Florence's (and Italy's) role as pioneer of capitalism in Europe that was the economic and social foundation of the Renaissance. Then let us also recall that Italy did not at all maintain its leading position, economically or socially. Italy did not produce a bourgeois democratic revolution, did not make the transition to a fully fledged capitalist state, did not even find the "leader" that Machiavelli called for in *The Prince* to unify the nation, until the Risorgimento in the mid-19th century and consequently experienced centuries of relative cultural decline—Giotto, da Vinci and Michelangelo gave way to Canaletto and Canova—while economic and cultural supremacy passed north to the Netherlands and England.

The early 16th century was thus a crucial turning point in the history of Italy, and also Germany as Marx and Engels were to explain, and therefore of Europe and the world. It was one of those moments when the door of history begins, tantalisingly, to open, inviting us to step through into a golden future, only to slam shut in our faces. The closest parallel I can think of is the 1920s and 1930s when the hopes aroused by the Russian Revolution were dashed and ended in the nightmare of Stalinism and fascism. Michelangelo's late works were produced in the early modern "Midnight of the Century" (the phrase is Victor Serge's). In fact the next major wave of the struggle, the international struggle of the bourgeoisie against feudalism, was only a couple of decades and a few hundred miles away—the Dutch Revolt began two years after Michelangelo's death—but neither he nor anyone else could possibly have had any sense of this at the time.

This raises the question of how much of the history I have been talking about Michelangelo would have been aware of and how it would have influenced his work. Clearly, he could not have been conscious of the terms that I have been using (feudalism, capitalism, bourgeoisie, etc) at all—this kind of analysis only becomes possible with Marx. Moreover, Michelangelo was a professional artist who depended, to live and to work, on commissions from Medicis and popes and who, in order to survive, had often to keep his counsel and sometimes make his excuses and leave. But we do know where his sympathies lay.

We know that the young Michelangelo was sympathetic to Savonarola, the Dominican priest and popular democrat who led Florence from 1494 till he was deposed by the pope and the Medicis and burned at the stake in 1498. We know that he was often in conflict with his Medici and papal masters and that he supported the Florentine Republic of 1527, leaving the city in disgust when Medici rule was restored. We know that in later life his "platonic" friendship with Vittoria Colonna in Rome involved much discussion of "Lutheran"-type ideas, which were regarded as heretical by the papacy. He would therefore most certainly have been sensitive to the changed political, moral and cultural climate. After all it resulted in the painting over of the genitals in *The Last Judgement* on the orders of Pope Paul IV in 1559!

But it so happened that Michelangelo produced, during these years, a series of major works, among the greatest in his whole output, which express with exceptional intensity this moment in history. These works are the so-called "slaves" or "captives". The first two, the *Dying Slave* and the *Rebellious Slave*, both from 1513, are still close on form and spirit to *David* and *Adam*. But then between 1519 and 1533 came *Atlas*, the *Young Slave*, the *Bearded Slave* and the *Awakening Slave*, who in age, size and physique are nearer to the Christ of *The Last Judgement*. They were all intended for the tomb of Julius II whose centrepiece was to be the awesome *Moses*, and they are all left "unfinished". Their unfinished character gives rise to one of those art-historical disputes that has not been, and probably cannot be conclusively resolved. Why are they unfinished? Are they unfinished because Michelangelo was obliged, by circumstances beyond his control, to leave them that way? Did he consciously, or unconsciously, choose not to finish them? In which case, are they really unfinished? If he really wanted to produce finished work, why did he not finish one of the series before starting on the next? My personal inclination is to believe they were deliberately left as they are because they are so powerful that way.

Anyway, conscious or unconscious, intended or unintended, the effect is the same—four giant figures struggling for freedom from the stone but still held captive by it. And they do not just capture the essence of that moment. They also make a powerful statement about human history and the struggle for human emancipation as a whole. For today, nearly 500 years later, we are still slaves fighting for our freedom, and still gripped by the rock of class society, alienation and "the muck of ages".

Now the question posed at the beginning of this paper—on what does Michelangelo's status as a giant of human history and culture rest—has received an answer. It is by no means a comprehensive answer—many aspects of Michelangelo, such as his architecture, and many of his works—have been neglected, but hopefully it grasps the main point. In his work as a whole Michelangelo expressed, more than any other artist, the hope and the dream of the Renaissance, and the despair and misery of the betrayal and crushing of that dream. And as always the art that penetrates most deeply into, and responds most powerfully to, the social relations and forces of its time is also the art that achieves the greatest "universal" appeal and validity.

References

Antal, Frederick, 1948, *Florentine Painting and its Social Background* (Routledge & Kegan Paul).

Berger, John, 1965, *The Success and Failure of Picasso* (Penguin).

Berger, John, 1972, "The Moment of Cubism', in John Berger, *Selected Essays and Articles* (Penguin).

Engels, Fredrick, 1883, *The Dialectics of Nature*, www.marxists.org/archive/marx/works/1883/don/ch01.htm

Gombrich, Ernst H, 1978, *The Story of Art* (Phaidon).

Gramsci, Antonio, 1971, *Selections from the Prison Notebooks* (Lawrence & Wishart).

Hadjinicolau, Nicos, 1978, *Art History and Class Struggle* (Pluto).

Hauser, Arnold, 1965, *Mannerism: The Crisis of the Renaissance and the Origin Of Modern Art* (Routledge & Kegan Paul).

Hauser, Arnold, 1999, *The Social History of Art* (Routledge & Kegan Paul).

Newman, Barnett, 1992, "The Sublime is Now", in Charles Harrison and Paul Wood (eds), *Art in Theory 1900-1990* (Blackwell).

Sala, Charles, 1995, *Michelangelo: Sculptor, Painter, Architect* (Terrail).

Schott, Rolf, 1975, *Michelangelo* (Thames & Hudson).

Symonds, J A, 1911, *The Life of Michelangelo Buonarroti* (Macmillan).

Vasari, Giorgio, 1991 [1550], *The Lives of the Artists* (Oxford University Press).

From deflected permanent revolution to the law of uneven and combined development
Neil Davidson

"Trotsky is the one for whom there is no room either in pre-1990 Really Existing Socialism or in post-1990 Really Existing Capitalism, in which even those who are nostalgic for Communism do not know what to do with Trotsky's permanent revolution".[1] Slavoj Žižek wrote these words at the beginning of the millennium and, in this case, he expresses a sentiment with which readers of *International Socialism* are likely to agree. The question of "what to do" with the concept of permanent revolution is one which this journal first addressed in a systematic way with the publication of Tony Cliff's major reappraisal of 1963, in which he augmented Trotsky's original concept with that of "deflected permanent revolution".[2] Cliff's article was part of a wider revisionist project. In the two years before his assassination in 1940, Trotsky made a number of claims about the world system and committed himself to a series of predictions about its future development. These included: that global capitalism had entered a period of permanent and irreversible decline, that the Russian Stalinist regime was an inherently unstable and historically

---

1:   Žižek, 2002, pp305-306. Thanks to Alex Callinicos, Joseph Choonara, Gareth Dale and Gonzalo Pozo for comments on the first draft.
2:   Cliff, 2003.

unique formation which was doomed to collapse, and that the coming revolutions in the colonial and semi-colonial world would be led by the working class, as the Russian Revolution had been in 1917.

In fact, following the Second World War capitalism entered the greatest period of growth in its history; Stalinist Russia not only expanded territorially through conquest, but its basic structures were independently replicated by Stalinist parties in the Third World; and—as this outcome suggests—the revolutions which occurred there were led not by the working class, but by elements of the middle class who then became the managers of a new bureaucratic state. Given these outcomes, some revision of Trotsky's final perspectives was inescapable but, short of abandoning them altogether, this could be done in one of two ways.

One way, ultimately adopted by adherents of what Isaac Deutscher called orthodox Trotskyism, was effectively to revise reality so that it corresponded with the theory—a necessary consequence of treating particular judgements by Trotsky as beyond falsification. In Alasdair MacIntyre's words, "It transformed into abstract dogma what Trotsky thought in concrete terms at one moment in his life and canonised this".[3] Canonisation involved two strategies of reality-avoidance. The first was the recategorisation of social classes: a party led by petty-bourgeois intellectuals and consisting of militarised ex-peasants could, for example, be described as representing "the Chinese working class" and its victory in 1949 hailed as a socialist revolution. But even those Trotskyists who treated Marxist class theory with greater seriousness than this could still avert their gaze from the truth with a second strategy, namely the adoption of an arbitrary formal definition of a "workers' state", where state ownership of the means of production became the only deciding factor, although the working class had neither led nor even participated in the revolution, did not in any sense control the new state and was subjected to a ruthless police dictatorship.

The second way, taken by Cliff and his initially small band of followers, was to revise the theory in the light of reality. Cliff held fast, not to specific judgements by Trotsky, but to the central tenets and methods of historical materialism that underpinned the latter's greatest achievements. Above all, Cliff cleaved to the self-activity of the working class, not as an optional if desirable extra, but as the indispensable core of Marxism as a theory of socialist revolution. In his autobiography Cliff recounted how, starting from this perspective, he "devoted a lot of time and effort to developing three interlinked theories to deal with the three areas of the world" where Trotsky's

---

3:    MacIntyre, 2008, p275.

predictions had proved false, "Russia and Eastern Europe, advanced capitalist countries, and the Third World": "The three theories were: state capitalism, the permanent arms economy, and deflected permanent revolution." This "troika", Cliff writes, "makes a unity, a totality, grasping the changes in the situation of humanity after the Second World War".[4]

Cliff was therefore responding to changes in the world capitalist system that orthodox Trotskyism refused to recognise; but there have been similarly dramatic shifts since Cliff concluded his reconsideration of the Trotskyist legacy. State capitalism still exists as a policy option for governments, as the quasi-nationalisation of banks during the financial crisis of 2007-8 has shown, but the era of state capitalism as a general tendency within the system ended between the emergence of neoliberalism in the mid-1970s and the fall of the Stalinist regimes in 1989-91. Vast sums are still wasted (in economic as well as moral terms) on arms, but military expenditure no longer acts to stabilise the system.[5] What then of the third component of the "troika"? Has deflected permanent revolution also become an essentially historical category?

In *International Socialism 126*, Leo Zeilig argued that deflected permanent revolution remains relevant today, despite the declining significance of the other component of the troika most closely related to it: "While the central role of the intelligentsia in the absence of a self-conscious working class subject is an absolute law in Cliff's theory, the importance of state capitalism for the deflected permanent revolution is neither absolute nor a requirement".[6] Zeilig applies the concept to Africa, a continent which, with the partial exception of Egypt, Cliff himself did not discuss, but the individual countries which Zeilig considers do fall into one of Cliff's categories, that of "deviations from the norm" of deflected permanent revolution.[7] The "norm" was established by those revolutions which had resulted in the most complete state capitalist outcomes under Stalinist leadership independently of Russia, particularly those in China and Cuba, although at the time when Cliff was writing in the early 1960s he could also have referred to North Vietnam, Albania or Yugoslavia. The "deviations" were those, actually the majority of cases, where the outcome was a mixture of state and private capitalism under radical nationalist leadership that may have been influenced by Stalinist ideas and organisational methods, but which often—as in the cases of Egypt or

---

4:   Cliff, 2000, pp42, 48.

5:   Pozo, 2010.

6:   Zeilig, 2010, p182.

7:   Zeilig, 2010, p163. The article is part of a growing and impressive body of work by the same author on the rich and complex history of African politics. See also Zeilig, 2007, Zeilig 2008, and Zeilig, 2009.

Iraq—oscillated between trying to incorporate the local Communist Party and trying to suppress it. With the very important exception of India, the most typical examples of the "deviations" were to be found in North Africa and the Middle East. Zeilig's use of the concept is illuminating in relation to those African states in which liberation movements were either completed (Ghana) or at least begun (Zimbabwe) within the post-war period of decolonisation which formed the context of Cliff's argument, but is it also the case that the theory can be applied to contemporary Africa and, by extension, the rest of the Global South?

I remain unconvinced. Not because I disagree with, for example, Zeilig's analysis of the recent events in the Democratic Republic of the Congo—quite the contrary; but rather because these seem to me to have little to do with permanent revolution, deflected or otherwise. Trotsky saw permanent revolution as a strategy which would enable the less developed countries to decisively break with feudal, tributary or colonial rule under working class leadership and move directly to socialism as components of an international revolutionary movement. Cliff saw deflected permanent revolution as the process which ensues when the working class does not carry through that strategy and another social force takes on the role of leadership, enabling the break with pre-capitalist modes of production or foreign domination to take place, but only in order for the countries in question to become parts of the capitalist world system. Although Cliff did not use the term, he effectively treated deflected permanent revolution as the modern version or functional equivalent of the bourgeois revolution.[8] Both the original and the revised concept therefore involved fundamental social transformations leading to either socialism (permanent revolution) or state capitalism (deflected permanent revolution).

Yet the term now tends to be used, as in Zeilig's article, to mean political events of far less significance. That this can be done without undue conceptual stretching suggests, at the very least, that there was always an ambiguity in Cliff's revision of Trotsky, which I think has two sources. One, which Cliff directly inherited from Trotsky, is the presence of an outstanding set of bourgeois revolutionary "tasks" which can be carried out by either the working class (permanent revolution) or the middle class "intelligentsia" (deflected permanent revolution). Much of the continued validity of both concepts therefore depends on how these tasks are defined and whether they are still outstanding. The other is the absence of any discussion of the

8:    Other writers in the International Socialist tradition have subsequently made this more explicit. See, for example, Callinicos, 1989, pp159-160, and Harris, 1978, pp261-282.

relationship between permanent revolution and the prior process of uneven and combined development, which was central to Trotsky's original conception. Nor did Cliff deal with the subject in later writings. Despite describing uneven and combined development as "the essence of the permanent revolution" in the first volume of his biography of Trotsky, the discussion is confined to a mere five pages across that work as a whole, all relating solely to Russia.[9] Yet, as we shall see, reintegrating the law of uneven and combined development with the strategy of permanent revolution will help answer many of the unresolved questions raised by its "deflection".

From bourgeois to permanent revolution

Trotsky was not alone in arguing that, by the beginning of the 20th century, the bourgeoisie was no longer capable of carrying out the revolution which bore its name.[10] Where he went far beyond his fellow-revolutionaries was in claiming that the Russian Revolution could lead, not only to the overthrow of absolutism, the establishment of representative government and the capitalist development of the productive forces, but to socialism itself. This was conditional, however, on the Russian Revolution being assisted by the revolutionary movement in the advanced West, whose own success could provide the material resources for socialist development that Russia lacked as an individual state. Trotsky was later to generalise this conception of permanent revolution, describing it as "the general trend of revolutionary development in all backward countries".[11] He also made what seemed at the time to be minor qualifications in relation to the two main social classes, but these contained possibilities, the realisation of which formed the background to Cliff's article.

On the one hand, Trotsky thought that even where foreign dominance was "concealed by the fiction of state independence" the ruling bourgeoisie was capable of resisting imperialism, at least up to a certain point.[12] This tended to be the case in countries which had never been formal colonies, or which ceased to be during the era of classic bourgeois revolutions. The most obvious examples of this were in the first and last destinations of his final exile: Turkey and Mexico. In this context he described the period of the 1930s as generally being one "in which the national bourgeoisie searches for

9:   Cliff, 1989, p128. For his entire discussion see Cliff, 1989, pp126-128 and Cliff, 1993, pp164-165.
10: See Day and Guido, 2009; Geras, 1976; Larsson, 1970, pp252-304; Löwy, 1981, chapter 2.
11: Trotsky, 1977b, p138.
12: Trotsky, 1976c, pp581, 582-583.

a bit more independence from the foreign imperialists" and that revolutionaries were "in permanent competition with the national bourgeoisie as the one leadership which is capable of assuring the victory of the masses in fight against the foreign imperialists". As the notion of "competition" suggests, although the organisations of the national bourgeoisie were in some senses "the Popular Front in the form of a party", they played a different role from the entirely reactionary popular fronts in Europe and North America: "It can have a reactionary character insofar as it is directed against the worker; it can have an aggressive attitude insofar as it is directed against imperialism".[13] Trotsky had written off the possibility of decolonisation without permanent revolution, seeing the relative freedom of states like Turkey or Mexico as exceptional; but what were the implications of states with a similar relationship to the world system (ie backward capitalism) multiplying, as they did from 1947 onwards with the creation of India and Pakistan?

On the other hand, Trotsky was also aware that the level of capitalist economic development, "the hierarchy of backwardness", varied enormously across what we now call the Global South.[14] As a result, the size of the working class and its ability to influence events was also subject to massive differentiation. Trotsky was the opposite of a utopian voluntarist and he accepted that a certain degree of social weight was necessary on the part of a working class before it could aspire to taking power; what was possible in India and China would not necessarily be possible in Equatorial Africa or Afghanistan. It was always necessary to establish working class organisational and political independence, but: "The relative weight of the individual and transitional demands in the proletariat's struggle, their mutual ties and their order of presentation, is determined by the peculiarities and specific conditions of each backward country and—to a considerable extent—by the *degree* of its backwardness".[15] However, even in those countries where the working class was much smaller than the Russian in relative terms, the global nature of the socialist project would enable them to overcome this obstacle. But what could the role of the working class be if the objective changed from international socialist revolution to national capitalist development?

Social or political revolution?

What were the "tasks" which Trotsky thought had to be accomplished in the process of passing from the bourgeois to the proletarian revolution?

13: Trotsky, 1979a, pp784-785.
14: Trotsky, 1976c, p582.
15: Trotsky, 1977b, p138.

In Cliff's summary, the bourgeoisie is "incapable of carrying out the thoroughgoing destruction of feudalism, the achievement of real national independence and political democracy", which he treats as the main tasks of the bourgeois revolution: "A consistent solution to the agrarian question, of the national question, a break-up of the social and imperial fetters preventing speedy economic advance, will necessitate moving beyond the bounds of bourgeois private property".[16] A more orthodox Trotskyist, Michael Löwy, similarly concluded from a study of Trotsky's works that what he calls the "democratic tasks" of the bourgeois revolution are "the agrarian democratic revolution", "national liberation" and "democracy".[17] These are potentially very demanding criteria indeed, many of which remain unmet throughout the entire Global South and indeed beyond today. In some places Trotsky seemed to realise that this was a problem. He was reluctant to describe the Japanese Meiji Restoration 1868, for example, as a bourgeois revolution, referring to it instead as "a bureaucratic attempt to buy off such a revolution", while at the same time acknowledging that the Meiji regime had accomplished in a matter of decades what it had taken Russia 300 years to achieve.[18] But if the notion of "tasks" were taken seriously in the case of the Japan, then this would mean that the bourgeois revolution was only consummated when agrarian reform and representative democracy were imposed by the US occupiers between 1945 and 1955. Unfortunately this introduces further problems since the American Revolution itself was presumably unfinished until the black population achieved full formal civil rights with the passing of the 1965 Voting Rights Amendment Act, the 1967 judgment in the case of Loving versus Virginia allowing "mixed" marriages, and so on.

The question of democracy is particularly important here, since with the partial exception of France, even the classic bourgeois revolutions did not lead to the installation of representative democracy. In fact, if we take bourgeois democracy to involve, at a minimum, a representative government elected by the adult population, where votes have equal weight and can be exercised without intimidation by the state, it is a relatively recent development in the history of capitalism. Far from being intrinsic to bourgeois society, representative democracy has largely been introduced by pressure from the working class, often involving the threat of revolution, and extended by pressure from the oppressed.[19] To insist that countries in the Global South

---

16: Cliff, 2003a, p188.
17: Löwy, 1981, p89.
18: Trotsky, 1972c, p291.
19: Acemoglu and Robinson, 2000, pp1182-1186; Therborn, 1977, pp4, 17.

are only completely capitalist when they have achieved stable representative democracy, apart from committing a category mistake (capitalism = economy; democracy = polity), is to expect a more complete outcome there than was achieved in the countries of the developed world. There are still important unresolved democratic issues in many countries, but they have nothing to do with the accomplishment or consolidation of capitalism.

This is what Cliff seems to have been implying in an important article from 1950 where he wrote of German unification "from above" during the 1860s: "The 'Bismarckian' path was not the exception for the bourgeoisie, but the rule, the exception was the French revolution".[20] The general conclusion was drawn by Alex Callinicos in this journal in 1982, when he noted the problem of making "an identification of bourgeois-democratic revolution with merely one of its cases", which is of course the French, "and making its specific features…necessary components of any 'genuine' bourgeois revolution": "Surely it is more sensible, rather than invoke the metaphysical concept of a 'complete and genuine solution' [to the tasks of the bourgeois revolution], to judge a bourgeois revolution by the degree to which it succeeds in establishing an autonomous centre of capital accumulation, even if it fails to democratise the political order, or to eliminate feudal social relations".[21] I agree with these conclusions, but they have certain implications for the theory of deflected permanent revolution that we have not considered. "Deflection" originally involved shifting from proletarian to bourgeois revolutionary objectives, but what can it mean if the real task of the bourgeois revolution has largely been accomplished on a global scale? In any case, "establishing an autonomous centre of capital accumulation" is scarcely an outcome which the working class can be expected to accomplish in the absence of the bourgeoisie!

The root of the problem is illustrated by the two main cases that Cliff discusses: China and Cuba. From the evidence of Cliff's autobiography, China seems to have been the main model for deflected permanent revolution; indeed he describes the 1963 article as being a "distillation" of his earlier book *Mao's China* (1957), with additional material on Cuba which, at that time, was the most recent addition to the roster of state capitalist regimes.[22] Before 1949 China stood historically before the completion of the bourgeois revolution: there was effectively no central state, the agrarian sector still contained tributary and feudal relations and it was subject to oppression by

---

20: Cliff, 1984, pp65-66.
21: Callinicos, 1982, p110.
22: Cliff, 2000, p227.

several competing imperialist powers. Cuba by 1959, on the other hand, was a bourgeois state—a very weak one, of course, overawed by the US and penetrated by organised crime, but it seems to be an abuse of language to say that it was in any sense pre-capitalist, nor was the working class striving for power in the 1950s in the way that the Chinese working class had in the 1920s. In order to understand the difference between these two revolutions, we need to establish an important distinction first made by Marx in the 1840s and later adopted by Trotsky: that between social and political revolutions.[23]

Political revolutions sometimes have social aspects and social revolutions always have political implications, but the terms nevertheless indicate an essential difference. Political revolutions are struggles within society for control of the existing state, but which leave the social and economic structure intact. These revolutions have been relatively frequent in history, from the Roman Civil Wars, which led to the abandonment of Republican rule for the Principate in 27 BC, to the Eastern European revolutions of 1989-91, which swept away the Stalinist regimes and began what Chris Harman called the "sideways" movement from Eastern state capitalism to an approximation of the Western trans-state model.[24] They may involve more or less popular participation, may result in more or less improvement in the condition of the majority, but ultimately the class that was in control of the means of production at the beginning will remain so at the end (although individuals and political organisations may have been replaced on the way), and the class that was exploited within the productive process at the beginning will also remain so at the end (although concessions may have been made to secure its acquiescence or participation). Social revolutions, however, are not merely struggles within existing society, but result in the transformation of one type of society into another and, as such, are extremely rare—so rare that we only know of two and one of these has not yet succeeded: the bourgeois revolution and the socialist revolution.

The relation between these two types of revolution is complex. Some revolutions which, taken by themselves, appear to be merely political revolutions, are in fact part of a more extended social revolution. In relation to the bourgeois revolution, the English revolution of 1688 has this relationship to the revolution of 1640; similar cases could be made for the French revolution of 1830 in relation to that of 1789 or, reversing the chronological order of importance, the American Revolution of 1776 in relation to the Civil War

---

23: Marx, 1975, pp419-420; Trotsky, 1937, p288. Much the clearest discussion of the subject is in Draper, 1978, pp17-21.
24: Harman, 1990, pp64-71.

of 1861-5. More importantly in the context of this discussion, some revolutions end up as political revolutions because they are failed social revolutions. In relation to the socialist revolution, this is clearly the case with the German Revolution of 1918. As Trotsky commented, "It was no democratic completion of the bourgeois revolution, it was proletarian revolution decapitated by the Social Democrats; more correctly, it was a bourgeois counter-revolution, which was compelled to preserve pseudo-democratic forms after its victory over the proletariat".[25] A similar case could also be made for the Portuguese Revolution of 1974—and indeed most of the so-called "democratic" revolutions to have taken place since, above all that of Iran in 1978-9.

China experienced a social revolution in 1949: it could have been the socialist revolution, if the movements of the mid-1920s had succeeded, but ended up instead as the functional equivalent of the bourgeois revolution instead—a lesser but still decisive systemic shift. Cuba only experienced a political revolution, which did not fundamentally change the nature of the economic system, and represented—using Harman's term, but reversing the direction of movement—a sideways shift from a highly corrupt market capitalist economy to one on the state capitalist model. This would have been more obvious if US paranoia about encroaching "communism" had not effectively forced the new Cuban regime to ally with Russia and adopt state capitalist forms of organisation—which was certainly not Castro's original intention. There were, in other words, two different types of revolution encompassed by the term "deflected permanent revolution" from the very beginning. As capital increasingly sweeps away even the remnants of previous modes of production and the social formations which include them, the pattern of revolutions has increasingly tended towards the "political" rather than the "social" type—the revolutions of 1989 in Eastern Europe; the subsequent displays of "people power" in the Philippines, Thailand and Serbia; and the "colour revolutions" in the former republics of the USSR. Capitalism endlessly reproduces differences in power and autonomy—the "unevenness" which I discuss below. Except in a handful of cases (Afghanistan, Nepal, Tibet) the unstable but structured inequality which results is not an unresolved issue from an earlier period, not a remnant of feudalism or colonialism, but a result of the normal operation of competitive accumulation expressed at the level of nation-states.

At least one leading thinker in the International Socialist tradition did argue that none of the cases of deflected permanent revolution involved social revolutions, although without using the latter term. Discussing the

---

25: Trotsky, 1969b, p131.

same examples as Cliff in an article for this journal written during the collapse of the Stalinist regimes, Harman noted:

In none of these cases was there a shift from one mode of production to another. In each case those who had control of the existing state apparatus used it to reorganise industry, reducing internal competition to a minimum to accumulate in the face of external pressures. That does not mean that there was never any opposition to such a move—"police" actions of various sorts were often taken against old, "private" capitalist interests who resisted the changes. But these were possible without any mobilisation of the mass of the population for full blooded social revolution, indeed in some cases without any mobilisation of the mass of the population at all.[26]

This perhaps goes too far, not only in respect of the Chinese Revolution of 1949, but a minority of the revolutions which followed it. Before the Ethiopian Revolution of 1974, for example, feudal social relations were still dominant and the state was the nearest to the European absolutist model of any remaining in the world.[27] Nevertheless, Harman's central point about the non-social nature of the revolution, like the majority of its predecessors, is correct, but does raise the question of whether retaining the term "deflected permanent revolution" has any benefits other than providing the consolations of familiarity. It is possible, of course, to explicitly detach it from the "tasks" of the bourgeois revolution, real or imagined, and instead relate it to the possibility of working class leadership in accomplishing democratic tasks (as in Thailand) or anti-imperialist struggle (as in Iraq) on the road to socialism—and this is more or less how the term tends to be used, but this has the danger of obscuring what is at stake.

Political revolutions, changes of regime by non-constitutional methods, are a fact of life in the Global South and likely to remain so, but these can take place without involving any independent working class intervention. If one Russian-backed gang of scoundrels replaces another US-supported collection of villains (or vice versa) in, say, Kyrgyzstan, and some working class people take part in accompanying demonstrations, this is not an example of deflected permanent revolution. There are of course very important recent examples where the working class has irrupted into what would otherwise been an inter ruling class dispute, thus opening up the possibility of social(ist) revolution, and again Iran in 1978-9 is the key

---

26: Harman, 1990, p38.
27: Halliday and Molyneux, 1981, pp62-74.

example, but their failure to seize power meant that the revolutions *remained* at the political level. Again this is not an example of deflected permanent revolution: Iran was a capitalist state, the working class was defeated and one wing of the bourgeoisie emerged triumphant over another on the basis of a different strategy for accumulation. The alternatives, of social revolution based on the working class or political revolution involving the ascendancy of a different section of the bourgeoisie organised by political Islamists, still pertain in Iran and also in Egypt, the two areas of the Middle East where new upheavals are most clearly being prepared—although as we shall see in due course, they are not alone. Before turning to the question of what is generating these potentially revolutionary situations, however, we need to address the nature of the class, or class fraction, which Cliff argued had replaced the working class, allowing the process of "deflection" to take place.

The incapacities of the bourgeoisie

Cliff identified the "revolutionary intelligentsia" as a substitute for the revolutionary bourgeoisie in the Global South. No summary can substitute for actually reading his exemplary analysis of this group, but the main characteristics that he ascribed to it are important to note here. As non-specialists, members of the intelligentsia can offer to represent the "nation" against other merely sectoral groups. The backwardness of their nation offends them, not simply as a matter of civic pride, but because in material terms it means they are unable to find work—or at least work in the state apparatus at a level appropriate to their education. As the traditional aspects of their society are increasingly destabilised by the irruption of capitalist development, they find it hard to maintain its values, but look instead to those of efficiency, modernisation, industrialisation, all of which are apparently embodied in the USSR. They claim to love "the people", but simultaneously feel guilty at their relative privilege and distrustful of those less educated or intelligent than themselves. Above all, they are hostile to democracy and strive to exclude the masses from their strategies of transformation, except in a subordinate or supportive role, which is why their preferred method is one of military struggle on a guerrilla or even conventional basis.[28]

Harman subsequently extended the argument in an important article on political Islam. Although Cliff's category was originally used with reference to "Stalinism, Maoism and Castroism", Harman now claimed that it was equally applicable to "the Islamist intelligentsia around Khomeini in Iran", who "undertook a revolutionary reorganisation of

---

28: Cliff, 2003, pp196-198.

ownership and control of capital within Iran while leaving capitalist relations of production intact".[29]

The brilliance of this collective portrait is not in doubt, but was the class fraction it describes a new development in the history of capitalism? The classical Marxist tradition was more sceptical than is generally thought about the extent to which the bourgeoisie had been at the forefront of revolutionary struggle, even in 1640 or 1789.[30] Trotsky tended to regard the petty bourgeoisie as the driving force behind successful bourgeois revolutions up to and including the French.[31] He also recognised, however, that other social groups had played this role, including feudal landlords in Prussia during the 1860s and—potentially at least—the working class in the Chinese Revolution of the 1920s. He did not, of course, claim that the bourgeoisie had never played a revolutionary role: simply that this was not a necessary condition for a revolution to qualify as bourgeois.[32] But in the cases where the bourgeoisie did lead, it is important to understand which sections were involved.

The bourgeoisie does not only consist of capitalists, in the literal sense of those who own or control capital. Hal Draper describes the class in this larger sense as involving "a social penumbra around the hard core of capitalists proper, shading out into the diverse social elements that function as servitors or hangers-on of capital without themselves owning capital".[33] The components of this "penumbra" are not, in fact, members of the petty bourgeoisie, who stand outside the capital-labour relationship and "earn their living by dint of their own labour and their own property", although they have often provided the foot soldiers for the struggle with feudal absolutism.[34] On the contrary: according to Perry Anderson, the peripheral membership of the outer bourgeoisie "is typically composed…of the gamut of professional, administrative and technical groups that enjoy life-conditions similar to capitalists proper—everything customarily included in the broader term 'bourgeoisie' as opposed to 'capital'."[35] Michael Mann has suggested that a variation of the schema erroneously ascribed to Lenin, whereby ideological leadership

29: Harman, 2010, p344.
30: Davidson, 2005, pp21-27. I discuss this issue in more detail in Davidson, 2011a, chapter 2.
31: Trotsky, 1976c, pp581, 583-584.
32: For discussions of this "consequentialist" position, see Callinicos, 1989, pp124-127 and Davidson, 2005, pp27-32.
33: Draper, 1978, p169.
34: Draper, 1978, p289.
35: Anderson, 1992, p112.

can only be brought to the working class "from outside", might in fact be relevant in relation to the bourgeoisie: "Left to itself the bourgeoisie was only capable of economism—in the 18th century of segmental manipulative deference".[36] It is in any case historically demonstrable that, down to 1848 at least, the most decisive leaderships tended to emerge from those sections of the bourgeoisie without direct material interests in the process of production, who were simultaneously less concerned with the destructive effects of revolutionary violence, but more able to overcome the competitive economic divisions within their class.

Are the leaders of the "deflected" revolutions so very different from those who led them between 1789 and 1848? Guevara trained as a doctor, but Robespierre was a lawyer, Danton a journalist, Roux a priest; only a very few, of whom Roederer was the most important, could seriously be described as capitalists. In some respects the parallels are nearly exact. As Eric Hobsbawm notes of the radicalism of students and intellectuals in 1848, "it was largely based on the (as it turned out temporary) inability of the new bourgeois society before 1848 to provide enough posts of adequate status for the educated whom it produced in unprecedented numbers, and whose rewards were so much more modest than their ambitions".[37] John Rees once observed that the intelligentsia "had, in an earlier incarnation, often been a crucial element of the practical leadership of the classical bourgeois revolutions", without however drawing any conclusions.[38] But if the above argument is correct, then the bourgeoisie's supposed abdication of its revolutionary role after 1848 was in fact simply an expression of the hostility which the core membership of this class had always displayed towards plebeian intervention, now heightened by the even greater threat posed by the working class.

The two real changes after 1848 lay elsewhere. One was that the non-capitalist sections of the bourgeoisie, which had previously given revolutionary leadership and which might have been less paralysed by fear of the working class, were increasingly integrated into a society in which their former frustrations and humiliations were rapidly becoming things of the past. The other was that sections of the existing ruling classes of Europe and Japan, such as the Prussian landlords to whom Trotsky refers, which had previously resisted revolution, now embraced a top-down version in order to make their states capable of military competition with their rivals—or in the case of Japan, to avoid the fate of colonisation and dismemberment that had befallen

---

36: Mann, 1993, p229.
37: Hobsbawm, 1975, p21.
38: Rees, 1999, p28; Rees, 2006, p155.

China. In the case of the colonial world after 1945, the core bourgeoisie had inherited the traditional fear of revolution from their predecessors, but the "revolutionary intelligentsia" were not in the position of their European equivalents after 1848 and far more closely resembled them before 1789: they could not look forward to wealth, power and recognition without a revolution. In some cases they did not need to take action for themselves because the process of transformation was initiated by an army coup.

This type of event, distantly related to the "revolutions from above" in Germany, Italy and Japan in the 1860s, had of course begun before the advent of Stalinism with the Turkish Revolution of 1919, and were led by groups which Ellen Kay Trimberger calls "autonomous military bureaucrats".[39] This is one area in which Cliff's account needs to be qualified as it is not entirely clear that "intelligentsia" is sufficiently broad a category to include the leading social forces involved in these revolutions, at least two of which, those led by Nasser in Egypt and Mengitsu in Ethiopia, were among the most important of the "deviations from the norm" of deflected permanent revolution. Military leaders, who are quite often junior officers, do of course have one important characteristic in common with members of the intelligentsia, in that they can also claim to represent "the nation" beyond mere factional interests. In the majority of cases where the military solution was not available, however, the intelligentsia needed to mobilise themselves. What is new in these situations was not therefore the existence or activity of a "revolutionary intelligentsia" hitherto unknown: both were already familiar from the history of the 19th century. It was rather that this class fraction felt able to take action in the knowledge that they did not need to fear the working class. Why not?

Cliff offers a number of reasons why the working class in the Global South did not play the role envisaged by Trotsky. Of these, the general influence of ruling class ideas and the illiteracy and inexperience of the workers are clearly relevant, but this was also true of Russia in 1917 and China in the 1920s; they are not in themselves an explanation. Other reasons have genuine explanatory power and remain extremely pertinent even today. Many workers in urban industry retain links to smallholdings in the countryside, to which they return in times of unemployment, making the permanent formation of class consciousness and organisation difficult. Conversely, those workers who are in stable employment can have relatively higher living standards than the rural masses, making the possibility of alliances with them less

---

39: Trimberger, 1978, pp4-5, 41-45. Trimberger identifies the Meiji Restoration as the first revolution of this type.

likely. Those trade unions or community groups which do exist are often led by non working class elements, "outsiders", with different interests and political goals, and are heavily reliant on support from the developmental state, which tends to impose an apolitical agenda acceptable to the regime. Both these leaderships and the personnel who run the state apparatus are influenced by Stalinist politics, the key subjective element in controlling and lowering the aspirations of the working class.[40] But many of these characteristics were also present in pre-revolutionary Russia: workers with links to the countryside; trade unions established by agents of the state; and industries where trade unions did not exist even before the ban which followed the Revolution of 1905.[41] Some deeper level of explanation is required.

The absence of the revolutionary party is clearly part of the explanation, but parties themselves can only have a meaningful existence where certain determinate conditions allow them to form and grow. Lack of revolutionary leadership can explain the outcome in China during the 1920s or in Iran in 1978-9, where major upheavals took place and Cliff's other inhibiting conditions were overcome, but not where such situations did not arise. At the end of his discussion of workers in the Global South, Cliff writes, "An automatic correlation between economic backwardness and revolutionary political militancy does not exist".[42] But Trotsky never argued that such an automatic correlation did exist; for him it was conditional and Cliff does not refer to, let alone discuss, the enabling condition which Trotsky saw as fundamental to its establishment: uneven and combined development.

From uneven to combined development

The radical *novelty* of what Trotsky meant by uneven and combined development is often underestimated. The most common mistake is to reduce it to, or confuse it with, the longstanding theory of uneven development.[43] The most famous (and certainly the most often quoted) passage in Trotsky's *The History of the Russian Revolution* is an expression of this position: "The privilege of historic backwardness—and such a privilege exists—permits, or rather compels, the adoption of whatever is ready in advance of any specified date,

---

40: Cliff, 2003, pp194-195.
41: Gatrell, 1994, p93; Koenker and Rosenberg, 1989, pp103-110; Schneiderman, 1976, pp69-140.
42: Cliff, 2003, p196.
43: For examples of these mistakes and a sketch of the history of the theory of uneven development, see Davidson, 2006a, pp10-20, and Davidson, 2009, pp10-11. For a more detailed discussion, see Davidson, forthcoming in 2011b, chapter 1.

skipping a whole series of intermediate stages".[44] But if all that Trotsky had proposed was a schema in which the "advantages of backwardness" allowed less developed nation-states to adopt the most modern available technologies he would have remained within the established limits of unevenness and, indeed, would not have distinguished himself from Stalinist usage of the same concept. As Ernest Mandel once wrote, part of the "magnificent theoretical achievement" represented by the law of uneven and combined development is precisely that it is "quite distinct from the law of uneven development familiar to all Marxists".[45] Why was the distinction necessary? What was missing from Trotsky's account of permanent revolution was any explanation for the *origin* of the revolutionary process, for the revolutionary militancy of the Russian working class and, by extension, at least some of the other working classes in the underdeveloped world.

Until the First World War uneven development had been a largely descriptive concept, without specific political implications. As Neil Smith notes, it "was first examined in any depth by Lenin, who tried to sketch some of the economic and geographical outlines of the process".[46] In *Imperialism: the Highest Stage of Capitalism* (1916) Lenin wrote, "The uneven and spasmodic development of individual enterprises, individual branches of industry and individual countries is inevitable under the capitalist system".[47] Essentially, he argued that by the beginning of the 20th century uneven development had acquired three main aspects. One was the process by which the advanced states had reached their leading positions within the structured inequality of the world system. During the late 19th century the "skipping of stages" had been the experience of several states, notably Germany, Italy and Japan. The pressure of military and commercial competition between the actual or aspirant Great Powers forced those which were still absolutist states based on the feudal mode of production—or at least those which were capable of doing so—to adopt the current stage of development achieved by their capitalist rivals, if they were to have any chance, not only of successfully competing, but of surviving at the summit of the world order. In very compressed timescales they had been able to adopt the socio-economic achievements of Britain to the extent that they became recognisably the same kind of societies, without necessarily reproducing every characteristic of the Anglo-Saxon pioneer: where backwardness remained

---

44: Trotsky, 1977a, p27.
45: Mandel, 1995, p1.
46: Smith, 1990, pxiv.
47: Lenin, 1964, p241.

it tended to be in the nature of the political regimes led by monarchs or emperors supported by a landowning aristocracy.

By the outbreak of the First World War membership of the dominant states was essentially fixed. What remained was the second aspect of uneven development: the ongoing rivalry between the great powers which involved them constantly trying to "catch up and overtake" each other in a contest for supremacy that would continue as long as capitalism itself. This rivalry led in turn to a third aspect: the developed imperialist states collectively, but competitively asserting their dominance over two other types, described by Lenin as "the colonies themselves" and "the diverse forms of dependent countries which, politically, are formally independent but, in fact, are enmeshed in the net of financial and diplomatic dependence", like Argentina and Portugal.[48] Colonial expansion prevented some of the societies subject to it from developing at all, and in the case of the most undeveloped, the peoples involved suffered near or complete extermination and their lands were taken by settlers. More often the peoples survived, but their social systems were immobilised by imperial powers interested in strategic advantage or plunder, or both.

Trotsky certainly took uneven development in these three senses as his starting point—as is suggested by the word order in the title of his own theory: "I would put *uneven* before *combined*, because the second grows out of the first and completes it".[49] How then does the concept of uneven and combined development differ from uneven development as such? The main difference is that it takes account of the internal *effects* of uneven development.[50] To explain the link between the advanced nature of Russian industry on the one hand, and the militancy of Russian workers on the other, Trotsky had to transcend the theory of uneven development, a process he did not complete until the early 1930s. The inability of uneven development to fully encapsulate these phenomena is what appears to have made Trotsky search for a new concept with which to supplement it. It took a political crisis to provoke this conceptualisation.

During the Chinese Revolution of 1925-7 the emergent Stalinist regime in Russia ordered the local Communist Party to subordinate its own organisation and demands to those of the bourgeois nationalists in the Guomindang. The ultimately disastrous outcome for the Chinese working class movement was the catalyst for Trotsky to generalise the strategy of permanent

---

48: Lenin, 1964, pp263–264.
49: Trotsky, 1979b, p858.
50: The only real forerunner here is Rosa Luxemburg in a brilliant article from 1896 on the Ottoman Empire—see Luxemburg, 2003, pp38-40.

revolution from Russia to sections of the colonial and semi-colonial world, not indiscriminately—since some were still untouched by capitalist development and had no working class of any size—but where conditions similar to those in Russia prevailed. Due to a common set of circumstances, the working classes in these countries had far greater levels of both consciousness and organisation than the proletariat in the more developed countries where Marxists had traditionally expected the socialist revolution to begin. Trotsky claimed that "the prediction that historically backward Russia could arrive at the proletarian revolution sooner than advanced Britain rests almost entirely upon the law of uneven development".[51] But uneven development was not the sole basis for this prediction, as we can see by contrasting actual Russian development with two possible alternatives.

One was the path of the advanced capitalist states. The pace of development was relatively faster in most of the countries that followed Holland and England, partly because of the urgency of acquiring the attributes of capitalist modernity, partly because the long period of experiment and evolution, characteristic of the two pioneers, could be dispensed with. In the case of Scotland in the 18th century or Prussia in the 19th century, this led to enormous tensions which resolved themselves in moments of class struggle foreshadowing the process of permanent revolution, above all in the 1820 general strike in the former and the 1848 revolution in the latter. But because these societies did make the transition to the ranks of the advanced societies, either as the centre (Prussia/Germany) or a component part of another national formation (Scotland/Britain) these moments passed with the tensions that caused them.

The other was the path of the colonies or semi-colonies. What Peter Curtin calls "defensive modernisation" was not enough to protect these societies from Western incursions. In the case of the Merinian monarchs of Madagascar, for example, "They not only failed to modernise beyond adopting Christianity and superficial European fashions, they failed to build a kind of society and government administration that would perpetuate their own power".[52] Colonial rule could even throw societies backwards, as in the case of British-occupied Iraq. Ruling through the Hashemite monarchy after 1920, the regime deliberately rejected any attempts at modernisation, except in the oil industry. Instead it reinforced disintegrating tribal loyalties and semi-feudal tenurial relationships over the peasantry. Peter Gowan describes the British initiatives as "the creation of *new* foundational

---

51: Trotsky, 1969b, p241.
52: Curtin, 2000, p150.

institutions of landownership in order to *revive* dying traditional authority relations, resulting in economically and socially regressive consequences, undertaken for thoroughly modern imperialist political purposes—namely, to create a ruling class dependent upon British military power and therefore committed to imperial interests in the region".[53]

A further group of states embodied "combination". These were unable to reproduce the level of development attained by the advanced capitalist states, but were nevertheless able to "unblock" themselves to the extent of making partial advances in specific areas. There were essentially three sub sets in this group. The first were feudal-absolutist or tributary states, like Russia or Turkey, which, under pressure from the Western powers, were forced for reasons of military competition to introduce limited industrialisation and partial agrarian reform. The second were still more backward states like China or regions like the post-Ottoman Arab Middle East, which had been broken by imperialist pressure, but which, instead of being colonised, were allowed to disintegrate while the agents of foreign capital established areas of industrialisation under the protection of either their own governments or local warlords. The third were colonial states like British India, and to a lesser extent French Algeria, where the metropolitan power was unwilling to allow full-scale industrialisation in case it produced competition for its own commodities, but was prepared to sanction it in specific circumstances for reasons of military supply or where goods were not intended for home markets. Tsarist Russia neither emulated the process of "catch up and overtake" among the advanced countries nor suffered that of "blocked development" within the backward ones, but instead experienced a collision between the two.

It was in relation to developments in China that Trotsky finally moved beyond uneven development. He continued to employ the term between 1928 and 1930, most importantly in the articles collected in *The Third International after Lenin*, and in *Permanent Revolution* and its various prefaces. In these texts his main emphasis is still distinguishing his use of uneven development from that of Stalin, for whom countries developed at different tempos and must therefore advance through a series of stages—including that of socialism—at their own individual pace. Trotsky highlighted instead the "unity" of the world economy and the "interdependence" of the imperial powers and the colonial and semi-colonial world. Unevenness in this sense means simultaneously that individual countries could leap over the capitalist stage of development, as Russia had done and as China might have

---

53: Gowan, 1999, p167.

done, but would still be unable to complete the transition to socialism while the world economy as a whole remained dominated by the capitalist mode of production: the international system was both a spur at one moment and a block at another.[54] Yet these important insights still did not address the question of how the first part of this process, the revolutionary moment, was possible. Trotsky needed a new concept, incorporating uneven development, but deepening its content.

It was in the first volume of *The History of the Russian Revolution* (1932) that he first outlines this new concept: "From the universal law of unevenness thus derives another law which, for want of a better name, we may call the law of combined development—by which we mean a drawing together of the different stages of the journey, a combining of separate steps, an amalgam of archaic with more contemporary forms".[55] The precise forms which combination took obviously varied depending on whether the country involved was a formal colony controlled by a single imperial power, like India, or one nominally independent, but actually subdivided between several warlords and imperial powers, like China. Clearly there were differences. Unlike Tsarist Russia, neither Imperial nor Republican China was in a position to stimulate capitalist industrial growth. Where similarities did exist was in the role of foreign capital and imported technology and in the limited geographical implantation of capitalist industry. Nevertheless it was possible to generalise in relation to the effects:

Historical backwardness does not imply a simple reproduction of the development of advanced countries, England or France, with a delay of one, two, or three centuries. It engenders an entirely new "combined" social formation in which the latest conquests of capitalist technique and structure root themselves into relations of feudal or pre-feudal barbarism, transforming and subjecting them and creating peculiar relations of classes.[56]

Uneven and combined development affects the totality of a national society, not merely the economy. Trotsky was not saying that forms characteristic of different stages of development simply coexist alongside each other in striking or dramatic contrasts, although that could be true. Nor was he just emphasising the existence of transitional modes of production, although he recognised that these could exist. Uneven and combined

---

54: Trotsky, 1969b, pp148-150, 252-260; Trotsky, 1974b, pp14-19.
55: Trotsky, 1977a, pp27-28.
56: Trotsky, 1976c, p583.

development usually involves what Michael Burawoy calls "the combination of the capitalist mode of production with pre-existing modes".[57] Jamie Allinson and Alex Anievas too have written of how the "logics of different modes of production interact with one another in consequential ways in backward countries".[58] But a process that permeates every aspect of society, ideology as much as economy, must involve more than this. The "articulation" of capitalist and pre-capitalist modes had, after all, been progressing slowly in the Russian countryside since the abolition of serfdom in 1861, and had led to many complex transitional forms, as Lenin documented.[59] None by themselves led to the type of situation Trotsky was seeking to explain: "At the same time that peasant land-cultivation as a whole remained, right up to the revolution, at the level of the 17th century, Russian industry in its technique and capitalist structure stood at the level of the advanced countries, and in certain respects even outstripped them".[60]

The detonation of the process requires sudden, intensive industrialisation and urbanisation, regardless of whether the pre-existing agrarian economy was based on feudal or capitalist relations. Burawoy is therefore right to describe uneven and combined development as a product of "the timing of industrialisation in relation to the history of world capitalism".[61] Here too the Chinese experience was important. Trotsky was quite insistent—perhaps over-insistent—on which mode dominated the Chinese social formation. He rejected Communist International claims that feudalism predominated in the Chinese economic base and political superstructure: "Of course, matters would be quite hopeless if feudal survivals did really *dominate* in Chinese economic life," he wrote in 1929. "But fortunately, survivals in general cannot dominate." Instead he emphasised the extent of market relations and influence of different forms of mercantile and banking capital. Rural social relations "stem in part from the days of feudalism; and in part they constitute a new formation", but within this formation:

> it is capitalist relations that *dominate* and not "feudal" (more correctly, serf and, generally, pre-capitalist) relations. Only thanks to this dominant role of capitalist relations can we speak seriously of the prospects of proletarian hegemony in a national revolution.[62]

57: Burawoy, 1985, p99.
58: Allinson and Anievas, 2009, p52.
59: Lenin, 1960, pp191–210.
60: Trotsky, 1977a, p30. And see, for example, Reiber, 1982, p224.
61: Burawoy, 1985, p99.
62: Trotsky, 1974b, pp159-160.

Whatever the extent of Trotsky's exaggerations, it is important—not least in relation to modern China—that uneven and combined development can take place where the capitalist mode was already dominant. The archaic and the modern, the settled and disruptive, overlap, fuse and merge in all aspects of the social formations concerned, from the organisation of arms production to the structure of religious observance, in entirely new and unstable ways, generating socially explosive situations in which revolution became what Georg Lukács termed "actual".[63] It is tempting to describe these as mutations, except that the inadequacy of the language led Trotsky to reject the biological metaphors in which stages of development had been described from the Enlightenment to the Third International in its Stalinist phase: "The absorptive and flexible psyche, as a necessary condition for historical progress, confers on the so-called social 'organisms', as distinguished from the real, that is, biological organisms, an exceptional variability of internal structure".[64]

These new combined formations gave rise to conflicts unknown in earlier historical periods. On the one hand: "The [backward] nation...not infrequently debases the achievements borrowed from outside in the process of adapting them to its own more primitive culture".[65] From 1861 Tsarism established factories using manufacturing technology characteristic of monopoly capitalism in order to produce arms with which to defend a feudal absolutist state.[66] On the other hand, by doing so they bring into being a class more skilled, more politically conscious than that faced by any previous absolutist or early capitalist states.[67] All subsequent non-Marxist theories of "the advantages of backwardness" assumed that technological transfers had a limited, or at least delayed, impact on other aspects of social life.[68] Against this Trotsky argued that these transfers could in fact quicken the pace of change more generally, so that they attained higher levels of development than in their established rivals. As an example of this he drew attention to the greater implantation of Marxist theory among the working classes of Russia and, later, China than in that of Britain. Thus, for Trotsky, the most important consequence of uneven and combined development was the enhanced capacity it gave the working classes for political and industrial organisation, theoretical understanding and revolutionary activity:

63: Lukács, 1970, chapter 1.
64: Trotsky, 1972b, p251.
65: Trotsky, 1977a, p27.
66: Treblicock, 1981, p208.
67: Trotsky, 1977a, p55. And see, for example, Gatrell, 1994, p15.
68: See, for example, Gerschenkron, 1962, pp127-128.

When the productive forces of the metropolis, of a country of classical capitalism…find ingress into more backward countries, like Germany in the first half of the 19th century, and Russia at the merging of the 19th and 20th centuries, and in the present day in Asia; when the economic factors burst in a revolutionary manner, breaking up the old order; when development is no longer gradual and "organic" but assumes the form of terrible convulsions and drastic changes of former conceptions, then it becomes easier for critical thought to find revolutionary expression, provided that the necessary theoretical prerequisites exist in the given country.[69]

But uneven and combined development can also work, as it were, in reverse: "debased adaptation" is not only a feature of backward societies. Here too the opening of the age of imperialism is decisive. Between 1870 and 1914, for example, imperial Britain, Germany and Japan all consciously emphasised the role of their monarch-emperors; in each case, the pre-existing symbolism of the crown being used to represent national unity against two main challenges: external imperial rivalry and internal class divisions.[70] But Trotsky saw this as a much more general phenomenon, necessarily caused by the need to maintain bourgeois hegemony over the exploited and oppressed in an era of revolution and which reached its apogee in the US:

It is considered unquestionable that technology and science undermine superstition. But the class character of society sets substantial limits here too. Take America. There, church sermons are broadcast by radio, which means that the radio is serving as a means of spreading prejudices.[71]

Trotsky's argument suggests two questions about the character of uneven and combined development. One is whether it applies to all periods in human history. Trotsky himself tended to think that it did. His claim that "the entire history of mankind is governed by the law of uneven development" can certainly be defended.[72] He later extended this, writing in *The Revolution Betrayed* (1937), "The law of *uneven* development is supplemented throughout the whole course of history by the law of *combined* development".[73] Whether this is equally defensible is, however,

---

69: Trotsky, 1972a, p199. See also Trotsky, 1977a, p33.
70: Cannadine, 1983, pp120-150; Bayly, 2004, pp426-430.
71: Trotsky, 1994, p257.
72: Trotsky, 1974b, p115.
73: Trotsky, 1937, p300.

another matter.[74] Trotsky did not attempt to demonstrate his claims for the transhistoricity of uneven and combined development, but Justin Rosenberg has attempted to do so with examples from the Russian state after 800 AD, which he claims show three aspects of combination.

First, "the course of Russian development was 'combined' in the sense that at every point it was causally integrated with a wider social field of inter-acting patterns of development".[75] By this he means that Russia was subject to "inter-societal causality", an environment in which the endless interplay of other states or social forces shaped its internal structure in a way that could never be completed. Second, combination also involved "structures" which "extended beyond Russia itself". Among such structures Rosenberg includes "regional political orders, cultural systems and material divisions of labour". The third, "yet deeper" dimension is the consequence of the first two, the creation of a "hybrid" social formation, "a changing amalgam of pre-existent 'internal' structures of social life with external socio-political and cultural influences". Consequently, there "never existed a 'pre-combination' Russia"; at every point its existence was traversed by these influences: "combined development identifies the inter-societal, relational texture of the historical processes within which the shifting meanings of the term 'Russia' crystallised and accumulated". In general terms, Rosenberg invites us to "abandon at the deepest theoretical level any notion of the constitution of society as analyti-cally prior to its interaction with other societies".[76]

The inseparability of the international from the social is, however, inscribed in historical materialism from the moment of its formation, notably *The German Ideology*. But in this moment, Marx and Engels were also clear that "history becomes world history" only as a result of capi-talism.[77] Why? Before capitalism all class societies, with the exception of those based on slavery, were based on variations of the same mode of pro-duction, involving surplus extraction from a class of peasants and taking either a "feudal" or "tributary" form depending on whether the main agent of exploitation was a class of local landlords or the state bureaucracy.[78] There were important differences between them, particularly in terms of how the ruling classes organised, but most pre-capitalist societies seem to

---

74: James Allinson and Alex Anievas also have concerns with claims for the transhistorical nature of uneven and combined development, although for different reasons from those expressed here. See Allinson and Anievas, 2009, pp62-63.

75: Rosenberg, 2006, p321.

76: Rosenberg, 2006, pp321-325.

77: Marx and Engels, 1976, pp50-51.

78: Haldon, 1993, pp63-69; Wickham, 2005, pp57-61.

have involved elements of both, with one or the other achieving dominance at different times. Those cases which were the purest examples of one variant or the other (for example, feudal England or tributary China) had quite different possibilities for capitalist development. Until that development took place, however, societies could borrow from each other, influence one another—particularly in the field of culture and philosophy—but were not sufficiently differentiated from each other for elements to "combine" to any effect. The very terms that Trotsky uses in describing combination—"archaic and more contemporary forms"—were unthinkable until capitalism defined what it meant to be "archaic".[79]

We therefore need to draw a distinction between Trotsky's general account of Russian development, which, as Rosenberg correctly says, was always subject to external influence, and the specific moment at which these influences were not merely successfully absorbed into an endlessly mutating social form, but set up a series of tensions which threatened to, and eventually did, tear the fabric of Russian society apart in 1917. The moment of uneven and combined development, in other words, only arrives with capitalist industrialisation and the historically unique society to which it gave rise. The immense difference between industrial capitalism and previous modes of production meant that, from the moment the former was introduced, combination became *possible* in a way that it had not been hitherto; but the structural dynamism of industrial capitalism compared with previous modes of production also meant that combination became *inescapable*, as all aspects of existing society registered the impact on them, to differing degrees, of this radically new means of exploitation. "In contrast to the economic systems that preceded it," wrote Trotsky, "capitalism inherently and constantly aims at economic expansion, at the penetration of new territories, the conversion of self-sufficient provincial and national economies into a system of financial interrelationships".[80] Rosenberg himself notes that, "for Trotsky, capitalism did not just change the world: it actually changed the overall nature of historical change itself".[81] I think he has insufficiently incorporated this insight into his own work.

The second question is whether uneven and combined development is a process necessarily confined to individual states. Rosenberg argues that, for Trotsky, "'combined development' was a phenomenon not of individual societies alone, but of the evolving international social formation as a

---

79: Trotsky, 1977a, p28.
80: Trotsky, 1974b, p15.
81: Rosenberg, 2007, p456.

whole".[82] In a discussion of Marx's original plan for the structure of *Capital*, he further claims that if we "neglect the significance of uneven and combined development" at the level of those determinants which apply to all societies, then the result will ultimately be either economic reductionism or a version of Realist International Relations theory in which states appear as sovereign actors seeking—insofar as they are able—advantage and security within the global system.[83] Colin Barker has reached similar conclusions to Rosenberg, suggesting that an "extended" concept of uneven and combined development is implicit in Trotsky's own work, "Only from the angle of world economy, of the *combined development* of the different countries within it, do words like 'advanced' and 'archaic' have any meaning, as measures of *coercive comparison* within a larger system of competitive transactions".[84]

I have more sympathy with these arguments since, as I have argued above, uneven and combined development is produced by the impact of different aspects of the international capitalist system (economic competition, military rivalry and colonial rule) on the societies constitutive of it. It is important, however, not to confuse the *sources* of a particular historical process with the process itself. Trotsky famously wrote, "Marxism takes its point of departure from world economy, not as a sum of national parts, but as a mighty and independent reality which has been created by the international division of labour and the world market, and which in our epoch imperiously dominates the national markets".[85] Uneven and combined development is a consequence of the world economy, but it is played out within the component parts of the states system: the territorial confines of these states are where the specific combinations take place. Indeed, it is difficult to see how any analysis of a "concrete situation" can be undertaken while remaining at the level of "the international". If the writers quoted in the previous paragraph are right, and what happened in Russia was merely an example of a universal process, then what remains of the "peculiarities" of Russian development which Trotsky took as the basis of his theory, and which he later extended to other areas of the colonial and semi-colonial world? If everywhere is subject to uneven and combined development then it clearly explains nothing in particular about Russia, or anywhere else for that matter, and we must search for another theory to achieve what Trotsky sought to do.

Uneven and combined development is a feature of certain societies:

82: Rosenberg, 2005, p41.
83: Callinicos and Rosenberg, 2008, p99.
84: Barker, 2006, p78. See also Allinson and Anievas, 2009, p54.
85: Trotsky, 1969b, p146.

unlike the world economy of which Trotsky spoke or the states system, whose interaction gave it birth; it does not constitute "an independent reality" greater than its component parts. Uneven development occurs at the international level, but it is meaningless to talk about combined development in this respect. The significance of the process is precisely the tensions and conflicts to which it gives rise within the territorial boundaries of particular states, not least because the state itself is a combined formation. In Russia after 1861, for example, the state apparatus remained staffed by members of the landed aristocracy, but these were not, as in England after 1688 and Germany after 1871, essentially agrarian capitalists, but feudal landlords presiding over a complex set of class relationships in various early stages to the transition to capitalism. The absolutist state nevertheless needed to industrialise in order to remain on a position of military parity with its rivals, but the reliance that it placed on the landlord class meant that industrialisation could not be financed through taxation or by using the appropriation of agricultural surpluses. This in turn compelled the state to borrow foreign capital, above all from France, with contradictory effect. Industrialisation took place rapidly and intensively, but without leading to the creation of a powerful native bourgeoisie. In order to sustain it the state needed to export grain in order to service its foreign debt repayments, leading, as grain prices fell, to greater pressure on the peasantry to deliver more grain without providing them with the means to increase productivity, thus leading to growing peasant unrest. And since industrialisation effectively coincided with the transition to capitalism, the proletariat was formed without intermediary stages, making it more volatile from the start, in a situation where the state could afford less in terms of making concessions over wages, conditions or political rights.[86]

Trotsky, who emphasised more than any of his contemporaries the reality of the world economy, was also the thinker who refocused attention from "the international" in general to its impact on individual nation-states. He never faltered in his belief that the socialist revolution could only ever be accomplished on a global basis, but was equally forceful in arguing that the strategies adopted by revolutionaries outside the developed West had to be based on an assessment of the extent of combined development and the specific forms which it took.

We can now return to the central absence in Cliff's revision of Trotsky. The theory of uneven and combined development explained what occurs when the process of "overleaping" takes place in the colonial or neo-colonial world, where it is impossible to fully "catch up" with, let

---

86: Looker and Coates, 1986, pp112-113; Schwartz, 2000, pp95-96.

alone "overtake" the developed West, but to do so instead in a fragmentary or partial way. But the resulting combined forms, because of their inbuilt social instability, paradoxically made revolutionary outbreaks more likely than in the developed world, with its greater levels of stability and reformist traditions. In other words, the presence of uneven and combined development made it possible for a strategy of permanent revolution to be pursued with greater likelihood of success; its absence made it, not inevitable, but less likely that such a strategy would be pursued in the first place, thus leading to the process of "deflection" highlighted by Cliff.

Conclusion

Permanent revolution, and consequently deflected permanent revolution may now be historical concepts, but uneven and combined development is not, with important implications for the possibility of socialist revolution beginning in the Global South. Following Trotsky, Tim McDaniel argues that there were four reasons why what he calls the "autocratic capitalism" of Tsarist Russia tended to produce a revolutionary labour movement. First, it eliminated or reduced the distinction between economic and political issues. Second, it generated opposition for both traditional and modern reasons. Third, it reduced the fragmentation of the working class, but also prevented the formation of a stable conservative bureaucracy, thus leading to more radical attitudes. Fourth, it forced a degree of interdependence between the mass of the working class, class-conscious workers and revolutionary intellectuals.[87] McDaniel claims that a comparable situation has arisen since only in Iran, but this seems to unnecessarily restrict the applicability of the model to situations which resemble pre-Revolutionary Russia closely in formal terms.[88] In fact, the relentless expansion of neoliberal globalisation, and the consequent irruption of industrialisation and urbanisation into areas they had previously bypassed, often under conditions of intense state repression, means that the responses identified by McDaniel are being reproduced places as distinct as China and Dubai.[89] But these are only the most extreme examples of a general trend that is the most characteristic of the current phase of capitalist development. Two points need to be made in relation to the process.

87: McDaniel, 1988, pp41-47.

88: McDaniel, 1988, p407.

89: Davis, 2007, pp53-54. Indeed, in the case of China, it might be said that the neoliberal turn after 1978 actually resumed the process of uneven and combined development originally detected by Trotsky in the 1920s, which had been consciously halted by a Maoist leadership only too conscious of the explosive effects of uncontrolled urban expansion. See Davidson, 2006, pp214-222.

One is that it is not limited to the Global South, but to the relatively undeveloped parts of the First and former Second Worlds. As Beverley Silver writes:

> Strong new working class movements had been created as a combined result of the spatial fixes pursued by multinational capital and the import substitution industrialisation efforts of modernising states. In some cases, like Brazil's automobile workers; labour militancy was rooted in the newly expanding mass production consumer durable industries. In other cases, like the rise of Solidarność in Poland's shipyards, militancy was centred in gigantic establishments providing capital goods. In still others, like Iran's oil workers, labour militancy was centred on critical natural resource export industries.[90]

Take, for example, the Italian Mezzogiorno, where Italian unification was followed by a pronounced process of deindustrialisation, which led to a steady drain of capital to the North, with a long-term reservoir of cheap labour-power, cheap agricultural products and a docile clientele in the South; here the process of uneven and combined development led to similarly high levels of militancy to that seen in countries characterised by more general backwardness, the key episode being the revolt of the Italian in-migrants against their living conditions and low pay during the "industrial miracle" of the late 50s and early 60s. What is interesting about the Italian example, however, is that the process has continued, in different forms until the present day.[91]

The second point to be made is that, in the Global South proper at least, the process is still unable completely to transform those societies. The state "containers" within which the process of uneven and combined development unfolds, including China, will never achieve the type of total transformation characteristic of the states that formed the original core of the capitalist world system, at least in any foreseeable timescale. One intelligent conservative commentator, Edward Luttwak, has referred to "the perils of incomplete imitation" whereby developing world ruling classes "have been importing a dangerously unstable version of American turbo-capitalism, because the formula is incomplete". What is missing? On the one hand, the legal regulation to control what he calls "the overpowering strength of big business", and on the other, the internal humility of the winners and

---

90: Silver, 2003, p164.
91: Ginsborg, 1990, pp223-9, 47-53; Hardt and Negri, 2000, pp287-289.

acceptance of the essential justice of their personal situation by the losers from the system.[92] Uneven and combined development is therefore likely to be an ongoing process, which will only be resolved by either revolution or disintegration. But in the meantime, China and other states like India and Brazil where growth has been less dramatic remain both inherently unstable in their internal social relations and expansive in their external search for markets, raw materials and investment opportunities. It is in this inherent instability that the possibilities for permanent revolution lie. This does not mean that wherever uneven and combined development exists today the working class movement will automatically adopt what Trotsky called the "boldest conclusions of revolutionary thought". In circumstances where Marxist ideas (and those of secular radicalism more generally) are either unavailable or discredited after the experience of Stalinism, movements will reach for whatever ideas seem to assist them in their struggle, regardless of their antiquity—but they will transform them in the process, contrary to what is asserted to the contrary by reactionaries in the West.

The late Fred Halliday once expressed his own disillusionment after the fall of the Soviet Empire, rejecting the revolutionary possibilities of uneven and combined development:

> The insight of Trotsky was that of locating the history, and revolution of any one country in a broader, contradictory context, in seeing how ideas, and forms of conflict, like forms of technology or economic activity, could be transposed to contexts very different from that in which they originated. The mistake of the Marxist approach was to conclude that, in the end, the combination would prevail over the unevenness. The unevenness, evident above all in the widening income gaps between rich and poor on a world scale, has continued to grow, and is replicated dramatically in an era of capitalist globalisation. But because of the fragmentary character of states, the spatial and political distributor of that unevenness, the combination, *the world revolutionary cataclysm*, did not occur.[93]

To this we reply: combination is not "the world revolutionary cataclysm", it is the objective enabling condition for it to take place. And if the cataclysm has not yet occurred, this is largely because of the absence of the missing subjective condition, which Trotsky recognised in 1917, and which Cliff highlighted back in the 1960s: the revolutionary organisation

---

92: Luttwak, 1998, pp25-26.
93: Halliday, 1999, pp320-321.

capable of giving focus to the social explosions which the process of uneven and combined development brings in its wake. In that respect, whatever else may have changed since both men wrote, the necessity for the party remains, if the incredible energies unleashed by uneven and combined development are not to be wasted yet again, with terrible consequences for the world and those who live in it.

References

Acemoglu, Daron, and James Robinson, 2000, "Why Did the West Extend the Franchise? Democracy, Inequality, and Growth in Historical Perspective", *Quarterly Journal of Economics*, www.people.fas.harvard.edu/~jrobins/researchpapers/publishedpapers/jr_west.pdf

Allinson, Jamie, and Alexander Anievas, 2009, "The Uses and Misuses of Uneven and Combined Development: an Anatomy of a Concept", *Cambridge Review of International Affairs*, volume 22.

Anderson, Perry, 1992 [1976], "The Notion of a Bourgeois Revolution", in *English Questions* (Verso).

Anievas, Alexander (ed), 2010, *Marxism and World Politics: Contesting Global Capitalism* (Routledge).

Barker, Colin, 2006, "Beyond Trotsky: Extending Combined and Uneven Development", in Dunn and Radice (eds), *100 years of Permanent Revolution: Results and Prospects* (Pluto).

Bayly, Christopher, 2004, *The Birth of the Modern World, 1780—1914: Global Connections and Comparisons* (Blackwell).

Burawoy, Michael, 1985, *The Politics of Production: Factory Regimes under Capitalism and Socialism* (Verso).

Callinicos, Alex, 1982, "Trotsky's Theory of 'Permanent Revolution' and its Relevance to the Third World Today", *International Socialism* 16 (spring).

Callinicos, Alex, 1989, "Bourgeois Revolutions and Historical Materialism", *International Socialism 43* (summer).

Callinicos, Alex, and Justin Rosenberg, 2008, "Uneven and Combined Development: the Social-relational Substratum of 'the International'? An Exchange of Letters', *Cambridge Review of International Affairs*, volume 21.

Cannadine, David, 1983, "The Context, Performance and Meaning of Ritual: the British Monarchy and the 'Invention of Tradition', circa 1820—1977", in Eric Hobsbawm and Terence Ranger (eds), *The Invention of Tradition* (Cambridge University Press).

Cliff, Tony, 1984 [1950], "The Class Nature of the People's Democracies", in *Neither Washington nor Moscow: Essays on Revolutionary Socialism* (Bookmarks), www.marxists.org/archive/cliff/works/1950/07/index.htm

Cliff, Tony, 1989, *Trotsky*, volume 1, *Towards October, 1879-1917* (Bookmarks).

Cliff, Tony, 1993, *Trotsky*, volume 4, *the Darker the Night the Brighter the Star, 1927-1940* (Bookmarks).

Cliff, Tony, 2000, *A World to Win: Life of a Revolutionary* (Bookmarks).

Cliff, Tony, 2003 [1963], "Permanent Revolution", in *Marxist Theory after Trotsky, Selected Works*, volume 3 (Bookmarks), www.marxists.org/archive/cliff/works/1963/xx/permrev.htm

Curtin, Peter, 2000, *The World and the West: the European Challenge and the Overseas Response in the Age of Empire* (Cambridge University).

Davidson, Neil, 2005, "How Revolutionary Were the Bourgeois Revolutions? Continued", *Historical Materialism*, volume 13.

Davidson, Neil, 2006a, "From Uneven to Combined Development", in Dunn and Radice (eds), *100 years of Permanent Revolution: Results and Prospects* (Pluto).

Davidson, Neil, 2006b, "China: Unevenness, Combination, Revolution?", in Dunn and Radice (eds), *100 years of Permanent Revolution: Results and Prospects* (Pluto).

Davidson, Neil, 2009, "Putting the Nation back into the 'International'", *Cambridge Review of International Affairs*, volume 22, number. 1.

Davidson, Neil, forthcoming in 2011a, *How Revolutionary Were the Bourgeois Revolutions?* (Haymarket).

Davidson, Neil, forthcoming in 2011b, *Violating all the Laws of History* (EJ Brill).

Davis, Mike, 2007, "Sand, Fear and Money in Dubai", in Mike Davis and Daniel Bertrand Monk (eds), *Evil Paradises: Dreamworlds of Neoliberalism* (Verso).

Day, Richard and Daniel Gaido, "Introduction", in *Witnesses to Permanent Revolution: the Documentary Record* (EJ Brill).

Draper, Hal, 1978. *Karl Marx's Theory of Revolution*, volume 2, *the Politics of Social Classes* (Monthly Review Press).

Dunn, Bill and Hugo Radice (eds), 2006, *100 years of Permanent Revolution: Results and Prospects* (Pluto).

Gatrell, Peter, 1994, *Government, Industry and Rearmament in Russia, 1900-1914* (Cambridge University).

Gerschenkron, Alexander, 1962, *Economic Backwardness in Historical Perspective* (Harvard University).

Geras, Norman, 1976, "Between the Russian Revolutions", in *The Legacy of Rosa Luxemburg* (New Left Books).

Ginsborg, Paul, 1990, *A History of Contemporary Italy: Society and Politics, 1943-1988* (Penguin).

Gowan, Peter, 1999, *The Global Gamble: Washington's Faustian Bid for World Dominance* (Verso).

Haldon, John, 1993, *The State and the Tributary Mode of Production* (Verso).

Halliday, Fred, 1999, *Revolution and World Politics: the Rise and Fall of the Sixth Great Power* (Macmillan).

Halliday, Fred, and Maxine Molyneux, 1981, *The Ethiopian Revolution* (Verso).

Hardt, Michael and Antonio Negri, 2000, *Empire* (Harvard University).

Harman, Chris, 1990, "The Storm Breaks", *International Socialism 46* (spring), www.marxists.org/archive/harman/1990/xx/stormbreaks.html

Harman, Chris, 2010 (1994), "The Prophet and the Proletariat", in *Selected Writings* (Bookmarks), www.marxists.de/religion/harman/

Harris, Nigel, 1978, *The Mandate of Heaven: Marx and Mao in Modern China* (Quartet).

Hobsbawm, Eric, 1975, *The Age of Capital, 1848-1873* (Weidenfeld and Nicolson).

Koenker, Diane, and William Rosenberg, 1989, *Strikes and Revolution in Russia, 1917* (Princeton University Press).

Larsson, Reidar, 1970, *Theories of Revolution: from Marx to the First Russian Revolution* (Almquist and Wiksell).

Lenin, Vladimir, 1960 [1899], *The Development of Capitalism in Russia*, in *Collected Works*, volume 3 (Foreign Languages Publishing House), www.marxists.org/archive/lenin/works/cw/volume03.htm

Lenin, Vladimir, 1964 [1916], *Imperialism, the Highest Stage of Capitalism: a Popular Outline*, in *Collected Works*, volume 22 (Foreign Languages Publishing House), www.marxists.org/archive/lenin/works/1916/imp-hsc/index.htm

Looker, Robert, and David Coates, 1986, "The State and the Working Class", in James Anderson (ed), *The Rise of the Modern State* (Harvester).

Löwy, Michael, 1981, *The Politics of Combined and Uneven Development: the Theory of Permanent Revolution* (Verso).

Lukács, Georg, 1970, *Lenin: a Study in the Unity of his Thought* (New Left Books), www.marxists.org/archive/lukacs/works/1924/lenin/index.htm

Luttwak, Edward, 1998, *Turbo-capitalism: Winners and Losers in the Global Economy* (Weidenfeld and Nicolson).

Luxemburg, Rosa, 2003 [1896], "Social Democracy and the National Struggles in Turkey", *Revolutionary History*, volume 8, number 3, *The Balkan Socialist Tradition and the Balkan Federation, 1871-1915*, www.marxists.org/archive/luxemburg/1896/10/10.htm

MacIntyre, Alasdair, 2008 [1963], "Trotsky in Exile", in *Alasdair MacIntyre's Engagement with*

Marxism: Selected Writings, 1953-1974, edited by Paul Blackledge and Neil Davidson (EJ Brill).

Mandel, Ernest, 1995, *Trotsky as Alternative* (Verso).

Mann, Michael, 1993, *The Sources of Social Power*, volume 2, *the Rise of Classes and Nation-States, 1760-1914* (Cambridge University Press).

Marx, Karl, 1975 [1844], "Critical Notes on 'The King of Prussia and Social Reform. By a Prussian'", in *Early Writings* (Penguin/*New Left Review*), www.marxists.org/archive/marx/works/1844/08/07.htm

Marx, Karl and Frederick Engels, 1976 [1845—1846], *The German Ideology*, in *Collected Works*, volume 5 (Lawrence and Wishart), www.marxists.org/archive/marx/works/1845/german-ideology/ch01a.htm#p27

McDaniel, Tim, 1988, *Autocracy, Capitalism and Revolution in Russia* (University of California).

Pozo, Gonzalo, 2010, "Reassessing the Permanent Arms Economy", *International Socialism*, 127 (summer), www.isj.org.uk/?id=660

Rees, John, 1999, "The Democratic Revolution and the Socialist Revolution", *International Socialism 83* (summer), http://pubs.socialistreviewindex.org.uk/isj83/rees.htm

Rees, John, 2006, *Imperialism and Resistance* (Routledge).

Reiber, Alfred, 1982, *Merchants and Entrepreneurs in Imperial Russia* (University of North Carolina).

Rosenberg, Justin, 2005, "Globalisation Theory: a Post-Mortem", *International Politics*, volume 42, number 1.

Rosenberg, Justin, 2006, "Why is there No International Historical Sociology?" *European Journal of International Relations*, volume 12, number 3.

Rosenberg, Justin, 2007, "International Relations—the 'Higher Bullshit': a reply to the Globalisation Theory Debate", *International Politics*, volume 44, number 4.

Schneiderman, Jeremiah, 1976, *Sergei Zubatov and Revolutionary Marxism: the Struggle for the Working Class in Tsarist Russia* (Cornell University Press).

Schwartz, Herman, 2000, *States Versus Markets: the Emergence of a Global Economy*, second edition (Macmillan).

Silver, Beverley, 2003, *Forces of Labour: Workers' Movements and Globalisation since 1870* (Cambridge University).

Smith, Neil, 1990 [1984], *Uneven Development: Nature, Capital and the Production of Space* (Blackwell).

Therborn, Goran, 1977, "The Rule of Capital and the Rise of Democracy", *New Left Review* I/103.

Treblicock, Clive, 1981, *The Industrialisation of the Continental Powers, 1780-1914* (Longmans).

Trimberger, Ellen Kay, 1978, *Revolution from Above: Military Bureaucrats and Development in Japan, Turkey, Egypt and Peru* (Transaction Books).

Trotsky, Leon, 1937, *The Revolution Betrayed: What is the Soviet Union and where is it going?* (Monad), www.marxists.org/archive/trotsky/1936/revbet/index.htm

Trotsky, Leon 1969a [1906], *Results and Prospects*, in *The Permanent Revolution & Results and Prospects* (Pathfinder), www.marxists.org/archive/trotsky/1931/tpr/rp04.htm and www.marxists.org/archive/trotsky/1931/tpr/rp08.htm

Trotsky, Leon 1969b [1929/30], *Permanent Revolution*, in *The Permanent Revolution & Results and Prospects* (Pathfinder), www.marxists.org/archive/trotsky/1931/tpr/index.htm

Trotsky, Leon, 1970 [1937], "Ninety Years of the Communist Manifesto", *Writings of Leon Trotsky [1937-38]*, edited by Naomi Allen and George Breitman (Pathfinder).

Trotsky, Leon, 1972a [1924], "For the Internationalist Perspective", in *Leon Trotsky Speaks* (Pathfinder).

Trotsky, Leon 1972b [1932], "In Defence of the Russian Revolution", in *Leon Trotsky Speaks* (Pathfinder), www.marxists.org/archive/trotsky/1932/11/oct.htm

Trotsky, Leon, 1972c [1933], "Japan Heads for Disaster" In *Writings of Leon Trotsky [1932-33]*. (Pathfinder).

Trotsky, Leon, 1974a, "Can a Counter-Revolution or a Revolution Be Made on Schedule?" In *The First Five Years of the Communist International*, volume 2 (New Park), www.marxists.org/archive/trotsky/1924/ffyci-2/25c.htm

Trotsky, Leon, 1974b [1928], "The Draft Programme of the Communist International—a Critique of Fundamentals", in *The Third International after Lenin* (New Park), www.marxists.org/archive/trotsky/1928/3rd/index.htm

Trotsky, Leon, 1976, *Leon Trotsky on China* (Monad).

Trotsky, Leon, 1976a [1928], "Summary and Perspectives of the Chinese Revolution", in Trotsky, 1976, *Leon Trotsky on China* (Monad), www.marxists.org/archive/trotsky/1928/3rd/ti09.htm#p3-03

Trotsky, Leon, 1976b [1928], "The Chinese Question after the Sixth Congress", in Trotsky, *Leon Trotsky on China* (Monad), www.marxists.org/archive/trotsky/1932/pcr/08.htm

Trotsky, Leon, 1976c [1938], "Revolution and War in China", in Trotsky, *Leon Trotsky on China* (Monad), www.marxists.org/archive/trotsky/1938/xx/china.htm

Trotsky, Leon 1977a [1932-3], *The History of the Russian Revolution* (Pluto), www.marxists.org/archive/trotsky/1930/hrr/ch01.htm

Trotsky, Leon, 1977b [1938], "The Death Agony of Capitalism and the Tasks of the Fourth International", in *The Transitional Program for Socialist Revolution* (Pathfinder), www.marxists.org/archive/trotsky/1938/tp/index.htm

Trotsky, Leon, 1979, *Writings of Leon Trotsky Supplement (1934-40)* (Pathfinder).

Trotsky, Leon, 1979a [1938], "Latin American Problems: a Transcript", in Trotsky, 1979, *Writings of Leon Trotsky Supplement (1934-40)* (Pathfinder).

Trotsky, Leon, 1979b [1940], "A Serious Work on Russian Revolutionary History", in Trotsky, *Writings of Leon Trotsky Supplement (1934-40)* (Pathfinder).

Trotsky, Leon, 1980 [1923], "The New Course", in *The Challenge of the Left Opposition (1923-25)* (Pathfinder), www.marxists.org/archive/trotsky/1923/newcourse/ch06.htm

Trotsky, Leon, 1994 [1924], "Radio, Science, Technology and Society", in *Problems of Everyday Life: Creating the Foundations for a New Society in Revolutionary Russia* (Pathfinder).

Zeilig, Leo, 2007, *Revolt and Protest: Student Politics and Activism in Sub-Saharan Africa* (I B Tauris).

Zeilig, Leo, 2008, *Lumumba: Africa's Lost Leader* (Haus).

Zeilig, Leo, 2009, *Class Struggle and Resistance in Africa* (Haymarket).

Zeilig, Leo, 2010, "Tony Cliff: Deflected Permanent Revolution in Africa", *International Socialism 126* (spring 2010), www.isj.org.uk/?id=641

Wickham, Chris, 2005, *Framing the Early Middle Ages: Europe and the Mediterranean, 400—800* (Oxford University Press).

Žižek, Slavoj, 2002, "Afterword: Lenin's Choice", in Vladimir Lenin, *Revolution at the Gates: a Selection of Writings from February to October 1917*, edited by Slavoj Žižek (Verso).

Socialism in the 21st century and the Russian Revolution

Simon Pirani

My book *The Russian Revolution in Retreat* will not "resonate with the tens of thousands of young people now open to socialist ideas", according to Kevin Murphy's negative review in *International Socialism 126*.[1] I hope he's wrong. In my experience, many young people who want to subvert and supersede capitalism in the 21st century read widely and think hard. Above all they want the truth. Often they study our history sceptically, not only to uncover stories of social movements that our enemies try to hide, but also to understand socialism's failures and to question authoritarian "socialist" orthodoxies.

The least that socialist historians of the Russian Revolution can do is to present information accurately and develop arguments and explanations on that basis. My book focused on a narrow time and space—Moscow between the end of the civil war in 1920 and Stalin's arrival in the Bolshevik leadership in 1924—and sought to draw conclusions about broader questions, including the changing political relationship between workers and the Bolsheviks who claimed to rule in their name. Kevin doesn't like these conclusions, but I think they work better than his backward-looking orthodoxy.

I argued that by 1924 the Bolsheviks had, essentially, politically expropriated the working class, ie pushed it out of the participatory decision-making central to my idea of movements towards socialism. "The

---

1:    Murphy, 2010, p204.

Bolsheviks' vanguardism and statism made them blind to the creative potential of democratic workers' organisations, intolerant of other working class political forces and ruthless in silencing dissent," I wrote.[2]

In the early years of the New Economic Policy (NEP), ie from 1921, this political expropriation was implemented not "simply by repression": the Bolsheviks effectively struck a deal with the majority of workers, that the party would ensure a steady rise in living standards, provided that workers raised productivity and kept out of political decision-making.[3] I argued that, while the "rolling-back of socialist aspects of the revolution, and the advance of Stalinism, were conditioned by many powerful factors over which the Bolsheviks had no control", such as the European workers' movements' failure to produce revolutionary change elsewhere, "perhaps different choices in 1921 would have made possible different types of resistance to the reimposition of exploitative class relations and the establishment of dictatorship".[4]

Kevin claims that I painted too negative a picture of the revolution's reversal. During the NEP (ie up to 1928), he writes, "Soviet workers continued to exercise control in production and the state instituted policies and legislation to defend workers and promote their self-organisation in factory committees, trade unions and the 700,000 strong proletarian women's movement".[5] Certainly the Bolsheviks passed laws on such vital issues as living standards, hours, health and safety, women's rights to divorce and abortion, education, etc. But workers' "control in production"? Really? Were the organisations that Russian workers had in 1917 believed would control production—soviets, trade unions and factory committees—doing so in the 1920s?

Take the soviets. They flowered in 1917 and weakened during the civil war. The first post-war soviet elections in 1921 were seen as an opportunity to rebuild. I described in my book how in Moscow this opportunity was missed, largely because the Bolsheviks rejected overtures of cooperation from a substantial non-party workers' grouping that won mandates from most big factories.[6] Reading the soviet's verbatim minutes and reports of its activity, I learned how, after the Bolsheviks spurned the non-party groups' proposals, live discussions gave way to formulaic speeches, resolutions were passed without amendment or discussion, and non-Bolshevik soviet delegates were victimised. I concluded that the

---

2:   Pirani, 2008, p235.
3:   Pirani, 2008, p235.
4:   Pirani, 2008, pp240-241.
5:   Murphy, 2010, p198.
6:   Pirani, 2008, pp96-107.

soviet became a "lifeless institution": Kevin admits this "may very well be the case", but then complains that I presented it as an "a priori assumption". [7] I didn't. I gave copious evidence.★ [8]

Kevin adds that in 1928 workers used the Ivanovo soviet to "lambast the regime's policy".[9] It's an inspiring story, but not relevant to the issue here, ie whether workers could use the soviets to shape their future, as they tried to do in 1917-18. While in 1921 there may have been an opportunity to revive such participatory democracy, by 1922-23 it had gone. To talk, as Kevin does, of workers having "control in production" after that date is meaningless.

What about unions? I argued that they were "emasculated", ie that power was stripped from the unions as "fora in which working-class collective political activity might develop".[10] Of course much damage had been done long before the period I researched—by the Bolshevik rejection from 1918 of all proposals for union and factory committee involvement in management, the economic catastrophe caused by war, and other factors. I began my research wondering about the extent to which workplace *political* activity—and not merely trade union activity directed at improving wages and conditions—revived after the civil war.

I invite readers to ignore Kevin's unsubstantiated claims that my research of factory committees was "scanty" and that I ignored the women's movement,★ and read my detailed accounts of changing workplace relationships, strikes, unemployed workers' actions, etc.[11] I found evidence that by 1922 bureaucratised unions routinely opposed strikes; had more unelected officials than elected ones; worked together with party and government to discipline and punish strike organisers; and became, despite some Bolsheviks' efforts to avoid it, heavily reliant on state funding. I concluded that unions had become dependent on the state and factory committees were getting integrated into management, in the context of the "social contract" described above.

Kevin writes that, as wages and conditions improved in the mid-1920s, workers customarily used official arbitration procedures, and that the Hammer and Sickle factory director complained the union was running the shops. OK. But how can he deduce from this that factory committees

---

7:   Murphy, 2010, p201.
8:   ★ indicates issues on which I have posted more detailed responses at www.revolutioninretreat.com/isjreply.pdf
9:   Murphy, 2010, pp201-202.
10:   Pirani, 2008, p155.
11:   Murphy, 2010, p200.

and women's organisations were "strengthened" or had "control"?[12] It all depends on what you mean by "strength" and "control".

For sure, as the economy revived, factory committees usually became better organised and better placed to negotiate with management. But *politically* the unions never returned to the vitality of 1917-18. The idea that factory-level organisations would participate in *political* decisions about the republic's future, or even strategic *management* decisions, was abandoned. On industrial issues, while workers could indeed use official procedures to change some things at factory level, they were largely deprived of the crucial weapons of striking, solidarity action and independent union organisation. And women's organisations were subject to two provisos: they had to be dominated by the Bolshevik Party, and they excluded women who lost their jobs (women were almost always laid off before men were).★ [13]

My disagreements with Kevin are not only about history, but about the movement to socialism. He thinks the limited concessions overseen by corporatist union structures were more important than the silencing of worker dissent and political "emasculation" of unions. I think the opposite.

What matters to me is that, by effectively outlawing dissent and binding the unions to the state, the Bolsheviks damaged working class creativity and political participation—notwithstanding their success, like various European social democratic parties, in improving living standards. Worse still, they claimed they were acting as "communists", helping to imbue swathes of the workers' movement internationally with ideas about a transition to "communism" via "leadership", a strong state, outdoing capitalism with industrial productivity, necessary sacrifice, etc. Sight was almost completely lost of ideas of a transition that supersedes alienation and alienated labour, that requires collective social participation, and that produces "mass communist consciousness" (Marx).

Socialists need to study all this, both to understand how our predecessors' emancipatory strivings were crushed, and to negate the aspects of their ideological legacy that pull us backward. That was my motivation for writing my book. During more than 20 years in a Trotskyist organisation, I used to see socialism as something that would use the Russian experience as a model. Now I think it's more complicated, and I hope readers will also aim for a more complicated view. The model needs to be taken apart and analysed to understand why it crashed.

For Kevin, things are simpler: socialist historians are pitted against

---

12: Murphy, 2010, pp200-201.
13: Pirani, 2008, pp161-162.

a "liberal" consensus united in a "mission...to connect the dots between 1917 and Stalinism"—in large part an amalgam he has dreamt up—and his complacent, two-dimensional task is to reiterate the Bolsheviks' positive achievements against their detractors.[14]

For example, in 1918 Lenin called the Soviet state a "workers' state with bureaucratic distortions". Kevin says that up to 1927-28 "the 'workers' state' part of Lenin's formulation...persisted", along with the "bureaucratic distortions".[15] For me, the "workers' state" is a cover-all formula that masks the very problems that need unpicking: the (inevitably) alienated character of wage labour in the Soviet state; the proliferation of forms of hierarchy and authoritarianism on the basis of this alienated labour, even in the absence of a recognisable ruling class; and the way that the Bolsheviks deceived themselves and many others that their control over the state gave it a "proletarian" character.

"The crucial question", Kevin writes, "was whether or not the working class could increase its authority on the 'bureaucratically deformed workers' state'."[16] I do not agree. To define problems in terms of the working class competing for "authority" in the state means to start from the wrong place. We need to understand socialism as the overturning and surpassing by the working class of all authority and all statehood, together with the social relations of production on which they are based.

Here much of the history of the Russian Revolution—not because of the people involved but because of the circumstances—can only provide mostly negative examples. "While Marx and Engels had envisaged that socialism would involve a movement towards a public power that supersedes politics, ie a negation of, an overcoming of, the state, the movement in Russia during and after the civil war was mainly in the opposite direction".[17]

Finally, Kevin's two-dimensional desire to defend the Bolsheviks ties him up in knots on the issue of repression. He rails against the "myth of early Soviet repression against striking workers".★ [18] What does he mean, "myth"? Didn't it happen? What about key turning points in the Soviet state's evolution, such as the repression of the Emergency Assembly of Factory Committees in Petrograd in 1918 or of non-Bolshevik soviets during the civil war? During the NEP repressive practices included the arrest, sacking and ostracising of strike leaders, and widespread arrests

---

14: Murphy, 2010, p197.
15: Murphy, 2010, p198.
16: Murphy, 2010, p202.
17: Pirani, 2008, p233.
18: Murphy, 2010, p199.

of members of non-Bolshevik, pro-soviet groups (Workers Truth, the Workers Group, anarchists, Left Socialist Revolutionaries, etc)—not to mention the suppression of the Kronstadt uprising. This forcible shutting up of political opponents was integral to the Bolshevik relationship with workers. It surely did not feel "mythical" at the time.

Kevin partly excuses Bolshevik repression on the grounds that its targets were anti-soviet. But many were not. He makes a telling mistake by claiming derisively that the Workers Truth group, formed by Red Army veterans who risked their necks to defend Soviet power, "argued for the overthrow of Soviet power".[19] They did not. Isn't it time, 90 years later, to abandon the sectarian Bolshevik mantra that "he who isn't with us is against us"?

Kevin's other argument is that repression in the 1920s was on a smaller scale than in the 1930s. He writes that "the entire Soviet prison population only exceeded 100,000 in 1925, with no more than a few thousand political prisoners".[20] In fact, prisoner numbers were probably significantly higher than he suggests—and there were shootings, too, which Kevin doesn't mention.* But the real problem is in Kevin's implication that, since the Bolsheviks jailed fewer people than Stalin's nightmarish dictatorship, they cannot have been such a bad bunch. I approach this issue differently.

What is important about the Bolsheviks' usually (but not always) careful, forensic repression of dissent, which concentrated on singling out activists—and, of course, had many, many times fewer victims than Stalin's— is that it disarmed the working class as a fighting force. It fitted with the Bolshevik world view, which by the mid-1920s vested hopes in the state, and abandoned in practice any sense that the working class was the motive force of history. By that time they were in a dead end. Let's not follow them.

References

Murphy, Kevin, 2010, "Conceding the Russian Revolution to the Liberals", *International Socialism* 126 (spring), www.isj.org.uk/?id=643

Pirani, Simon, 2008, *The Russian Revolution in Retreat, 1920-24: Soviet Workers and the New Communist Elite* (Routledge).

19: Murphy, 2010, p199.
20: Murphy, 2010, p199.

Sexism and sex work:
A response to Dale and Whittaker

Jess Edwards

The previous issue of this journal carried an article by Gareth Dale and Xanthe Whittaker arguing that sex work is fundamentally the same as other forms of wage labour in capitalist society.[1] They argue that the primary response of revolutionary socialists to the growth of the sex industry should be to organise sex workers in their workplaces and fight for unionisation. They point to the work of the International Union of Sex Workers (IUSW), now a branch of the GMB union in Britain.

Dale and Whittaker seem to be, at best, ambiguous in their opposition to the sex industry. They are led to this position because their article reduces the question of sex work to that of economic exploitation. Their arguments misrepresent and misunderstand the role of women's oppression and how this relates to sex work.

Jane Pritchard's original article,[2] to which Dale and Whittaker were replying, rightly argued that Marxists have a unique position in a debate that is largely polarised between abolitionist feminists (who want to see sex work abolished by law) and feminists who argue for the unionisation of sex workers. We seek to combine a fight against an oppressive industry with supporting the rights of those people working within it.

1: Dale and Whittaker, 2010, p187.
2: Pritchard, 2010.

Oppression and exploitation

Throughout their article Dale and Whittaker emphasise the economics of sex work at the expense of its political aspects. Sex workers, they argue, sell their labour power in the same way as other workers in capitalist society. They quote one sex worker who describes her work as producing "assembly line orgasms" and as being "repetitive manual labour".[3] Take a minute to think about the reality of being the producer of "assembly line orgasms". Could this "repetitive manual labour" be the reason why 68 percent of prostitutes suffer from post-traumatic stress disorder?[4]

Limiting the debate to the labour process misses the central point: that sex work is a product of women's oppression, the roots of which are located in the rise of the family within class society. Capitalism's need for labour power to be privately reproduced in the home, and the corresponding ideology that perpetuates the family as a norm, gives rise to alienated relationships between men and women where sex and sexuality is distorted and degraded. That is why the Russian revolutionary Alexandra Kollontai described prostitution as "the shadow of the family".[5]

Dale and Whittaker tend to present women's oppression as an external force that merely conditions how work takes place in the sex industry. For instance, they argue that oppression is a factor that undermines the conditions that sex work takes place under.[6] They also say that "the sex industry is overtly involved in women's oppression as are the advertising and fashion industries. Conversely, women's oppression is involved in sex work".[7] But oppression is not separate from and external to sex work. It is part of the explanation for sex work. The industry further reinforces sexism in wider society, helping to shape how men and women view themselves and each other. This is why we cannot simply have a trade union response. The "raunch culture" of the modern sex industry affects all women and men in society.[8] Faced with a rise in sexism, surely we must have more to say about sex work than "Organise the sex workers".

Dale and Whittaker's reductionism leads them to compare sex work to other forms of employment in which large numbers of women are involved such as nursing and social work. They argue that sex work "belongs to a category of high-touch, personal-interaction service work

---

3: Dale and Whittaker, 2010, pp184-185.
4: Quoted in Baryard, 2010, p141.
5: Kollontai, 1921.
6: Dale and Whittaker, 2010, p188.
7: Dale and Whittaker, 2010, p185.
8: Levi, 2005.

that is associated with care and/or desire, and as such is coded as naturally women's work and held in low regard".[9]

If this were the case, why would anyone on the left oppose the sex industry and not also oppose the NHS? Jobs in the health service are shaped by women's oppression—they are seen as caring professions that are better suited to women, and nursing in particular is badly paid as a result. But these areas of work are not in themselves products of women's oppression in the way that sex work is. A socialist society would still involve health-care. It would not involve sex work.

Equating sex work with care work suggests a further logical conclusion: that the sex industry performs a socially useful function. For example, the organisation TLC for Disabled People[10] argues on its website, "Sex workers not only bring joy into the world, but also rescue disabled people from personal anguish, sexual purgatory, and touch deprivation. (Keen to register as a sex worker? Just go to the Profiles section of the site.)"[11]

But Whittaker and Dale seem to go even further than seeing sex work as socially useful. They suggest that sex work represents a challenge to the institution of the family. They state that prostitution, rather than being the flip side of the family, actually represents "its negation".[12] They quote Sophie Day, who argues that the selling of sex "confounds the separation between a public economy and a private realm of socially significant relationships. In this view, the realm of the market is contaminated by women who live their lives in public, and the realm of the home is likewise threatened by the introduction of money and economic thinking".[13]

Do Dale and Whittaker hold this position—that sex work is not only a threat to the family but also to some of the fundamental structures of capitalist society? If so, then presumably socialists shoud be encouraging people to enter the sex industry. In fact, this is precisely what the IUSW does. Their website advertises the sex industry, giving advice for those wishing to start work as sex workers and advertising the "best" providers. The IUSW even goes as far as to have the bosses of those "good providers" as leading spokespeople of the union. Douglas Fox, owner of the Christony Companions Escort Agency, one of the largest escort agencies in Britain, is also a leading figure in IUSW. His agency website proudly carries the logo of the GMB.[14]

9:    Dale and Whittaker, 2010, p187.
10:   The IUSW provides a link on its website.
11:   www.tlc-trust.org.uk
12:   Dale and Whittaker, 2010, p189.
13:   Quoted in Dale and Whittaker, 2010, p189.
14:   http://toomuchtosayformyself.com/2009/01/09/the-great-iusw-con/

This is where a purely trade union response to the sex industry has led: a major national trade union advertising a company that rents out women by the hour. No socialist should support this.

Sex work is damaging

When discussing prostitution, Dale and Whittaker argue that "an individual's core identity—whatever it is—may well include their sexuality but surely cannot be capacious enough to include all sexual acts in which they engage". This approach risks falling into a postmodern pick and choose conception of identity. They seem to argue that how we "perceive" ourselves is the key.

They write that some sex workers "feel as though they are selling their selves" while others simply see it as selling services.[15] Is their claim that if some sex workers do not feel oppressed, then they are not? If a worker says that they do not "feel exploited" at work, does this mean that they are not exploited? Our analysis of sex work should not be based upon how some sex workers view their work. It must be based on concrete analysis of social and economic relationships.

Dale and Whittaker write that prostitutes are able to "deploy techniques that enable them to live in two bodies".[16] They present this as an argument for why prostitution is not damaging to people working as prostitutes. But the "splitting of the self", as they put it, must surely be a horrendous form of alienation, forced upon the sex worker through the degradation involved in their work, and not a positive coping strategy which protects the sex worker's "core being" from damage.

They write about how the men who use prostitutes are often "far from domineering" and they quote a sex worker who says, "The punters may be sad and inadequate but for the most part they are grateful and respectful." They also quote from a survey that found that most clients of sex workers are not derogatory about them. But whether sex work damages sex workers is not a question of how some of their clients view them. A man paying a woman for sex gets the things he pays for from the woman. The woman's own sexual desire is not taken into account because she is there purely to provide a service. It is this that governs the relationship between client and sex worker, not the level of politeness exercised by the former. Besides, it is not just for the individual sex worker that this relationship is damaging; the sale of sex as a commodity feeds into the general objectification of women in wider society.

15: Dale and Whittaker, 2010, p186.
16: Dale and Whittaker, 2010, p187.

How we fight today

Dale and Whittaker's arguments have serious implications for how we fight for liberation today. If a lap dancing club is set to open, should socialists oppose it on anti-sexist grounds or see it as a great opportunity for a unionisation campaign? Is it right or wrong for Job Centre Plus to advertise pole dancing jobs?

A political rather than a trade union approach would see socialists uniting with campaigners against women's oppression who want to stop the growth of Spearmint Rhino. A political approach would be to say that pole dancing should never be seen as a job to advertise to young unemployed women.

In seeking to avoid the normalisation of the sex industry we must, of course, be careful not to fall in behind the right wing moralists. It is absolutely right that sex work should not be criminalised, as this only makes the conditions that sex work takes place in more dangerous.[17] If some sex workers can organise to improve their conditions, then we should support this, as Pritchard makes clear in her original article. However, socialists must look beyond trade union concerns. This is not lining up with bourgeois moralists as Dale and Whittaker suggest.

Our ethics are guided by the fact that we want to end oppression and exploitation and create the world anew. To seek to organise sex workers at the expense of raising arguments against the sex industry does not help achieve that aim. It runs the risk of legitimising an industry that reinforces the oppression of women.

To take a firm stance against the existence of the sex industry is not, as Dale and Whittaker argue, to provide only "lukewarm" support for the women within that industry.[18] On the contrary, it is the best way of fighting for the rights of those women, as part of a fight for women's rights in general. To argue that we should prioritise organising sex workers, simply because they are workers, is to fall into a different kind of moralism, one which ignores political considerations.

We are fighting for a world where the notion that sex can be bought with money is an alien concept and where economic considerations are removed from sexual relationships. This would be a world where sexual relationships are prompted by nothing other than "the abandon of young love, or by fervent passion or by a blaze of physical attraction or by a soft

---

17: See, for instance, Choonara, 2008.
18: Dale and Whittaker, 2010, p184.

light of intellectual and emotional harmony".[19] We can best achieve this through a political struggle for liberation, not as mere "trade union secretaries" but as "tribunes of the oppressed".[20]

References

Baryard, Kat, 2010, *The Equality Illusion: The Truth about Men and Women Today* (Faber).

Choonara, Esme, 2008, "Prostitution: The Government Puts Women In Danger", *Socialist Worker* (1 March), www.socialistworker.co.uk/art.php?id=14280

Dale, Gareth, and Xanthe Whittaker, 2010, "A Response to the Sex Work Debate", *International Socialism 127* (summer), www.isj.org.uk/?id=664

Kollontai, Alexandra, 1921, "Prostitution and Ways of Fighting it", speech to the third all-Russian conference if the heads of regional women's departments, www.marxists.org/archive/kollonta/1921/prostitution.htm

Lenin, 1961 [1902], *What Is To Be Done?*, in *Collected Works*, volume 5 (Moscow), www.marxists.org/archive/lenin/works/1901/witbd/

Levi, Ariel, 2005, *Female Chauvinist Pigs: Women and the Rise of Raunch Culture* (Simon & Schuster).

Pritchard, Jane, 2010, "The Sex Work Debate", *International Socialism 125* (winter), www.isj.org.uk/?id=618

19: Kollontai, 1921.
20: Lenin, 1961, chapter 3.

Book reviews

Skipping stages

Esme Choonara

Richard B Day and Daniel Gaido (eds),
**Witnesses to Permanent Revolution:
The Documentary Record**,
(Haymarket, 2011), $36

"The revolutionary centre is moving from the West to the East," writes German socialist Karl Kautsky in 1903 in the first article in this collection. It is an apt opening for a groundbreaking book that documents some of the huge debates that took place in the socialist movement in Russia and beyond in the years 1903-1907.

This was the era of growing agitation against the Russian Tsar, the disaster of Russia's war with Japan and of course the first Russian revolution of 1905. Questions about economic development, class forces and revolutionary agency were posed concretely and with urgency. And for most of the authors represented in this collection, the answer lay at least in part in the theory of permanent revolution.

This theory is most associated with Leon Trotsky. Yet while the editors of this remarkable collection in no way underestimate Trotsky's unique contribution, they also make clear that his work emerged from the wider debates he was part of.

The editors, Richard B. Day and Daniel Gaido, have collected and translated some of Trotsky's little known articles from this period alongside pieces by Russian

revolutionaries Parvus (who Trotsky credited with being the key influence on the development of his theory), Plekhanov and David Ryazanov and by German socialists Karl Kautsky, Rosa Luxemburg and Franz Mehring. Several of the articles appear in English for the first time or have been retranslated from the original for this volume. What emerges is a lively debate about the roles of different classes, the nature of revolution and the basis of Marxist theory itself.

One theme that runs throughout the book is the lessons of the 1848 European revolutions which in the early 1900s clearly still felt quite contemporary. Marx had learned from the 1848 revolutions that the bourgeoisie was no longer a revolutionary class as it had been in the Great French Revolution. Instead the bourgeoisie had shown that it was terrified of the revolutions it helped to initiate, and turned to shoddy compromise with the old order and vicious repression of the working class forces that had helped to lead the revolutions.

In 1850 Marx and Engels drafted an address to the members of the Communist League which argued that workers needed to fight for political organisation independent from other class forces. They wrote that the workers' "battle cry must be: the permanent revolution".

Witnesses to Permanent Revolution shows how Marx's theory was applied by a new generation to the experience in Russia, an absolutist state that was still economically backward compared to

Western Europe. It was a largely feudal country and the question of the peasantry had loomed large in socialist debate for many years. However, as many of the writers here testify, Russia had imported some of the most advanced forms of capitalist production into the cities, creating powerful concentrations of workers.

These workers had already shown their power in mass strikes in the 1890s, but the question remained as to what sort of revolution could Russia expect and what sort of strategy the left should pursue. If Russia was still a feudal society, did it have to have a capitalist revolution and a period of capitalist development before socialist revolution was possible? This was certainly the orthodoxy among many Russian Marxists at the time. It was a view put forward most stridently by Plekhanov, who argued that workers should form a bloc with the bourgeoisie.

Lenin strongly disagreed that workers should form a bloc with the bourgeoisie. But he too accepted that there would need to be a "democratic revolution" before a socialist one. He argued that the workers' key ally should be the peasants and that they should fight together for the "revolutionary-democratic dictatorship of the proletariat and the peasantry".

The only work by Lenin that is included in this collection is a short introduction to one of Kautsky's articles. But Lenin is repeatedly quoted in the editors' comments, mostly to point out his errors and to give context to those arguing for permanent revolution. Intriguingly, the editors also then include one passage to suggest that Lenin may in fact have agreed to some degree with Trotsky and the others who called for an "uninterrupted revolution". Lenin was wrong on the question of permanent revolution—both in terms of the character of the revolution and the role of the peasantry. He rectified his position

decisively in practice, if not explicitly in theory, in the 1917 revolution. But the scattered references to Lenin throughout this collection leave a slightly unfathomable and unsatisfactory picture of Lenin's evolving thought and tactics.

In contrast to Plekhanov and Lenin, all the other authors represented in this book believed to varying degrees that the unique position of workers in Russia raised the possibility of permanent revolution—revolution led by the workers and going beyond democratic demands. Much of their argument was based on the development of Russia's different classes. For example Luxemburg points to the speed of the economic transformation of Russia and the sudden birth of a working class. She also argues that liberalism in Russia has not grown out of progressive forces as it did in Western Europe but out of the agrarian aristocracy.

Unsurprisingly, Trotsky was the clearest on the political role of the different classes. He lays out his position in an article written in November 1905, "Social Democracy and Revolution". Comparing the role of various classes in 1905 to those in the 1848 revolutions, he explains:

"The class dismemberment of a bourgeois nation has gone much further in our country than in Prussia and Austria in 1848. Our liberal bourgeoisie turned out to be counter-revolutionary even before the revolution reached its culmination. At every critical moment, our intelligentsia democrats displayed their impotence. The peasantry as a whole represents spontaneous insurrection—but it can be put into service of the revolution only by a force that will take state power into its own hands. That leaves the proletariat." (p555)

Both Trotsky and Kautsky in different ways explore how even if the working class were to set out to achieve a purely democratic reform of Russian society, the logic of coming to power would compel them to implement measures that would move towards socialism. Workers could not maintain political power without starting to challenge for economic power.

Many of these discussions started before 1905, but the revolution had a massive impact, not least by establishing the mass strike as a weapon of revolutionary struggle. And while much of the writing in *Witnesses to Permanent Revolution* stresses the global dynamics of the system that made workers' revolution a possibility in Russia, there is also a sense of the impact of the 1905 revolution internationally. Luxemburg and Kautsky, for example, saw the use of mass strikes and the upsurge in Russia as a chance to re-energise the German SPD which was coming under the conservative influence of a large trade union bureaucracy.

It is Trotsky's articles from 1905 that really stand out in this collection. It is an absolute joy to read his polemics on how to split the army and the picture he paints of how workplaces can become centres of resistance that spread the struggle. And it is fascinating to see in Trotsky's writings collected here the foundations for his seminal writings on permanent revolution, *Results and Prospects* and his later riposte to Stalin, *Permanent Revolution*.

The theory of permanent revolution represented a wider challenge to a deterministic view of Marxism and of history and class struggle. Several authors look at how the late economic development of Russia meant it was not destined to follow the same prolonged stages of industrialisation as Western Europe. It was the mixture of old and new in Russia that created new possibilities. The question was whether the workers' movement could seize them. And that, as Parvus, Trotsky and Luxemburg make clear, was a

question of politics and of class struggle.

Trotsky slates those that appeal to "objective social development" to deny the possibility of workers' revolution in Russia. He points out that his critics are missing the interaction of economic with social and political factors—the class struggle. This of course was not to say that workers' revolution was guaranteed success. Permanent revolution is a theory of what is possible, as Trotsky himself explains in the collection. But it is a chance that must be taken and a fight that must be waged. As Luxemburg put it, "It is a poor leader and a pitiful army that goes into battle only when it knows in advance that victory is in its pocket." (p566)

Sometimes reading debates between figures on the left, involving historical references readers may not be familiar with, can be a daunting or even demoralising experience. But the brilliant and precise annotating of this collection, along with a short introduction to each piece, makes every article accessible to a wide range of readers.

Editing is of course always a political role, and at times I found myself in disagreement with Day and Gaido's emphasis or evaluation. I felt they overestimated the contribution of Ryazanov—clearly a talented and principled revolutionary Marxist, but hardly the precursor of Trotsky's theoretical insights that the editors claim for him. Similarly, while they are right to reclaim the revolutionary Kautsky from the renegade he later became, they overplay the clarity of some of his work on Russia.

But none of this detracts from the fact that Day and Gaido have done a fantastic service with this immense collection. *Witnesses to Permanent Revolution* is a fascinating and thought-provoking book and one that genuinely sheds new light on past debates about socialism that can help to inform the future.

Labour theory of value?

Estelle Cooch

Donald Filtzer, Wendy Z. Goldman,
Gijs Kessler and Simon Pirani (eds),
**A Dream Deferred: New Studies in
Russian and Soviet Labour History**
(Peter Lang, 2008), £52.70

The great American poet, Langston Hughes asked "What happens to a dream deferred? Does it dry up, like a raisin in the sun, or fester like a sore and then run?" This book, which takes its title from Hughes' poem, aims to address those deferred and conflicting dreams that plagued the world's first socialist revolution in Russia in 1917.

The collection of 16 essays was brought together following the Labour History of Russia and the Soviet Union: Work in Progress conference in Amsterdam in March 2005 with the aim of "discovering the scholars working in Russian/ Soviet labour studies" and according to the editors of the book, charting new directions for study entirely.

The first aim has undoubtedly been met. The 16 essays present differing and at times contentious views about Soviet labour history with a bias towards the first half of the twentieth century (only two of the essays discuss anything after Stalin's death in 1953). Whether or not the essays chart new directions for the future however is less clear. In several cases new archival evidence has prompted entire reinterpretations of previously assumed analyses. Wendy Goldman's essay "Terror in the Factories" considers the implications of the Kirov murder in 1934 and is outstanding. Diane Koenker's essay considering "Soviet Work Leisure

Travel in the 1930s" offers an analysis of an often overlooked element of Soviet life and Donald Filtzer's essay on the 1947 food crisis sensitively deals with the devastating effects of capitalist economics and food distribution, lessons that remain just as relevant today. Several of the essays are less successful. An essay by Simon Pirani entitled "Mass Mobilisation versus Participatory Democracy: Moscow Workers and the Bolshevik Expropriation of Political Power" reiterates the sometimes bizarre conclusions of liberal historians and fails to further discussion of a post-revolutionary society.

The book is split into three parts : Workers and Workers' Politics, Workers and Work: Coercion and Incentives and Family, Food and Work, Strategies for Survival. One essay by Sarah Badcock in the first part of the book discusses the attitudes of workers in Sormovo, a town near the major Russian city of Nizhny Novgorod. Following the October Revolution Badcock notes that "the Bolsheviks were the most numerous party in the Sormovo soviet after the September elections". Despite this seemingly quite important recognition, thereafter there is hardly a mention of Bolshevik activists or indeed the debates in Sormovo that allowed for Bolshevik gains in the elections. Instead, just pages later, there is a vague allusion to "the self-confidence, consciousness and wealth of the Sormovo workers' organisation" not being mirrored elsewhere, with no mention of the roles of any Bolshevik party members. For Badcock little progress could be made after the October Revolution without the consent of the Socialist Revolutionaries and Mensheviks, whom she deems to be the "moderate socialists". Consequently when workers were not active with the SR's or Mensheviks political allegiances get dismissed as "amorpheous and ill defined".

This sits neatly with Simon Pirani's conclusions that as early as 1923 working class political activity was being "severely restricted" by a social contract between employers and workers that ceded decision-making power in exchange for consistent improvements in living standards. Pirani highlights the campaign to confiscate church valuables and the trial of the Socialist Revolutionaries in June 1922 as two key turning points in replacing participatory democracy with coerced mass mobilization. By 1921, according to Pirani, the plenums of the Moscow Soviet had transformed from a participatory body into a "lifeless course of lectures". Pirani's denunciation of the confiscation of church valuables as "an offensive underpinned by state repression" presents the campaign led by the GPU secret police as little more than unorganised violence led by armed thugs. The complex reasons behind the campaign, that five million died during the famine that precipitated it and the fact that no object necessary for worship was ever removed are not deemed relevant by Pirani. He simply concludes on behalf of historians everywhere that the campaign was "agreed by historians to have contributed little to the relief effort". The reality was much more complex. One source tells us, "The amount of surplus wealth taken from the church was enormous, and yet so much remains that its loss is hardly noticeable to the visitor".*

Many of Pirani's conclusions are addressed by Kevin Murphy's impressive article on strikes during the Early-Soviet Period of 1922-32. Murphy expands on his work in the much-praised book *Revolution and Counterrevolution: Class Struggle in a Moscow Metal Factory*. He presents a picture of a post civil war society with much to play

* Hecker, J F, *Religion and Communism*, 1933, London

for. Unlike Pirani who seems to imply the ascendancy of Stalin to leadership was assured by the early 1920s, Murphy highlights the differing features of the early and late 1920s. Between 1922 and 1928 only six GPU reports mention the arrest of strikers and only five reports mention other strikes in which force was used or threatened. The Rates Conflict Commission (RKK) which acted as an arbitration committee forming collective agreements handled cases involving over thirteen thousand workers. Contrary to the assumptions of many historians, in 65 percent of cases the commission sided with workers. Similarly when it came to outright repression, Murphy found in only 9.4 percent of cases did arrest or threat of being fired prevent strike action.

The interesting insights that Murphy provides are mirrored in articles by Wendy Goldman, Diane Koenker and Donald Filtzer. Goldman's article on the Kirov murder deconstructs the popular notion that the murder was purely the "portal to the Great Terror" and notes how local party committees carried on "business as usual" until at least the autumn of 1936. Goldman's findings strengthen the view that the terror was launched and directed from above, in contrast to the view propagated by traditional Cold War historians that placed working class organisations at the centre of the terror. Goldman presents evidence that even throughout the 1930s during the the Moscow show trials some workers questioned, "Why must we forget the merits of Trotsky, Zinoviev and Kamenev in the civil war?" Another worker told a party organiser, "Trotsky was a brilliant, prominent person who made great contributions which the party is hiding and not discussing." Of the 9.1 percent of party member expelled from local groups between July and December 1935, a marginal 2.8 percent were expelled for Trotskyist-Zinovievite opposition. Goldman excellently represents the conversations and debates that went on within the Russian working class in the midst of the purges. She highlights those workers who stood up and said in reference to Trotsky, "Perhaps they wanted to make a second revolution. Lenin said that everyone will be free, but in reality there is not freedom." Time and time again those who locally propped up Stalinist policies questioned whether or not their hardworking comrades should be punished for voting for Trotskyist resolutions the decade before. Elements of Goldman's analysis are arguable, but as a whole the essay is riveting. There are other essays within the book that provide evidence for new debates and ask new questions entirely. Koenker's essay on leisure trips as an incentive in the Soviet Union highlights the differences between the gains outlined in the 1922 Labour Code (that allowed workers paid vacations long before the rest of Europe followed suit) and the superficial incentives during Stalin's rule and after.

A Dream Deferred is an ambitious book that throughout asks and answers exciting and new questions about Russian labour history. The suppression of such studies that followed the degeneration of the revolution under Stalin makes such research even more necessary. There is much to question in the book, much to debate, but just as much to praise. It is fitting to consider the end of Langston Hughes' poem: "Maybe it just sags like a heavy load. Or does it explode?" It remains a sad fact that the distortion of the legacy of the Russian revolution continues to sag like a heavy load on socialist activists, but equally its legacy still has the power to explode by motivating and inspiring activists today. It is that legacy that we continue to fight for.

Other worlds are possible!
Beccy Reese

Mark Bould and China Mieville (eds), **Red Planets, Marxism and Science Ficiton** (Pluto Press, 2009), £19.99

This collection of essays provides a critical analysis of science fiction (SF) within the media of film and novels. The genre, which involves exploring the possibility of worlds structured in ways different to ours, appeals to many who are inspired by the slogan "another world is possible". One of the challenges facing socialists is to show that a world without capitalist relations is not impossible. For this reason, SF has radical potential for thinking differently about the world.

Of course this is not to suggest that SF can only be progressive. Indeed as Bould points out in his introduction, "A group of SF writers...originally proposed the Strategic Defence initiative to Ronald Reagan in the early 1980s and these writers...advise the US Department of Homeland Security on the so-called War on Terror".

The first essay takes Holbein's painting *The Ambassadors*, which features a distorted skull superimposed on a stately portrait, as a starting point to elaborate a fundamental quality of SF. By distorting reality our perspective on our own time and space is altered. It is this that gives SF the ability to throw light on our current times by shifting us to a different perspective. The recent TV show Battlestar Galactica showed empathy with suicide bombers on US television, through the prism of a war between man and machine. (It is a shame that none of the contributors discuss television within this genre given the speed with which this medium is able to respond to the present.)

Matthew Beaumont takes us through this idea from a great number of viewpoints although in the end really gives us little beyond this basic idea to chew on.

An examination of how art might function in future utopia societies, using Ursula Le Guin's *The Dispossessed* and Kim Stanley Robinson's *Blue Mars* as examples, demonstrates how SF provides an opportunity to explore what might occur with the removal of the capitalist profit motive. It can be difficult to imagine art that is neither a a commodity that needs to make a profit nor a pleasure to be consumed.

One area that causes much debate among those concerned with literary theory is how to define SF. One definition, by Darko Suvin, is a constant point of reference in this collection. Suvin says science fiction is "a literary genre whose necessary and sufficient conditions are the presence and interaction of estrangement and cognition distinguished by the narrative dominance or hegemony of a fictional 'novum' validated by cognitive logic."

In the latter essays Milner refers to this barely intelligible definition as "archetypically academic" and Mieville takes it apart by examining whether the reader and the author really believe the fiction to be possible and what happens to Suvin's definition if they don't.

Jorgensen's essay "Towards a Revolutionary Science Fiction" urges a shift in thinking about SF from imagined futures ("coded expressions of history") to real possibilities ("actualisation of history"). He comes to the conclusion that SF is a useful tool which can create revolutionary thinking. As an example he looks to Ursula Le Guin's *Left Hand of Darkness* in which a human species exists that has no sex drive. Reading this novel "as a concrete scientific suggestion to engineer a human society that is not warped by libidinal investments" allows us consider the difference between our current reality and a possible, believable alternative. This essay argues that SF is good for thinking with, which is fairly self-evident for any revolutionary who enjoys playing around with "what if" ideas that SF throws out.

This collection ensures that SF is not simply dismissed as being dominated by special effects, shiny spaceships and kooky aliens. But it's a shame that it's fascinating ideas are too often tangled up in academic jargon.

A fiery polemic
Gareth Dale

*Alex Callinicos, **Bonfire of Illusions: The Twin Crises of the Liberal World**, (Polity Press, 2010), £14.99*

A book's dedication rarely relates closely to its content but this is an exception. Dedicated to the memories of Chris Harman and Peter Gowan, its twin themes are their lifelong preoccupations: capitalist crisis (Harman) and US imperialism (Gowan).

In the first part, Callinicos examines the causes of the Great Recession. He divides them into three spheres. One is long-term overaccumulation and profitability decline. Capitalism's 1950-73 "golden age" was not followed by stagnation, but the lower average profitability of subsequent decades explains the harsh programmes of restructuring and wage repression that came to be known as neoliberalism. But neoliberal restructuring couldn't restore profit rates to levels capable of supporting sustained rapid global growth.

China's rise occupies a pivotal position in Callinicos' second sphere: the unstable and structurally imbalanced global financial system. China and its East Asian neighbours gained a competitive edge by keeping wages low, creating a "savings glut", and depressing the value of their currencies through the accumulation of large dollar reserves. That the US could attract colossal chunks of East Asia's savings can be read as a sign of its continued economic strength. That so many of its liabilities now lie in foreign hands can be read as a sign of weakness. Dollar recycling from China and other surplus countries enabled interest rates in the West to remain low, and this underlay events in the third sphere: the dependence of the economies of the West in the late 1990s and 2000s upon credit bubbles. With subdued wage growth, demand came disproportionately through spending by the rich and credit-driven spending by the poor—fuelled in part by predatory lending by banks. The trigger for the Great Recession, the bursting of the credit bubble, was indissolubly bound up with the other causes. Had profit rates been robust in the 2000s, expansion would not have been so bubblesome; had wages climbed in step with productivity, demand growth would not have relied upon credit mania.

The Great Recession has brought the neoliberal model into crisis. Not only has it arrived at the culmination of three decades of neoliberal ascendancy, but its major contributory causes include two of neoliberalism's core commitments: wage repression and financialisation. By the latter, Callinicos is referring to three features in particular. One is the increased weight of finance. Another is the integration of a broader array of actors—including industrial firms and consumers—into financial markets. The third is the rise of shadow banking (hedge funds and private equity firms) and the proliferation of financial instruments, notably derivatives.

In tracing the part played by credit derivatives Callinicos draws upon Dick Bryan and Michael Rafferty's Capitalism with Derivatives. In their account, derivatives dismantle any asset into constituent attributes and establish price relations between different sorts of capital. They enable the law of value to operate more forcefully and ubiquitously, as the intensity of competition between bits of capital is ratcheted up, enforcing the requirement that each asset yields its due return. The pressure to deliver "competitive" levels of wages and productivity to match global benchmark rates of return on capital places additional burdens on labour. Bryan and Rafferty predicted in 2006 that derivatives "have made it likely that any financial crisis will have a more pervasive and speedy impact than was previously the case", a forecast that was amply borne out shortly after the ink had dried.

Using a delightfully absurd metaphor, Bryan and Rafferty describe the system of financial derivatives as "a flexible, floating monetary anchor" for the global financial system, similar to the role once played by gold. Callinicos concurs that the derivatives system provides a foundation of the financial system but does not see derivatives as a new "gold", for, unlike Bryan and Rafferty, he disputes that they assume the role of money. Instead, reading Marx through David Harvey, he insists that the contradiction between money as measure of value and as means of exchange is an intrinsic feature of capitalism's laws of accumulation as manifested, crucially, in the tension between the sustaining of accumulation through credit creation and the need to preserve the quality of money. Derivatives function as a measure of value but not as a means of circulation.

So much for the causes of the Great Recession. What of its nature? Callinicos argues that it was a moment of revelation of the underlying crisis of accumulation. Its acuteness stems from the fact that a generalised economic crisis arrived together with a major financial crash. Indeed, it is this that invites comparison with Great Depression, although in the recent crisis massive state intervention served to ensure that a slump on the scale of the 1930s was avoided. Had states permitted inefficient capitals to fail, an even sharper slump would have occurred, but the devaluation of capital would have helped to restore conditions for sustained growth. Instead, they shored up unprofitable banks and other firms deemed "too big to fail", and helped to restructure and rescue industrial corporations such as GM and Chrysler. The problem with this strategy is that it leaves chronic overcapacity, as witnessed worldwide in certain sectors (such as automobiles), and most gravely in the section of the world economy that is recovering most rapidly, China. One should beware, therefore, of reading too much into the signs of recovery. The long-term crisis of overaccumulation and profitability, Callinicos predicts, is set to continue.

If the economic future is unstable, what of the geopolitical? Once upon a time there was talk of a sunny liberal future in which a benign and powerful US hegemon, backed by a strong EU, oversaw trends towards global governance and democracy. This geopolitical illusion has been smouldering for some time, but Callinicos identifies the Georgia-Russia war of 2008 as a pivotal conflagration. It was fought and won by Russia against an erstwhile colony whose overtures to Nato were perceived as threatening it with encirclement, while Washington could only look on helplessly. The limits to US power were revealed—Russia succeeded in splitting Nato's European members over the issue. Meanwhile, Europe's other international organisation, the EU, has been snared in contradictions. And in Asia, the limits to US power have been probed by the Iraqi and Afghani resistance forces, and face the

looming challenge of China.

Hegemonic decline doesn't happen overnight and its pace should not be exaggerated. US GDP is growing faster than many of its economic peers, not to mention its political rivals (Russia, Venezuela). The US will remain the world's dominant economy for decades to come; Obama has successfully relegitimated US militarism; and Washington will continue to act as supreme "broker", capable of orchestrating power relations across the globe. Nevertheless, the system is tending towards multipolarity, and relations between states will as a result become more fluid and unpredictable. 2008 won't be the last time in which Washington's "imperial overstretch" is manifested in impotent rhetoric as Russia's borderlands blaze. Beijing-Washington tensions will be a recurring feature—even in Latin America, as Chinese trade links begin to honeycomb US influence, eroding the pillars of the Monroe Doctrine.

So what of the prospects for progressive change? Some harbour hopes for a return to the "embedded liberalism" of the postwar age, but for Callinicos that is but another illusion. That regime was built upon vigorous growth rates and the conceding of considerable economic autonomy to nation states, but the former seems unlikely and the latter can be ruled out due to the globalised nature of production. In the long term, he holds out for democratic planning. En route thereto, a number of measures can be taken, including nationalisation of the commanding heights, wealth redistribution, and a universal direct income. Illusions in neoliberalism, let alone the market, are deeply entrenched, and, despite the book's title, Callinicos does not pretend that they will be reduced to ashes under the impact of the crisis. That will require protracted political and ideological struggles.

Pick of the quarter

The latest issue of *New Left Review* (II, 64) has some interesting pieces. In a careful analysis, Peter Nolan and Jin Zhang show what a high mountain China must climb, even though it has overtaken Japan as the second largest economy in the world. They argue that, during the era of globalisation, "well-known firms with superior technologies and powerful brands have emerged as 'system integrators'" that dominate individual sectors. These firms are based very largely in the North. Following the financial crisis, "there is deep uncertainty about the future structure of the global political economy", say Nolan and Zhang. But in the short term, and despite all the boosterism about the BRICs, the process of Northern-dominated concentration and centralisation of capital has continued.

Slavoj Žižek offers his own take on the eurozone crisis, in the course of which he makes some good theoretical and political points. And there is a fascinating interview with Adolfo Gilly—historian of the Mexican Revolution, veteran of many great Latin American movements, and onetime follower of the weirdest of all orthodox Trotskyists, J Posadas.

The new issue of *Historical Materialism* (18.2) leads with Kees Van Der Pijl's Isaac and Tamara Deutscher Prize Lecture, in which he outlines his attempt to extend historical materialism to embrace international relations. Ben Fine has an important article, "Locating Financialisation". It is dense and difficult, but it offers a far-reaching critique of Costas Lapavitsas's argument that contemporary finance has developed an independent base of exploitation, as well as Fine's own analysis of financialisation. His arguments largely dovetail with those put forward in this journal

In a timely piece of publishing, September's *Monthly Review* contains an article called "Chemical Catastrophe: From Bhopal to BP Texas City" by Tomás Mac Sheoin.* Comparing the deadly accidents at Bhopal in India and the Texas City refinery, Mac Sheoin exposes the extent to which cost-cutting and the drive for profits caused both disasters. His conclusion, that we are likely to see more such incidents in the future, is hard to argue with in the wake of the BP oil spill.

Andrew Kliman's "Lies, Damned Lies, and Underconsumptionist Statistics" is a spirited polemic against underconsumptionist theories of the present economic crisis. It is available for free from the Marxist-Humanist Initiative website.†

Finally, the July issue of *Socialism and Democracy* contains an article by Paul Blackledge entitled "Marxism, Nihilism and the Problem of Ethical Politics Today". The article picks up many of the ideas discussed in his articles "Marxism and Ethics" and "Marxism and Anarchism" in previous issues of this journal.

AC & JJ

---

* www.monthlyreview.org/100901macsheoin.php
† www.marxisthumanistinitiative.org/economic-crisis/lies-damned-lies-and-underconsumptionist-statistics.html